CLASSICAL COMMUNICATION
for the
CONTEMPORARY COMMUNICATOR

CLASSICAL COMMUNICATION
for the
CONTEMPORARY COMMUNICATOR

Halford Ryan
Washington & Lee University

Mayfield Publishing Company
Mountain View, California
London • Toronto

Library of Congress Cataloging-in-Publication Data
Ryan, Halford Ross.
Classical communication for the contemporary communicator /
Halford Ryan.
p.   cm.
Includes bibliographical references and index.
ISBN 1-55934-033-9
1. Public speaking. 2. Oral communication. 3. Oratory.
I. Title
PN4121.R9   1991   91-21417
808.5'1—dc20   CIP

Manufactured in the United States of America
10 9 8 7 6 5 4 3 2 1

Mayfield Publishing Company
1240 Villa Street
Mountain View, California 94041

Managing editor, Linda Toy; production editor, April Wells; copyeditor, Loralee Windsor; text and cover designer, Susan Breitbard. Photos for Chapters 1–6 and of Patrick Henry, Frederick Douglass, Henry Ward Beecher, and Harry Emerson Fosdick by permission of The Bettman Archive; photos of Richard M. Nixon, Jimmy Carter, and Barbara Bush by permission of UPI/Bettman. The text was set in 10/12 Goudy and printed on 50# Text White Opaque by The Maple-Vail Book Manufacturing Group.

Text Credits

The author and publisher gratefully acknowledge permission to reprint material from the following copyrighted sources.

Beecher, Henry Ward, "Woman Suffrage Man's Right," February 2, 1860, Beecher Family Papers, Manuscripts and Archives, Yale University Library.

Bush, Barbara, "Choices and Change," Wellesley, Massachusetts, June 1, 1990, *Vital Speeches of the Day*, July 1, 1990, p. 549.

Fosdick, Harry Emerson, "My Account with the Unknown Soldier," Riverside Church, New York, November 12, 1933, Fosdick Papers, Burke Library, Union Theological Seminary, New York City.

Nixon, Richard M., "My Side of the Story," September 23, 1952, *Vital Speeches of the Day*, October 15, 1952, pp. 11–15.

Ryan, Halford Ross, *Harry Emerson Fosdick: Persuasive Preacher*, Greenwood Press, 1989.

Ryan, Halford Ross, *Henry Ward Beecher: Peripatetic Preacher*, Greenwood Press, 1990.

Ryan, Halford Ross, "Senator Richard M. Nixon's Apology for 'The Fund.'" *Oratorical Encounters: Selected Studies and Sources of Twentieth-Century Political Accusations and Apologies*, Greenwood Press, 1988.

Contents

Preface

The basic course in speech communication has traditionally been a stand-up-and-give-five-speeches course. Whether elected or required and whatever its title, the fundamentals course is often an undergraduate's only exposure to one of the oldest disciplines in academia. Yet the historical antecedents of this art have often been given at most a passing mention in courses devoted to public speaking. The classical canons, which were developed by theorists and have been used by practitioners throughout the history of Western public address, have rarely been made accessible to the modern student. Nor have texts of noteworthy speeches, which illustrate the techniques of rhetoric, generally been presented for study.

Aristotle defined rhetoric as "the counterpart of Dialectic."[1] The Greek word *antistrophe*, which is translated as "counterpart," signified the turning away from the chorus in a Greek play. E. M. Cope noted that the antistrophe communicated the sense that rhetoric and dialectic were analogous although different, that there were "general resemblances and specific differences."[2] Aristotle's imagery communicates the departure point for this work, which, as an antistrophe, is a turning away from the status quo.

Beginning students in public speaking can master the rudiments of the Greek and Latin rhetorical traditions. This includes Aristotle's *Rhetoric*, Corax and Tisias, the Sophists, the logographers or speech writers, Isocrates, and Plato's *Gorgias* and *Phaedrus*. The *Rhetorica ad Herennium*, Cicero's various works, and Quintilian represent the Roman tradition.

I use the classical canons of oratory to organize the book. In many instances the canons have been used for the criticism of rhetoric but not employed to teach it. The scholarly criticism of the art of public speaking, in which to some degree most of the classical canons are used as common topics for rhetorical foci, can also be applied fruitfully to teaching. As originally intended, the canons can help the student speaker learn how to conceive, write, practice, and deliver a speech.

Rhetorical criticism and persuasive speaking can be convertible. After being introduced to the rudiments of classical rhetoric, students can detect many of these devices in addresses that contain them. Conversely, having studied these techniques in model addresses, students can then use them, in conjunction with their own creativity, to make distinguished persuasive speeches.

The thesis is that students can compose more artful communications if they study and emulate rhetorical techniques that have been used by successful speakers. Therefore, seven classical and contemporary speeches are included for study. These speeches were selected on the basis of their illustrating one or more of the rhetorical techniques discussed in the chapters. The texts are: Patrick Henry's "Give Me Liberty," which contains numerous rhetorical questions and uses the classical pattern; Frederick Douglass's "What to the Slave is the Fourth of July?" which illustrates many classical techniques; the Reverend Henry Ward Beecher's "Woman's Suffrage Man's Right," which demonstrates several kinds of rhetorical adaptations to the audience; the Reverend Harry Emerson Fosdick's "The Unknown Soldier," which is a model of speech organization and refutative rhetoric; Senator Richard Nixon's "My Side of the Story," which contains many of the rhetorical devices and two of the organizational patterns discussed in this book; President Jimmy Carter's "The Panama Canal Treaties," which is an example of the classical pattern ill-adapted to its rhetorical purpose; and Barbara Bush's commencement address at Wellesley College, which illustrates audience adaptation in the epideictic genre. Although the relative greatness of some of these addresses might be debated, the speeches cover the gamut of Western speaking, they represent the techniques discussed in this book, and they demonstrate, if one must apply that criterion, successful public persuasions. Moreover, I quote throughout the book appropriate passages from other speeches, which are not printed as entire texts, to illustrate different speakers' rhetorical techniques. Although these examples are culled primarily from contemporary communicators, I use quotations from historical speakers occasionally.

Classical Communication for the Contemporary Communicator admittedly aims high. The focus is on producing a polished persuasion. This does not imply that the student speaker, after attaining a level of artistry, is insensitive to the needs of the audience. Martin Luther King, in "I Have a Dream," and Jesse Jackson, in "Rainbow Coalition," fused an elevated style and an energetic delivery, neither of which were pedestrian, to an urgent concern for the body politic at important junctures in U.S. history. Neither does this suggest that most students will eventually become senators, presidents, or major public figures. It is to say that students will encounter in their life's work rhetorical situations in which they will have to prepare a talk, make a professional presentation, perhaps deliver a formal speech, or compose a compelling written communication, not to mention their speeches for the classroom, oral reports in other classes, and written papers. It is to say that students can master the rudiments of rhetorical criticism so that they can evaluate their fellow classmates' and other speakers' persuasive discourse. It is to say that proficiency in speaking is desirable, and significant achievement in the discipline is even more advantageous. A liberally educated person should be able to speak with distinction and to distinguish the chaff from the wheat in his or her own and other communicators' speeches. With an emphasis on the former goal, but not forgetting the latter, the techniques in this book should enable students, and later productive adults, to encounter these problems with a measure of success.

As indirect yet invaluable contributors to that measure of success, the following reviewers have my gratitude for their thoughtful comments: Gary Collier,

California State University, Chico; Thomas Conley, University of Illinois; William R. Dresser, Denison University; Richard Katula, DePaul University; William and Kari Keith, University of Louisville; Joseph L. McCaleb, University of Maryland; and Jeran M. Ward, Lewis and Clark College.

Notes

1. Aristotle, *Rhetoric,* translated by W. Rhys Roberts (New York: The Modern Library, 1954), 1354a1.
2. Edward Meredith Cope, *The Rhetoric of Aristotle with a Commentary* (Cambridge: University Press, 1877), I: 2.

To the Student

Before you embark on the study and practice of public speaking, you ought to know its strengths and limitations.

The ancients defined rhetoric as the art of persuasive discourse. An art comprised certain techniques and teachable skills that a student could learn. These skills for persuasive speaking seemed to work most of the time; one trained in the art could presumably craft a more persuasive speech than one who lacked systematic instruction. However, mastery in the art did not always guarantee success, for even the most carefully crafted speech may fail to persuade. Ministers and politicians continually confront the successes and failures of their art of public discourse.

The ancients mapped rhetoric's verbal strategies and tactics, and the results are still employed today. Many of the ideas have been given new names, perhaps in an effort to disguise the debt owed to their originators. This textbook openly uses the ancient's terms, and gives rightful credit to their ideas by illustrating the original sources of their insights.

The ancients thought of rhetoric as a utilitarian art that functioned in two ways. If the art produced the structure and analysis of persuasive speaking, it also provided the ability to analyze a speech. Thus, while this book is intended primarily to teach how to write and deliver an address, you will also be learning how to evaluate spoken discourse. In our society you are constantly being bombarded by broadcasts from politicians, preachers, advertisers, and so on. As you learn how to persuade others, you will also learn how others persuade you.

The ancients led the way in using rhetorical criticism to help to teach the art of speaking. They often offered good and bad speakers of their day as exemplars. This textbook follows in their footsteps, using examples of both successful and unsuccessful persuasions to illustrate the techniques of rhetoric. This practice will help you establish a foundation for rhetorical criticism, which can be defined as a reasoned explanation of why a speech succeeded or failed. Thus, the trained speaker in the art of rhetoric should be able to construct a persuasive speech and should also be able to analyze another speaker's speech.

The selection of speeches quoted in this book is wide-ranging and diverse. Most students probably have watched the recent presidential campaign debates and have seen enough documentary programs about historic U.S. presidents to have some familiarity with presidential speaking, which is represented in several of the examples. But lesser-known Americans have also addressed audiences, and these speakers need to be quoted, too. Hence the range of quoted speakers is historical as well as contemporary, famous as well as unknown, black as well as white, women as well as men, for all these persons have contributed to American public address. This range of communicators will also give you some idea of the important roles that speakers have played in the history of the United States.

The development of a systematic ethical scheme for public address is beyond this textbook's purpose. However, the ethical concerns of rhetoric are important considerations. From ancient to modern times, thoughtful individuals have recognized that rhetoric is a powerful tool. Some critics hold that rhetoric is immoral because it can be and often has been employed for evil ends. (Adolph Hitler is a prime example.) Other critics believe that rhetoric is amoral. Like an automobile or a revolver, rhetoric can be used or abused. Whatever philosophical position one takes on the ethics of rhetoric, certain verities remain from ancient times to the present: Lies, distortions, half-truths, misstatements, and misrepresentations have no place in the moral practice of public speaking.

CHAPTER 1

The Classical Heritage of Rhetoric

Plato (427–347 B.C.). A Greek philosopher in the Academy and author of the *Phaedrus* and *Gorgias*, Plato taught the ethics of persuasive discourse and the analysis of the audience.

Abraham Lincoln, in his famous "House Divided" speech in Springfield, Illinois, June 16, 1858, spoke the rationale for this chapter: "If we could first know where we are, and whither we are tending, we could better know what to do, and how to do it." If the present is a precursor of the future, as Lincoln argued it was, then the past was the precursor of the present, and it behooves the student to understand the classical heritage of rhetoric. How the pioneers and practitioners of public speaking developed the art of persuasion is the subject of this chapter.

HISTORICAL AND MODERN CONTEXTS

The ancient Greeks and Romans have dominated the intellectual development of the West for 2000 years. Most of the English language is derived from classical Greek and Latin. From the ancients we derived our public architecture, the theory of a legislative body consisting of upper and lower houses, the practices of democracy and freedom of speech, our belief in the importance of a liberal arts education, and the concept of the citizen-speaker. These ideas were developed in the short span of about three centuries before, and one century after, the birth of Christ.

The practice of giving prepared, persuasive speeches began in ancient Greece for a variety of reasons. The Athenians founded the first democracy in which free male citizens, eighteen years of age and older, could participate directly in the government of Athens. Although all could vote, only those who could afford to do so were able to participate in the day-to-day governance of the

1

city-state. Citizens learned that by speaking persuasively in the assembly, one could convince other citizens to vote as one desired.

A second arena in which Athenians quickly recognized the utility of the spoken word was the legal system. There were no lawyers in the courts of ancient Athens; citizens had to prosecute others or defend themselves by themselves. In a civil or criminal suit, one either succeeded or failed, so it profited one to try to sway the judge or jury by learning to speak persuasively. A third arena that required public speaking talents was the public festival. On such occasions, much like our Fourth of July, Columbus Day, and Memorial Day, Athenian citizens gathered to listen to a speech as part of a civic or a religious celebration. The better speech makers were called on to do the honors, and a great speech could be a stepping stone to a career in the legislative assembly.

As the Greek city-states declined in wealth and power in the third and second centuries before Christ, the Romans began to dominate the Western world culturally and politically. Because Rome eventually developed a republican form of government, speaking became as prized in Rome as it was in Greece. Although more elitist than the Greek assembly, the Roman Senate was still a place where one could bend other senators to one's will through oratory. Rome instituted the practice of professional pleaders, much like our modern lawyers, so that one could also make a career in public speaking. Eloquent layspeakers still appeared at public functions, and even the lowliest Roman citizen might be expected to deliver a eulogy at a close relative's funeral.

The Romans used and honed the Greek rhetorical tradition. They also added new concepts as they further developed the craft of public persuasion. With the rise of imperial Rome and the consequent loss of a republican form of government, speaking in the legislature and in the courts became primarily ceremonial because the emperors banned free speech. Nevertheless, the concept of the citizen-speaker was developed and perfected in ancient Greece and Rome, and it is an idea that still functions in the United States of America.

The ancients faced some problems, the solutions to which we now take for granted. How can the speaker best go about writing a speech? Is there a systematic method? What should be the substance of the speech? Should a speech be organized, and if so, how? Does word choice matter? Should language be ordinary or uncommon? How should the speech be delivered? Does delivery really matter, and can skills in delivery (if there are such skills) be taught?

In addition to these practical questions, which faced each prospective speaker, the Athenians and the Romans considered some educational and philosophical problems. For instance, they pondered whether speaking can be taught. And if speech can be taught, what is its academic place? Is it a skill, akin to cookery; is it real knowledge, such as a geometric proof; or is it an art, such as painting and sculpture? Assuming that public speaking can be taught, what is the best way to teach it? Should one learn by trial and error, as one learns a skill; should one master a set of rules, as one masters arithmetic; or should one learn principles that can be adapted to varying situations, which allows creativity in an artistic endeavor? Along these lines, the ancients questioned whether preparation and practice helped one to be a more compelling speaker, and they wondered whether one could or should improve one's own speeches by studying other model speeches.

The ancients also pondered why some speakers were successful persuaders while others were not. They sought the factors that explained success, because they reasoned that this knowledge would help a speaker at any level of expertise become a more successful persuader.

The Athenians and the Romans also worried about the ethics of speaking. Some realized that a crafty speaker might sway the assembly to enact legislation that it should not enact or that an innocent defendant who was a weak or unconvincing speaker might be judged guilty. Then, as now, the critics realized that these miscarriages could and did occur. But other commentators questioned whether such occurrences indict the art of speaking or whether the blame should be placed on the speaker who used the art of rhetoric for evil ends. Some Greek and Roman critics even advocated that it was a civic duty to gain mastery over the spoken word and use it to expose unethical speakers. Thus a moral speaker can use an amoral rhetoric to condemn an immoral speaker.

The ancients were not immediately able to answer these questions, many of which still confront twentieth-century speakers. And they did not all agree on many of the answers that were proposed over the years. Yet they made valuable contributions to the art of public speaking that still guide the teaching and practice of rhetoric.

The best way to understand the ancient's contributions is to examine how the practice of public speaking developed. That is the subject of the rest of this chapter. But to make some sense of about four hundred years of classical rhetorical theory, it might help to have some major themes in mind. What follows is a kind of preview and distillation of the classical heritage of rhetoric.

- A student speaker should master the five **canons,** or principles, of the art. An application of the techniques of rhetoric does not guarantee success, but the student trained in rhetoric should be able to prepare and to deliver better communications than the untrained person. The student should also realize that an important part of knowing the rules of the art is knowing when to break the rules and when and how to adapt them for a particular speaking situation.

  Knowledge of the techniques of rhetoric also enables the student to be a better and more critical listener. The presence or absence of proofs for an argument, whether the speech is organized cogently or arranged haphazardly, whether the language has stylistic merits or is pedestrian, and whether the speech is delivered forcefully or weakly are considerations that enable a listener to evaluate the worth of public address. This analytical power of assessing speech is useful in and out of the classroom. It equips men and women to discharge their duties as American citizens by contributing intelligently and ethically to public discourse, either as critical listeners or as critical respondents to other speaker's assertions.

- Knowing and being able to apply the classical canons of rhetoric are necessary but not sufficient for effective public speaking. The ancients realized that rhetoric could instruct a speaker how best to present the case, but they also demanded that the speaker have a case. This entails presenting reasons, proofs, and analyses that rest on solid research and evidence. Indeed, the trained speaker-critic can present the best proofs to the audience, and can detect and confute weaknesses in the speeches of others.

- The speaker should always keep the audience in mind. After all, the audience decides whether it is persuaded. The capable and honest speaker employs rhetoric at its finest level when advocating the best interests of the audience. Although individuals might quibble over what "the best interests of the audience" means, lies, deceits, half-truths, and misstatements have no place in the ethical scheme of a speaker who would speak well. It is the function of the speaker-critic to expose those who would speak unethically.

- The tenets of classical rhetoric are accessible to the modern student. Although the Greeks and Romans did not have colleges and universities as we conceive them today, they did instruct students in the art of rhetoric. If anything, they instructed their students at a younger age than is the norm for contemporary students.

- Polished public speaking is an attainable goal for the contemporary communicator. Men and women have spoken, and continue to speak, eloquently and persuasively throughout the history of the United States, as the speeches that are anthologized in the Appendix and the quotations from other speeches in this textbook will attest. The common thread is that all these men and women mastered the art of oral communication. Some learned the craft by trial and error, and some by copying other successful speakers. In most instances, however, they learned how to speak when they took courses in rhetoric, debate, and public speaking.

- The historical and philosophical context of rhetoric relates to the context of contemporary public speaking. Since the ancients developed the practice of rhetoric, three major foci have characterized the study and practice of public address: the speaker, the speech, and the audience. Which of these foci are stressed determines what the student will study and how the student will speak.

George Kennedy outlined three strands in the fabric of rhetoric that correspond neatly to the traditional foci of speaking:

1. **Technical rhetoric** is concerned with the speech, is practical, and "shows how to present the subject efficiently and successfully."[1] This kind of rhetoric was practiced especially in the law courts but was also applied in civic life. The subject of technical rhetoric is, more often than not, political issues.

2. **Sophistic rhetoric** is concerned with the speaker, who is conceived as "an ideal orator leading society to noble fulfillment of national ideals."[2] **Epideictic,** or ceremonial, rhetoric appears to find a comfortable place in this category. This strand is characterized by the liberally educated speaker who can best address the audience as the good citizen speaking well.

3. **Philosophical rhetoric** is concerned with the kinds of audiences and the speech's effect on the audience. The arena is **deliberative oratory** or legislative rhetoric. Kennedy believed philosophical rhetoric stressed "what hearers should believe and should do."[3] In a way, there is a sense of moral duty in philosophical rhetoric.

These strands often so intertwine that they become indistinguishable. But if one requires a concise ordering of this book's rhetorical strands, to use Kennedy's terminology,

> The emphasis is on technical rhetoric,
> in a deliberative setting,
> toward a philosophical end.

THE GREEK TRADITION

The rise of rhetoric as a tool to defend or prosecute at the bar and to advance oneself in the legislative assembly was linked to the democratic form of government in Sicily. That is not to say that citizens under the king did not plead their cases or that there was not a kind of deliberative oratory in the king's aristocratic councils. But in the Sicilian democracy, where free males over the age of eighteen constituted the government, judges decided cases and the people determined their own destiny.

Corax of Sicily

In about 467 B.C., the Sicilians overthrew Hieron, their king, and established a democracy. Lawsuits arose over land disputes after the fall of the tyrant. Because Sicily was still a Greek state rather than Roman, its court system did not have lawyers to plead cases; each citizen prosecuted or defended his own case. In the spirit of an entrepreneur, Corax of Sicily conceived a set of precepts for citizens to use in the courtroom.

Thus Corax became the first to affirm that practice and training in public address and an organizational strategy helped to make one a more persuasive speaker.

Corax wrote down his precepts and called the book *Techne,* the Greek word for technique. This prototype for textbooks in public speaking was the first theoretical Greek book on rhetoric, or any academic subject, for that matter, and was the basis for Corax's teaching of the craft for money. Corax reasoned that training in speaking was better than no training at all, and that cogent structure and proof made a speech more persuasive than chaos and assertion.

Corax advocated arranging one's speech in five parts. The introduction aimed to obtain a favorable hearing from the audience by making the listeners receptive to the speaker and the speech. The narrative communicated the facts of the case, and, whenever possible, slanted them to show the speaker as a just and honest man. The arguments presented the analytical proofs of the case. In the arguments section, which was perhaps the most important part of the speech, the speaker marshalled all the reasons for his case. In the refutation or subsidiary remarks the citizen-speaker apparently had three choices: (1) to refute his opponent's arguments against his case; (2) to attack his opponent's case; or (3) to combine the two approaches. The conclusion, or **peroration,** would summarize the speech and appeal for a favorable verdict from a jury of fellow citizens.[4]

Tisias was a contemporary of Corax, and was one of Corax's students. Tisias evidently composed his own *Art of Rhetoric,* but it, too, is lost and he is remembered best for a lawsuit he had with Corax.

Corax had an advertising gimmick to induce citizens to take his course in public speaking: He guaranteed the product. The *Techne* was supposed to ensure success to its purchaser. After taking Corax's course, Tisias refused to pay for it. Corax took Tisias to court and argued that the fee must be paid either way: If he won, the fee should be paid; if he lost, the fee should also be paid because Tisias's success would demonstrate that Corax's fee had been earned. Equally cagey, Tisias countered with his own rhetorical appeal: If he won, he need not pay; if he lost, he should not pay because his failure would demonstrate that Corax's *Techne* had proven worthless.

Exasperated with this kind of argumentation, the court threw out the case with the judicial notice, "bad crow, bad eggs." The wry humor becomes evident when one learns that *corax* is the Greek word for crow; hence the court allowed that a bad crow, Corax, had hatched a bad egg, Tisias. Ironically, Tisias did not have to pay.[5]

Although it is unclear whether Corax and Tisias actually prepared students for political oratory, there is no evidence to suggest that they did not. A reasonable inference can be made that individuals who wished to polish their speaking skills in the legislative assembly might have consulted them for advice and training. For instance, the organizational pattern that Corax taught for use in the courtroom is also suited to attacking or defending a piece of legislation. The introduction could refer to the bill; the narration could develop the historical need, or lack thereof, for the proposal; the arguments could adduce reasons for, or against, the legislation; the refutation could attack the opponents' reasoning and evidence; and the peroration could appeal for action.

Corax and Tisias were representative of the technical strand of rhetoric. They were interested in its practical uses, and they responded to the needs of free citizens for polished public persuasions in a new democratic society.

The Sophists

Concurrently with Corax and Tisias a group of men known as **sophists** traveled through Greece teaching male citizens who could afford to pay the required fees. They were called sophists, based on the Greek word *sophos* (wisdom), because they were the wise men or teachers of their era. Their students mastered economics, ethics, and politics; they learned how to compose speeches; and they determined how to write with correct word choice and appropriate grammar. Whereas men such as Corax and Tisias had been concerned primarily with rhetoric, the sophists provided a comprehensive education in which public speaking played an important, but not primary, role. At their best, these teachers exemplified **sophistic rhetoric** because they aimed to produce the educated citizens who could best lead the state.

The sophists were the Greek prototypes of modern teachers and professors. They taught the kinds of knowledge that would help their pupils become better citizens and, to be sure, gain material advantage in the world. They taught the range of subjects that we now call the liberal arts: mathematics, politics, economics, history, law, literature, fine and practical arts, and rhetoric. The art of persuasive speech underlay all these subjects, whether at the bar, before the legislature, or in animated discussions with one's friends.

Protagoras of Abdera, a city northeast of Athens, was one of the earliest sophists. Protagoras taught in Greece from about 455 B.C. to 415 B.C. He introduced the idea that most questions were debatable, that for every position there was a counterargument. Protagoras's idea is the basis for an adversarial legal system with prosecuting and defense attorneys, for academic and political debating, and for the concept of the devil's advocate. He taught public speaking and debating, and he required pupils to master the art of dialectic, or the art of questioning and answering.[6]

It is an accepted rule in contemporary life that to win friends and influence people one should remember people's names. The originator of that concept was Hippias of Elis. Hippias taught from about 430 to 400 B.C. Among the subjects he taught was the study of mnemonics. Claiming that he could remember fifty names and recite them back in the order they were given, he taught his students the techniques one could use to remember things and recall them. For instance, one might remember a speech by likening it to a house: The atrium would be the introduction; the living room, the narration; the dining room, the arguments; the kitchen, the refutation; and the pantry, the conclusion.[7]

We assume that the sophists taught their pupils skills in delivery, although Thrasymachus of Chalcedonia, who taught from about 430 to 400 B.C., was one of the few teachers to write anything on how to deliver a speech. Thrasymachus believed that skills in delivery made the speech more convincing. For instance, he advised his students to employ rhythm, or vocal pacing, in the voice to effect persuasion. He also taught his students to vary their pitches and inflections, and to couple them with gestures to tap the audience's emotions.[8]

Perhaps the most famous sophist was Gorgias of Leontini, Sicily. Gorgias was born in the early fifth century B.C. and lived almost a hundred years. He was probably a student of Tisias. Gorgias went to Athens from Sicily as the head of a delegation in 427 B.C. to secure aid from Athens in a war the people of Leontini were having with the people of Syracuse, Sicily. Gorgias was such a powerful orator and so impressed the Athenians that his addresses would have lasting consequences for the study of rhetoric.

Although a sophist, Gorgias was better known as a teacher of rhetoric and as a practicing speaker. He was best known for composing and delivering encomiums for celebrations and festivals. An **encomium** is a speech of praise. The ceremonial speech, unlike the forensic speech that aimed at justice and the deliberative speech that aimed at expediency, functioned primarily as entertainment for the Athenian populace. The encomium was intended primarily to demonstrate the speaker's ability to craft an elegant address. Gorgias excelled in this art. He developed a grandiose style that dazzled the listener with rhythm and rhyme, figures of speech, and ostentatious vocabulary. In a sense, his speeches were more poetry than prose, more delightful than practical, because his ornamental language charmed more than persuaded his audiences (except that he was a gifted ceremonial speaker).

Foremost among the sophists was Isocrates (436–338 B.C.). Although early in his life he wrote speeches for clients to deliver in court, Isocrates later changed careers and became a professional educator. Isocrates was the first Greek to found an institution of higher learning. He established a school in Athens to prepare students for a political life in the Greek city-state. Isocrates's school differed from those of other sophists because he did not travel but made his students come to him and remain with him for an extended time.

Isocrates contributed to rhetorical and educational theory in two notable ways:

1. He theorized about a question that has fascinated teachers since ancient times: Does nature or nurture determine prominence in a student? Isocrates believed that outstanding speakers were born with a natural ability, but he conceded that practice and a thorough mastery of one's subject matter could make even a mediocre speaker more persuasive. This instructional theory is the underpinning of the liberal arts education in which men and women are trained to think and speak in a free and open society. Isocrates's idea that education, training, and practice could make a productive citizen, or a successful speaker, is a democratic belief distinctly contrary to the aristocratic conviction that only certain individuals, usually of noble birth, can achieve eminence and distinction.

2. In an effort to distinguish himself and to diminish the excesses of Gorgias's grand style, Isocrates developed the periodic sentence. The periodic sentence is constructed so that it withholds its complete meaning until the very end, thus adding suspense to the speech and holding the listener's attention. Perio-

dicity is usually accomplished by withholding an important noun or verb until the end.[9]

The following example from Franklin D. Roosevelt's First Inaugural Address illustrates not a periodic sentence but the periodic style. Only after a series of balanced sentences that began with the same five words did FDR unveil the key thought in a climactic sentence.

> It can be helped by preventing. . . . It can be helped by insistence. . . . It can be helped by the unifying of relief activities. . . . It can be helped by national planning. . . . There are many ways in which it can be helped, but it can never be helped by merely talking about it [applause].[10]

Before leaving the sophists, it is important to recapitulate how they viewed the art of rhetoric. Critics complained that the sophists and their students could easily make the truth appear the untruth, that evil could be championed. Adolph Hitler is the prime example of this kind of ability in the twentieth century. The sophists would have responded with a "yes, but" argument. Rhetoric, they said, was amoral. Speakers could use it to obtain good purposes or evil ends. But the praise or blame belonged to the speaker who exploited rhetoric, not on the art itself. Moreoever, students skilled in the art of rhetoric can also advocate truth and expose error. The long line of humanistic speakers in American history is too lengthy to enumerate, but for every Hitler there was a Franklin D. Roosevelt; for every racist a Frederick Douglass or Martin Luther King, Jr.; and for all those who would deny women the right to vote, an Elizabeth Cady Stanton or Susan B. Anthony.

The Logographers

Like modern Americans, the ancient Athenians were a litigious lot. But while Americans employ lawyers to plead their cases, the Athenians gave their own speeches in prosecution or defense. This was required by Athenian law. Because success at the ancient bar (as at the modern one) often depended on who could best persuade the jury, there arose a group of individuals who could be paid to write speeches for their clients to deliver in court. These men were known by their contemporaries as **logographers,** from the Greek words *logos,* which means word, and *grapho,* which means write. The modern term is *speech writer* or (with a somewhat negative connotation) *ghostwriter.*

Most of the logographers wrote speeches for courtroom speaking, although some also composed speeches for clients to deliver in the legislative assembly just as modern speech writers compose rhetorical discourse for political (and corporate) clients. But the logographers did not deliver the addresses they wrote; like their modern counterparts, they were masked, as Lois Einhorn has noted, behind their clients.[11]

We know little about the logographers' general activities except that they composed speeches for pay. But we can assume that they enacted ancillary roles as necessary to compose effective speeches. They probably knew and advised their clients about points of the law; they probably interviewed witnesses with an eye to strengths and weaknesses in testimony; and they probably advised clients on skills in delivery.[12]

The first logographer was Antiphon, who was born around 480 B.C. and was executed for treason in 411 B.C. for his part in a conspiracy to overthrow the democratic government in Athens. Antiphon primarily wrote speeches for the courtroom, but he also composed speeches for clients to use in the *ekklesia* (legislative assembly). Antiphon wrote most of his speeches in a plain style, that is, a kind of everyday conversational manner. His word choice was slightly elevated from the street-corner variety, but he was concerned to make the client appear to be an ordinary person.

Antiphon authored "On the Murder of Herodes," which is an existing speech in defense of a person charged with a cold-blooded murder. It was a difficult persuasive task, not only because the defendant was from a city that had revolted against Athens, which the Athenians would have held against him, but also because the deceased had disappeared at sea on the same ship as the defendant, which aroused strong suspicions of foul play. The speech that Antiphon wrote wove the facts into a long narrative that stressed his client's innocence, argued the probabilities in the case, and complained at length about the nature and haste of the trial. In modern terminology, the defendant claimed he was being railroaded. The verdict is unknown, but Kathleen Freeman, although granting that suspicion of the defendant's guilt was strong, believed the decision was not guilty.[13]

Lysias was perhaps the most famous of the Athenian logographers although he was never an Athenian citizen but a resident alien. Born around 459 B.C., Lysias came to writing speeches in a roundabout fashion. The owner of a factory that manufactured shields for the Athenian army, Lysias led a comfortable life until 404 B.C., when the so-called Thirty Tyrants seized power in Athens. Casting about for scapegoats and money, they seized on Lysias and other resident aliens to satisfy popular frustrations and to confiscate their wealth and property. Lysias barely escaped with his life. With the overthrow of the tyrants, Lysias returned to Athens and began writing speeches for litigants. As a crafter of words he more than regained his previous fortune.

Lysias solved a problem that had long vexed logographers. Because many logographers wrote speeches in the same fashion for everyone, the speeches tended to sound the same. The Athenians were perceptive people, and litigants' use of language inappropriate to their stations in life frequently drew attention to itself. Athenians asked themselves, if the litigant's case was just, why did he have to have a logographer to dress it up? The fact that he had employed a logographer might be a betrayal of the case's weakness.

Lysias developed the concept of **ethopoiea.** He observed "that a purveyor of words for others, if he would serve his customers in the best way, must give the words the air of being their own." The Greek noun *ethos* means character, and the verb *poeio* means to make or do. Thus *ethopoiea* meant that Lysias made the character of the speaker apparent in the style of the speech.[14]

Along with the concept of revealing a speaker's character in the speech, Lysias's ability lay in what Kathleen Freeman called "the art that conceals art." Lysias strove to hide his craft from the audience as much as possible. Eschewing the florid style of other logographers, Lysias composed his addresses in an ordinary style that did not draw attention to itself or to the fact that the speech was ghostwritten.[15]

Lysias's speech, "On the Killing of Eratosthenes the Seducer," is an intriguing defense of the accused murderer of Eratosthenes. Euphiletus, the defendant, slew his wife's lover and used the defense that Athenian law allowed such a murder because seduction defiled the family and state. He was brought to trial by the wife's relatives, who claimed that Euphiletus created the situation so that he could accomplish a cold-blooded murder. Lysias had his client repeatedly demonstrate how his murdering Eratosthenes was actually a service to the state! The verdict is unknown, but Kathleen Freeman believed that, although the Athenians were probably repulsed by Euphiletus's savage act of binding Eratosthenes and then knifing him while he begged for his life, the jury probably acquitted him because of his appeal to the sanctity of the home.[16]

Demosthenes (384–322 B.C.), known more as an orator, also wrote some speeches for clients. Demosthenes was forced into the business when his guardians stole his inheritance. But his first love was politics so he turned his talents to speaking. In the waning years of the independent Greek city-states, Demosthenes delivered speeches against Philip of Macedonia who was trying to conquer the Greeks. These "Philippics" quite rightly warned the Athenians against Macedonian mastery. In 338 B.C., the Greeks lost their independence to Philip at the battle of Chaerona, and Alexander the Great subsequently maintained Macedonian control over Hellas.[17]

Demosthenes was a student of Isocrates and overcame through hard work (as his teacher said one could) two distinct disadvantages:

1. Demosthenes stammered, so he practiced with a pebble in his mouth to force correct articulation.
2. He had a naturally weak voice, so he went to the sea shore and recited poetry over the sound of the waves.

A classical joke has a fellow Greek tell Demosthenes, as he is practicing a speech on the shore, that people would understand him better if he took the rocks out of his mouth.

Most of the logographers represented the technical strand of rhetoric. They were concerned with the practical aspects of rhetoric and the success of their clients. Ethical questions about rhetoric—whether one should compose a speech for a guilty man or impart knowledge and technique that would enable a client to use rhetoric for evil ends—evidently did not overly trouble the logographers because (like the sophists) they viewed rhetoric as amoral. Isocrates and Demosthenes, however, were the best of the logographers, because they spoke for the ideals of the Greek city-state.

Before condemning the ancients for their apparent disregard of ethical matters, it might behoove the twentieth-century student to question contemporary practices. Given the assumption that one is innocent until proven guilty, no one seriously objects to a defendant's right to professional counsel. And although some critics complain about politicians' use of speech writers, the American people continue to elect officials who require assistance in writing speeches. However, contemporary audiences are apparently very concerned when a communicator uses other speaker's thoughts without attribution, or uses lies and distortions. Such unethical speaking has cost candidates their chances in the presidential primary races. One Greek, Plato, would have been pleased with the standards to which the American people usually hold their public persuaders.

Plato

Plato lived from 427 to 347 B.C. He was a student of Socrates (470–399 B.C.) and later founded his own school, known as the Academy. In the history of persuasive discourse, Plato contributed most to the philosophical strand of rhetoric. Plato was more concerned with the ethical implications and the truth and justice of discourse than he was in teaching others how to write and deliver speeches.

Plato wrote a number of dialogues or philosophical conversations, which illustrated the art of dialectic, or discovering truth through questions and answers. The dialogues have been called Socratic, because they featured Socrates versus one or more antagonists who represented the antithesis of Socrates's philosophical position. The dialogues have also been called Platonic, because Plato actually wrote them, although they were supposed to be representative of Socrates's bent and flavor.

Plato composed two Socratic dialogues devoted to rhetoric. The first one (written around 387 B.C.) was entitled *Gorgias* and featured several rhetoricians versus Socrates. The most famous protagonist was the sophist Gorgias of Leontini, after whom the dialogue was named. In it, Plato argued that rhetoric should be used only for just ends.

In the *Gorgias* Plato leveled several charges against rhetoric and the sophists who taught it. First Socrates got Gorgias to admit that "rhetoric produces persuasion . . . in the listener's soul." Plato regarded a speaker's imparting knowledge to an audience more important than persuading them, so he made Gorgias acknowledge that a speaker, more than a doctor, could persuade a crowd on the subject of health; Gorgias even had to admit that *crowd* was a euphemism for the ignorant, for people who really knew medicine would follow the doctor's, not the speaker's, prescriptions. However, Plato did accede to Gorgias's observation that the speaker, not the craft, was responsible for the effects of rhetoric. This was an important distinction, because Plato deplored those who misused rhetoric more than he disparaged rhetoric itself. Thus, Plato affirmed the amorality of rhetoric.[18]

Plato's second complaint was that rhetoric was not a systematic discipline. "I say that it is not an art," Socrates advised Gorgias, "but a knack, because it is unable to render any account of the nature of the methods it applies and so cannot tell the cause of each of them." Moreover, Plato scorned rhetoric by holding that it was "a branch of flattery," which was akin to cookery for the stomach and cosmetics for the face.[19]

But Plato's real misgiving about rhetoric was that having the knack did not necessarily produce justice. Unlike the sophists, who held that their rhetoric was amoral, Plato maintained that "the true orator" would always try to achieve "the engendering of justice in the souls of his fellow citizens and the eradication of injustice, the planting of self-control and the uprooting of uncontrol, the entrance of virtue and the exit of vice."[20]

Focusing more on Plato's complaints about rhetoric, twentieth-century critics have often missed the point that in the *Gorgias* Plato granted that rhetoric had a valid function as long as it served "the ends of justice, and for that alone." In a sense, Plato was at once close to and far from his sophistical counterparts. Both antagonists seemed to agree that rhetoric could be moral or immoral. But Plato held that a just man would never use rhetoric for wrong purposes. In a practical sense, Plato would apparently have required a logographer to determine his client's innocence before writing a speech of defense. But what if the client really were innocent and the logographer mistakenly thought him guilty?[21]

George Kennedy wisely observed that "Philosophical rhetoric is thus an ideal, beyond the possibilities of the Greek city." He might easily have added that it is beyond the possibilities of any city anytime. Nevertheless, Plato's ideal that rhetoric should be employed only for justice remains a goal toward which speakers should strive.[22]

In his second dialogue devoted to rhetoric Plato questioned how a speaker swayed an audience. This query was addressed in the *Phaedrus*, which was written around 370 B.C.

Plato granted that a persuasive speech should be organized in a rational fashion. He mentioned a preamble, a narrative, testimony, proofs, probabilities, a confirmation, and supplementary confirmation, but inexplicably he did not mention a conclusion. It is interesting to note that Plato did not invent this organizational pattern but borrowed it from his sophist predecessors. But in giving the pattern his imprimatur, he inadvertently validated the sophist's reasoning that arrangement affects an audience's reception of a speech.[23]

The major contribution that Plato made in the *Phaedrus* was to argue that the rhetorician must analyze the audience to discern what arguments would persuade its members. Although Plato did not venture to state how his theory of audience analysis would work, he did at least point rhetoricians in the right direction. They should try, he said, to discover how speeches influence listeners' minds, or souls, to use Plato's words. He perceived that a given kind of speech should persuade a certain type of person: "he must apply *this* kind of speech in *this* sort of manner in order to obtain persuasion for *this* kind of activity [emphasis in the original]." Plato also included in his theory of persuasion the arrangement and adornment of the speech, and the advice that an orator should address clever minds with complex communications and simple souls with simple speeches.[24]

The idea that a speaker should analyze the audience was a master stroke for the ages. Plato's concept continues to operate in twentieth-century communications. The public opinion polls, to which officeholders and office seekers constantly refer to discern what issues they should discuss or duck, are an example of Plato's principle. However, Plato would doubtless deprecate this use of his dictum.

For all its importance, the idea of audience analysis had a serious pragmatic flaw. Assuming that one addressed a single conservative with one kind of speech and a liberal with another, Plato's theory would work. But if an orator faced an audience composed of a spectrum of political stances, it is unclear how the speaker could satisfy all these auditors, for an argument to the conservatives would probably succeed in alienating the liberals, and vice versa. George Kennedy perceived the problem inherent in Plato's theory: "How can an orator know the souls of his audience in any full sense? . . . How can he keep from enflaming one at the same time he calms another?"[25] Indeed, Plato's idea has plagued some modern speakers. Some critics hold that contemporary politicians dilute their communications to appeal to the lowest common denominator. Hence, the sorry state of public discourse today, but Plato would have had the last word—"I told you so."

Aristotle

Aristotle, a pupil of Plato's in the Academy, was the most important figure in classical Greece to write a definitive work on rhetoric. Part of this may be because other authors' works have not survived, while Aristotle's did. Aristotle lived from 394 to 322 B.C. Early in his life he resided in Macedonia, where he tutored King Philip of Macedonia's son, who later became Alexander the Great. Aristotle returned to Athens and taught in a covered walkway attached to the public gymnasium, which was called the Lyceum.

Aristotle's work on public speaking was the *Rhetoric*. The treatise, which some critics believe was Aristotle's lecture notes, was written or compiled over a period of time, so it is difficult to give precise dates, but 330 B.C. is a reasonable date by which to assume the *Rhetoric* was probably in its finished form.[26]

Aristotle conceived rhetoric as the power to observe the persuasive elements inherent in a speaking situation. If one possessed this ability, one should be able to write and deliver a compelling speech. His famous definition of rhetoric is: "Rhetoric may be defined as the faculty of observing in any given case the available means of persuasion." The means of persuasion were the logical extension and codification of Plato's idea that the speaker should know and name the various elements that persuade different listeners. Unfortunately, Aristotle did not define *persuasion,* but he used the Greek word *pistis,* which means faith, trust, proof.[27]

Three Kinds of Proof   Aristotle asserted that three kinds of proofs persuaded an audience. His claim has not been refuted and it stands secure today. He held first that belief is achieved by the speaker's personal character, or ***ethos*** [1356a5]. Aristotle divided ethos into three constituent parts: a speaker's good sense, good moral character, and goodwill [1378a8]. This kind of persuasion was achieved through the speech's revelation of the speaker's personality. Aristotle affirmed Lysias's idea that a successful logographer could make the speaker's character apparent and persuasive in an address. Aristotle thought ethos was the most important means of persuasion a speaker possessed [1356a13]. This belief is the basis for many speeches of apologia or self-defense in which public figures attempt to clear charges against their characters.

Aristotle held that the second persuasive proof occurred when the speaker stirred the emotions of the audience. The classical term was ***pathos.*** Aristotle recognized that emotions such as anger, pity, fear, shame, jealousy, and greed aroused the audience to accept the speaker's address. **Emotional appeals** are potent persuaders for both good and evil ends. Unfortunately, Hitler appealed to anti-Semitism and racist rhetoric flourishes today in negative campaigning. But Elie Weisel pricked the nation's conscience during the Bitburg Cemetery controversy in 1985 when President Reagan honored a German cemetery that contained the remains of Nazi SS troops. And black speakers use Martin Luther King's birthday to urge a fulfillment of his dream.

Aristotle's third element of proof was ***logos,*** or logical proof. Aristotle believed that people were persuaded by the "truth or an apparent truth [1356a19]." Like Plato, his teacher, Aristotle would have preferred that speakers use correct reasoning, but Aristotle's approach to life was more pragmatic than Plato's, and he wisely observed that skilled speakers could persuade by appealing to proofs that seemed true.

Although the three proofs can be separated for discussion, they often blur and merge. For instance, Democrats demonstrate their good sense, goodwill, and good moral character to a partisan audience by deprecating the trickle-down theory of tax cuts for the rich. Note the emotive connotations of the words *trickle-down, tax cuts,* and *the rich,* which are Democratic catchwords. Conversely, Republicans reveal their ethos by advocating tax relief as sound economic sense.

Three Categories of Discourse   Aristotle evidently liked tripartite divisions because he also partitioned discourse into three catagories. Forensic speaking was practiced in the law courts. Epideictic oratory was sort of a catchall category that covered what we would now call ceremonial speaking. Deliberative persuasion was delivered in legislative assemblies. Aristotle believed these kinds of oratory treated definitive matters and dealt with specific periods. The chart below indicates his distinctions:

Kind of oratory	End or goal	Time period
Forensic	Justice	Past
Epideictic	Praise or blame	Present
Deliberative	Expediency	Future

Aristotle's tripartite division was neat to a fault. Although it is generally useful to keep his differentiations in mind, it is worthwhile to note that he did not account (how could he?) for such modern speech forms as sermons, inaugural addresses, campaign speeches, political debates, sound bits, and after-dinner speeches—although some believe that these kinds of speeches fall into the epideictic category. Moreover, although it is generally true that deliberative speakers address impending legislation, they often treat past and present problems to urge future action.

Style and Organization   Aristotle did not deign to discuss delivery for he felt it was not "an elevated subject of inquiry [1403b38]." But he did consider style. A good style had to be appropriate and clear. In terms of clearness, Aristotle advised the speaker to use everyday common words. He defined appropriateness by negation: It was neither mean nor elevated [1404b3]. Later on he stated that language was appropriate if it expressed emotion and revealed character [1408a10]. Another facet of Aristotle's conception of style can be appreciated by understanding his distinction between oral and written language. He said the written language was more finished, more proselike, whereas spoken language "better admits of dramatic delivery [1413b20]."

Aristotle used divisions similar to Corax's speech organizational pattern. Aristotle's divisions were the introduction, the narration, the arguments, and the epilogue (like Corax's conclusion). Aristotle believed that the material contained in Corax's refutation belonged in the arguments, but whether it did is not the point. Aristotle's genius lay in the fact that he advised a speaker to adapt the pattern to the particular persuasive problem. He went beyond a rote formula. Normally a speaker would first state the case and then refute the adversary's analysis. However, if the opponent's case was particularly strong, Aristotle recommended refuting the antagonist's case before advancing one's own [1418b8-20].

Concerning humor or jesting, Aristotle gave credit to Gorgias of Leontini for correctly observing "that you should kill your opponents' earnestness with jesting and their jesting with earnestness [1419b4]."

Even Aristotle's prescription for ending the speech sounded a bit sophistical. The four functions were to make the audience disposed toward you, exaggerate or downplay the salient facts, excite the appropriate emotions, and refresh the audience's memory. To illustrate a forceful conclusion and to terminate the *Rhetoric*, Aristotle quoted Lysias's peroration for his own speech: "I have done. You have heard me. The facts are before you. I ask for your judgment [1420b5]."[28]

Deductive Argument: Enthymeme and Syllogism   Aristotle is also credited with conceptualizing what we might now call the logic of rhetorical appeals.

He termed such rhetorical reasoning the ***enthymeme,*** which means literally "in the mind." The speaker persuaded by relying on a premise that was in the minds of the listeners, or by inviting the audience to complete the chain of reasoning. This can be illustrated by the 1984 presidential campaign in which Republicans charged that Walter Mondale was going to raise taxes. GOP persuaders wisely played on a premise that is deeply imbued in many voters' minds: They are against taxes. The argument that many listeners doubtless made in their own minds— perhaps subconsciously—was something like: "I will not vote for someone who will raise taxes. Mondale will raise taxes. I will not vote for Mondale." And they did not.

Aristotle believed the enthymeme was "a sort of syllogism [1355a8]." A famous categorical **syllogism** is:

> All men are mortal [major premise].
> Socrates is a man [minor premise].
> Therefore, Socrates is mortal [conclusion].

General Douglas MacArthur argued a categorical syllogism in his famous "Don't Scuttle the Pacific" speech before a joint meeting of Congress on April 19, 1951. In speaking about his firing by President Harry S. Truman for insubordination in not following the president's orders, MacArthur glossed over the fact of insubordination and focused instead on Truman's unpopular handling of the Korean war. MacArthur argued this syllogism:

> All wars require a military victory.
> The Korean conflict is a war.
> Therefore, the Korean conflict requires a military victory.

Of course, MacArthur did not have to prove all the premises. He relied on the enthymemes that Americans want military victories (not a stalemate, which was Truman's policy), and that the Korean conflict was clearly a war (the Truman administration called it a "police action"). There was little wonder that Congress thundered its approval after MacArthur's famous completion of the argument: "In war there is no substitute for victory." Later, during the Vietnam war, conservatives used the same syllogism:

> All wars should be won.
> Vietnam is a war.
> Therefore, Vietnam should be won.

Albeit logically sound, by the end of the early 1970s, few Americans believed in the major premise, and Vietnam, like Korea, ended without a military victory of the kind associated with the two world wars.

Although a speech could be presented as a syllogism, Aristotle realized that most speakers did not develop or prove all of their premises, and few people would be able to follow "a long chain of reasoning [1357a4]." Instead, speakers constructed their speeches by using the enthymeme. That is, they relied on the fact that the audience already believed the main premise of the argument. It remained for the speaker to complete the argument.

When the Reverend Henry Ward Beecher argued for woman suffrage (see Appendix), he used several enthymemes. Take the following example in which opponents to woman suffrage argued that in voting a woman would be indelicate. Here is the complete syllogism these opponents might have argued:

> Women should not be allowed to be indelicate.
> Voting is indelicate.
> Therefore, women should not be allowed to vote.

Beecher replied: "What is there in depositing a vote that would subject a woman to such peculiar exposure? A woman, dropping a letter into the post office, is made more public, and is fully as indelicate, as in depositing her vote." Beecher built his refutation on a premise the audience already believed: Women are allowed to mail a letter. Since voting is so similar to mailing a letter, voting should be allowed.

Inductive Argument: Example   Aristotle's other contribution to the analysis of how speakers persuade was to note that speakers argued by example. Whereas the enthymeme relied on **deduction,** which meant that the speaker argued from general premises to specific conclusions, arguing by example relies on **induction.** Induction means that the speaker cites several examples or instances in order to prove a general point. In Patrick Henry's famous "Liberty or Death" speech, he persuaded his audience gathered at Richmond, Virginia, by example. First he gave the example of British military activities in the colonies, which were meant to subdue the colonists. He presented additional examples of petitions, supplications, and remonstrances that had been slighted by king and parliament. These examples inductively demonstrated that Virginians had no other alternative than to fight the British. In his "Panama Canal Treaties" speech, President Jimmy Carter also argued by example. He cited the names of prominent politicians and military leaders who supported the treaties. Since these important people supported the president, Carter invited his listening audience to induce from those examples that average Americans should also support their president.

Accusation and Defense   Aristotle also discussed a speech set that he had observed. The speech set consisted of a **kategoria,** or speech of accusation, and an **apologia,** or speech in defense. Isocrates and Plato also conceived of speeches of accusation and apology, and Aristotle observed that "One man accuses the other, and the other defends himself, with reference to things already done."[29] Thus the speech set could be an instance of forensic oratory with prosecution and defense; it could take place in a legislative assembly wherein one citizen would attack another's proposal, which would motivate a defensive response; and it could also be employed in an epideictic setting wherein a speaker could blame another citizen for wrongdoing, after which the citizen thus attacked might deliver a defense in a later epideictic situation.

This speech set also occurs in contemporary communications. For example, when Senator Richard Nixon was attacked for maintaing a political slush fund, he bought radio and television time to defend himself. He delivered his apologia, often called the "Checkers" speech, in 1952. His speech and a rhetorical criticism of the classical devices that he used in his defense is included in the Appendix.

Aristotle's Influence on Rhetorical Tradition   Aristotle's *Rhetoric* was and is perhaps the most important classical work on the art of persuasion. His oratorical genres and modes of proof, especially the logical appeals of the enthymeme and example, have figured prominently in persuasive speaking from classical times to the present. Thus, Aristotle represents the philosophical strand of rhetoric because he was interested in rhetoric's role in political and judicial situations, but he also gave attention to the technical strand in that he suggested how a speech should persuade the audience.

THE ROMAN TRADITION

Although the Greeks were the first to be interested in rhetoric, the Romans, who supplanted the Greeks in political power if not in cultural attainments, also contributed to the body of important rhetorical works. And their important works have affected the conception and practice of rhetoric down to the present day. The three major Roman authors were Cicero, Quintilian, and an unknown author who composed the work to which we now turn.

Rhetorica ad Herennium

The author of the *Rhetorica ad Herennium* is unknown. For almost a thousand years it was thought to be an early work of Cicero's, but it has become clear that this is not true. The original title is uncertain, and its date is unknown, although it was probably written around 80–90 B.C. Nevertheless, the book is the oldest complete Latin treatment of the art of persuasive speaking, and it represents the technical strand.[30]

The *Rhetorica ad Herennium* incorporated Aristotle's ideas and elements of the Greek tradition, but it went considerably beyond them. The author based his book on Aristotle's three genres of oratory—epideictic, deliberative, and forensic, or judicial. As might be imagined, although deliberative and ceremonial speaking were not slighted, the author concentrated heavily on judicial speaking because that was the kind of oratory aspiring young Romans would most likely practice. The *Rhetorica ad Herennium*'s major contributions to persuasive theory were its codification of the Roman **classical canons of rhetoric**; its clarification of the arrangement of a speech; and its penetrating analysis of delivery, which Aristotle had considered beneath his notice.

The Five Classical Canons   First of all, the *Rhetorica* identified the five classical canons, which are the basis for this textbook. **Inventio** was the act of devising proofs and words that would make the speech convincing. **Dispositio** was the arrangement and ordering of language for effect. **Elocutio** was the adaptation of suitable words for the speech. **Memoria** was the retention of the words in their correct arrangement. **Actio** was the graceful regulation of the voice and gestures.

As far as can be determined, under this scheme *memoria* was the retention in the mind of the words that were produced by the first three canons. The speaker remembered the invented language, its arrangement, and its style. As the fifth and last canon, *actio* was evidently envisioned as a kind of afterthought. How one delivered the finished speech was apparently set apart from the task of remembering the speech itself. Yet, the traditional classical scheme of delivery's succeeding memory is not serviceable.

The ancients seemed to be in a pedagogical dilemma. Given the fact that all major authorities prescribed various rules to follow in delivering the speech, it seems that the speaker should retain those rules. In fusing bodily action to words, the speaker would have to remember when to gesture, how to emphasize an anaphora vocally, how fast to speak in the introduction, and conclusion, and so on. In short, if the speaker must remember the arrangement and style of the speech, then it seems that the speaker should remember how to deliver the speech. The ancients appeared to stop short of that logical connection between remembering words and remembering their delivery.

However, in *De Partitione Oratoria* Cicero seemed to reverse the canons of memory and delivery. He noted that delivery, including voice management and gestures, as well as the speech itself, were all in the keeping of memory. Thus, Cicero made memory the last canon [1, 3]. Quintilian, although he chose the traditional order, was aware that there were differences in opinion among ancient authorities as to whether memory was the last canon [III, 3, 1–14].

The position taken in this textbook is that the canon of *memoria* arches over the other four canons. That is, the speaker needs to remember what is to be said and how it is to be spoken. Pedagogically that means that the student speaker practices the speech to retain its form and substance as well as its delivery.

Unlike the Greeks, who were speculative, the Romans were practical. Sounding a bit like Isocrates, who recommended study and practice, the *Rhetorica ad Herennium* noted that a student could master the five canons by three means: theory, imitation, and practice [I, ii, 3].

The modus operandi of this textbook is derived from the *Rhetorica ad Herennium*. This textbook gives you the theory of persuasive speaking. It gives you texts of successful speeches that employed classical concepts, which you can follow to the degree you deem desirable. It remains for you to practice the tenets of rhetoric to deliver a compelling speech.

The Six-Part Pattern of the Speech   In the *Rhetorica ad Herennium*, Corax's five-part pattern was increased to six. These parts are as follows. The **exordium** was the introduction. The **narratio** was the narration. The **divisio** was the division of the speech; this was the addition to Corax's original five parts. The *confirmatio* was the arguments section, and the **confutatio** corresponded to the refutation. The **conclusio** was the summary or conclusion of the speech [I, iii, 4].

The author recognized that an effective introduction should make the audience attentive, receptive, and well-disposed toward the speaker and the speech. For instance, a speaker could arrest the audience's attention by referring to an important subject of concern to the audience and relating it directly to the speaker's topic. The author stressed that the exordium should not be too long lest the audience tire before the speaker moved to the main part of the speech!

After the introduction made the audience receptive, the narration should continue that interest and attention. To keep the speech moving, the narration should be brief, clear, and plausible. The author reminded the speaker to stick to the facts of the case, not to wander off course, and to remember that "the shorter the Statement of Facts, the clearer will it be and the easier to follow" [I, ix, 15].

The division of the speech can be viewed as a cumbersome appendage or as a brilliant addition. On the one hand, it is one more section to remember, and it seems to interrupt the logical progression of the narration to the confirmation. On the other hand, the author was aware of the needs of the audience when recommending a division. For the sake of clarity, which was one of Aristotle's criteria for a compelling style, a speaker should indicate the areas of agreement and disagreement with an opponent or the audience. This would minimize misunderstanding and help the speaker establish as much common ground with the audience as possible.

The author's explication of the confirmation, confutation, and conclusion is similar to Corax's conception, which has already been discussed and does not need to be repeated here. However, the author did make some telling observations about how the speaker should apply the six-part pattern.

Applying the Six-Part Pattern   Although the *Rhetorica ad Herennium* is filled with the rules of rhetoric that a speaker should follow, its writer recognized that precepts could be broken in order to adapt to different rhetorical situations. Indeed, the author asserted that the highest practice of the art is to know when to break the rules: "It is often necessary to employ such changes and transpositions when the cause itself obliges us to modify with art the Arrangement prescribed by the rules of the art" [III, x, 17].

For instance, the author advised that if a previous speaker had wearied the audience with verbosity, one might skip the introduction, and perhaps even the narration, and go immediately to a strong argument in the confirmation to regain an audience's attention. Later the speaker could weave into the speech the parts of the introduction and narration that were initially omitted. (Here the canon of memory would be invaluable because the speaker would need to know the speech so well that he or she could adapt on the spot.)

The author also advised the speaker how to arrange arguments. In both the confirmation and confutation sections, the speaker should begin and end each part with a strong argument and place weaker arguments in the middle. The analysis of the audience on which the author based this precept was remarkably keen:

> [T]he strongest arguments should be placed at the beginning and at the end. . . . those of medium force. . . . should be placed in the middle. For immediately after the facts have been stated [in the narration] the hearer waits to see whether the cause can by some means be proved, and that is why we ought straightway to present some strong argument. . . . it is useful, when ceasing to speak, to leave some very strong argument fresh in the hearer's mind [III, x, 18].

The author of the *Rhetorica ad Herennium* also made some significant contributions to the conceptualization of style and delivery. In fact the writer's analysis of *elocutio* and **pronuntiatio** is so insightful that chapters 4 and 5 on style and delivery will discuss these findings in more detail. Suffice it to say here that in terms of *elocutio*, the author detailed three kinds of style: the grand, the middle, and the simple. As for *pronuntiatio*, the author introduced the idea of the conversational manner of delivering a speech. The freshness and appropriateness of this concept conceal the fact that the author wrote about the conversational mode over 2000 years ago.

Another Roman author—the scourge of Latin students who have to translate his famous speeches against Catiline—wrote about rhetoric at about the same time as the *Rhetorica ad Herennium* was produced. We now turn to this most famous Roman orator and writer on rhetoric.

Marcus Tullius Cicero

Cicero was a seasoned speaker. He practiced law and became quite wealthy from his pleading, which enabled him to have villas throughout Italy; he was elected to the consulship, which was the highest elective office in ancient Rome; and he was a member of the Roman Senate where he delivered the famous speeches that led to the execution of Catiline for treason. The effectiveness of Cicero's persuasive speeches can be gauged by the following fact. When he was executed by would-be dictators Marc Antony, Lepidus, and Octavian for his part in attempting to keep Rome a republic, Cicero's hands, which had gestured so eloquently, and his head, which had spoken so persuasively, were cut from his body and nailed to the speaker's rostrum in the Roman forum where he had often delivered speeches.

Throughout his political career Cicero found time to compose several important treatises on rhetoric. Early in his career Cicero was interested in the technical strand of rhetoric, but later in his life he turned to the sophistic strand to consider the attributes of an ideal speaker.

Cicero completed his first work on rhetoric in his late teenage years. *De Inventione (On Invention)* was written when he was between fifteen and eighteen years old and was published around 90 B.C. The work was supposed to comprise a complete treatment of the five rhetorical canons, but Cicero completed only the two books on invention. In *De Inventione* Cicero simply transmitted much of the rhetorical theory that has already been discussed and there is no compelling reason to repeat this. However, Cicero added a few insights.

Constitutio or Status   Cicero is generally associated with the idea of *constitutio*. In fact this idea was not initiated by Cicero; its originator was Hermagoras of Temnos, a Greek rhetorician in the second century B.C. However, little of Hermagoras's writings have survived, so Cicero is generally credited with a full explication of the doctrine. In any case Cicero believed that controversies on which people speak and debate always involve a question about *constitutio*, which means the place or ground for a dispute. Cicero later used the Latin word *status*, which is closer to the Greek word **stasis,** the term that Hermagoras used, when referring to *constitutio*. We shall continue to use the word *status*.

The first status is **coniecturalis,** whether a fact *is*. For instance, few would argue against the fact that numerous contemporary Americans roam the streets and sleep wherever they can. **Definitiva** denotes a definition of the fact. Some people define the people mentioned above as homeless, others counter that they are bums. **Generalis** denotes a value, class, or quality. Some people maintain that the street people deserve public assistance; others counter they should be forced to work, and still others argue that many of them should be returned to the mental institutions from which they were ejected in the mid-1980s to reduce state and federal social budgets. **Translativa,** which was appropriate to judicial oratory, indicates a transfer to another court or jurisdiction. If certain individuals can be termed *homeless* and if they merit aid, a jurisdictional argument can arise over whether the problem belongs to individual cities, counties, or states or to the federal government. Cicero's status system is useful in trying to determine the grounds for the dispute so that the speaker can build arguments or refute the opposition at the very point of contention.

Cicero's Contributions to Rhetorical Theory   Cicero added a seventh part to the six-part speech pattern of the *Rhetorica ad Herennium*. The **digressio,** or digression, was an aside of some unconnected material that the speaker added for effect. Thus the seven parts were introduction, narrative, division, arguments, refutation, digression, and conclusion [I, 20–109]. Although Cicero himself named the digressio and allowed that a speaker could use it, he believed that it should not be listed as a separate part because he disapproved of digressing from the main purpose of the speech [I,97]! His reasoning is well taken and will be followed in this textbook.

Cicero's reliance on the tradition of the *Rhetorica ad Herennium* can also be appreciated in his tripartite division of an effective exordium. A convincing exordium should make a listener "*benivolum, attentum, docilem*" [I, 20] or, as I translated the Latin, "well disposed, attentive, and teachable."

De Oratore (*On Oratory*), written in 55 B.C., is perhaps Cicero's most famous work on public speaking. Cicero modeled it after Plato's *Gorgias* and *Phaedrus*, making it a dialogue in which various persons discussed the nature of public address. *De Oratore,* in three books, functioned primarily as a sophistical discussion of Cicero's theories of rhetoric. For instance, Cicero believed that all great speakers must have knowledge of the subjects on which they would persuade and that great speaking was a gift of nature—as are the speaker's voice, visage, and physical form—but that one's speaking can be improved by art and drill.

Cicero believed that the practice of persuasive speaking had preceded its theory, that is, writers observed and studied natural eloquence in speakers and then constructed their theories of rhetoric. In a beautiful Latin construction of **chiasmas,** or word inversion, Cicero observed (the chiasmas is underlined): "*sic esse non eloquentiam ex artificio, sed artificum ex eloquentia natum*" or, as I translated the Latin, "thus it is not eloquence from theory but theory from eloquence born" [I.146].

In *DeOratore* Cicero did not treat in detail the technical aspects of rhetoric as he had in *De Inventione*. He did, however, outline the three aims of speaking: "*aut docendo aut conciliando aut permovendo*" or, as I translated the Latin: "either teach or win over or move deeply" [II, 310].

Theories of Style   As for style or *elocutio,* Cicero added two ingredients to Aristotle's criteria of clarity and appropriateness. Cicero counted four qualities. He believed a good style should be (1) correct, (2) intelligible, (3) embellished, and (4) appropriate. In a sense, Cicero added only embellishment because correctness really meant speaking in precise Latin [III, 37]. In order to master the elements of an effective style, Cicero advised students to read the great orators [III, 39]. This text follows his advice by providing in the Appendix great speaker's texts for study.

Cicero composed three works in 46 B.C. In one way or another, the three books centered on whether a great speaker should use ornate and elegant language (which Cicero favored) or employ a **plain style.** This quarrel was the Attic-versus-Asian controversy.

The Atticists were critics who believed that speakers should employ a plain style of public address. The **Attic style** used little verbal ornamentation and rhythm in speaking, used emotional appeals sparingly, and used clear and ordinary words. The Attic style was thought to represent the purest form of Attic or Greek speaking, and Atticists held that it should be preferred by Roman speakers.

In juxtaposition to the Attic style was the **Asian style.** It was called Asian because when the Greeks, under Alexander the Great, encountered grander speaking styles in the conquered lands of the Asian subcontinent, they adopted a more florid form of speaking. The Asian style used grandiose words and more rhythmic speaking, tended to be verbose rather than succinct, and relied heavily on emotional appeals for effect. The Atticists believed that the Asian style represented a debauched style of speaking in Rome.

Cicero favored the Asian style of speaking. He believed his career testified to the efficacy of the Asian style in both Roman politics and the law courts.

Brutus, written early in 46 B.C., was his first salvo in the Attic-Asian controversy, for in it he attacked the Atticists. Not to be outdone, the Atticists tried to discredit the position Cicero took in *Brutus,* although the exact nature of their attack is unknown because the speeches or written works no longer exist.

Perhaps as a partial response to these attacks, Cicero composed a short work in 46 B.C. entitled *De Optimo Genere Oratorum (On the Best Kind of Orators).* In this brief work, which was to be an introduction to his translation of two speeches by Aeschines and Demosthenes, Cicero recapitulated some of his major themes. With regard to the controversy, Cicero held that the best Greek speakers (meaning himself) used an ample, ornate, and copious style.

Of note here is that Cicero reiterated his tripartite function of the speaker: "The supreme orator, then, is the one whose speech instructs, delights, and moves the minds of his audience."[31] Cicero evidently envisioned that the speaker should accomplish all three goals in an address because he used the connective, *et* (and) *"et docet et delectare et permovet."* It is worth noting that while Cicero used the connective *and* here, he used *or* in *De Oratore;* thus there is some question whether the speaker should accomplish one or more of these goals, or all of them in a given speech.

The *Orator,* written late in 46 B.C., was a kind of offensive-defense as Cicero continued to refute the Atticists. In the *Orator,* Cicero argued that the successful speaker should be able to employ the three kinds of style as appropriate, but he still maintained that the grand style exemplified the persuader's highest attainment.

Cicero's Later Works   Brief mention is due Cicero's *Topica,* written around 44 B.C. At the request of a friend, Cicero composed the *Topica* to explain Aristotle's work of the same name. The *Topica* referred to certain topics that one could argue primarily in legal cases, but that could be applied to epideictic and deliberative speeches as well. For our purposes, Cicero reiterated the idea of *status* [93] (remember that in *De Inventione* he had used the Latin term *constitutio*) to denote the points of contention. These were conjecture, definition, and quality. (For some unknown reason, Cicero deleted *translativa,* the appeal to a different jurisdiction.)

The last important work that Cicero composed on the theory of speaking was *De Partitione Oratoria (On the Division of Oratory).* Written in 46 B.C., the work was intended to be Cicero's detailed instructions to his son, Marcus Tullius, on the study of rhetoric. The book is conceived as a dialogue between the elder and younger Ciceros, with the son, who was about nineteen years old, asking the questions and the famous father answering them.

In *De Partitione* Cicero made two major points that are worth remembering:

1. He recapitulated the five canons of rhetoric: invention, arrangement, style, delivery, and memory.
2. He took the seven-part organizational speech pattern that he had outlined in *De Inventione,* and collapsed the divisions to four.

To his son in *De Partitione Oratoria,* he recommended the introduction, the narration, the proof, and the conclusion. Cicero stated that the introduction and conclusion were to influence the audience's mind whereas the narration and the
proof functioned to establish the case [4]. Later in the work Cicero stated that
proving the case consisted of two parts, the confirmation and the refutation [33];
hence, he kept the refutation but conceived it as a subset of proving one's case.
Although there may be some merit in envisioning the parts of the speech in this
manner, the position taken in this textbook will be the Greek's five-part or
Cicero's earlier conception of the six-part speech pattern.

Cicero was killed in 43 B.C. by soldiers under the command of Marc Antony.
The justification was a proscription, a Roman euphemism for legal murder. But
Cicero's speeches survived, and his rhetorical theory was preserved and perpetu-
ated by the last great Roman theorist, Quintilian, to whom we now turn.

Marcus Fabius Quintilianus

Quintilian was born sometime between A.D. 30 and 40 in Spain, which was then
a Roman province. Around A.D. 50, Quintilian's father took him to Rome to
study. Quintilian became a lawyer, but his greatest and enduring fame was based
on his teaching of rhetoric. Quintilian was appointed the head of the state school
of oratory by the Emperor Vespasian, and the Emperor Domitian awarded Quintilian the equivalent of a modern medal of honor.

Quintilian's contribution to the study of public speaking was his *Institutio
Oratoria,* which was published in the early first century A.D., just before his death
in A.D. 96.[32] The work comprised twelve books. Quintilian's rhetoric stressed the
technical strand by discussing artistic devices, the sophistic strand in educating
the speaker, and the philosophical strand in discussing how the art should be
employed for the good.

Quintilian endeavored in his work to combine educational and rhetorical
topics. For instance, as a teacher, he believed in the concept of *in loco parentis,*
wherein the teacher or college should act in place of the parent [II, 2, 5], and he
was against the practice of flogging students because schoolchildren could be easily victimized. (Those who favor corporal punishment or paddling in secondary
schools should especially read Book I, Chapter 3, paragraphs 13–18.) As a rhetorical theorist, he mainly transmitted the classical heritage: He accepted the five
canons of rhetoric and the three divisions of oratory, and he made only a few
minor adjustments to Cicero's status theory.

With regard to the five canons of rhetoric, Quintilian made a most saga-
cious observation when he held that the canons were interdependent. Before
Quintilian, one senses that a speaker invented arguments, then arranged them,
then styled them, then memorized them, and finally delivered them. Quintilian
seemed to suggest that an integral relationship existed among the canons, that
they were not so easily compartmentalized as other theorists might have implied.

Quintilian even went so far as to suggest that invention included arrangement [I, Prooemium, 22; III, 3, 2; VI, 5, 1].

Quintilian's greatest contribution to the study of rhetoric was his conception of the ideal orator. According to Quintilian "*Vir bonus dicendi peritus,*" (the good man skilled in speaking) was the ideal speaker. [IV:12,1] This was Marcus Cato's definition of the good speaker, and Quintilian stressed the "good man" part of the definition. Quintilian believed foremost that the speaker should be an ethical communicator with a firm moral character and knowledge of all that was just and honorable [XII, 2, 1]. Quintilian's conception was model, for there have been bad men skilled in speaking (Adolph Hitler, for example) and good men not skilled in speaking (President Herbert Hoover, for example). But the ideal has been attained, in the nineteenth century by Daniel Webster, perhaps the greatest American orator, and Elizabeth Cady Stanton, the leading women's rights advocate of the era, and in the twentieth century by President Franklin D. Roosevelt and Congresswoman Barbara Jordan. Indeed, Quintilian laid the intellectual groundwork for the modern liberal arts education that prepares the "good man" and for courses in speech that prepare men and women to be "skilled in speaking."

CLASSICAL INFLUENCES ON THE THREE STRANDS OF RHETORIC

Summarizing 400 years of classical rhetoric is a Herculean task. Yet it can be done by relating the classical influences on the three strands of rhetoric.

The Greek tradition, represented by Corax, the sophists, and the logographers, were interested primarily in how the speech persuaded an audience. They focused on the proofs for a speech, and they offered the classical organizational pattern as the best method to present the speaker's reasons. They also thought that the art of rhetoric was amoral.

Isocrates, Plato, and Aristotle were also committed to the sophistical strand in that they believed a speaker should be educated in what we would call the liberal arts. Rhetoric could be abused, but they preferred that the enlightened speaker would use persuasion ethically.

Plato took his concerns a step further into the realm of philosophical rhetoric. He envisioned that rhetoric should be used for only moral and truthful purposes. Aristotle agreed with Plato, but pragmatically conceived rhetoric itself to be amoral.

The Roman theorists seem to fall into two camps. They appear to have evolved, as the Greeks did, from technical to sophistical to philosophical rhetoric.

The author of the *Rhetorica ad Herennium* and the early Cicero were primarily concerned with the technical strand of rhetoric. Their contributions included the five canons of rhetoric, including a more complete analysis of style and delivery than the Greeks had offered.

The sophistical strand was exemplified by the later Cicero and then Quintilian. Both men were interested in the education and training of the speaker.

Quintilian was a Roman who gave considerable attention to the philsophi-
cal strand of rhetoric. He was not a Plato of the Roman world, but he did envision
that the well-trained and educated speaker should speak the truth.

Notes

1. George A. Kennedy, *Classical Rhetoric and Its Christian and Secular Tradition
    from Ancient to Modern Times* (Chapel Hill: The University of North Caro-
    lina Press, 1980), p. 16.
2. Ibid., p. 17.
3. Ibid.
4. Richard C. Jebb, *The Attic Orators* (London: Macmillan, 1876), I: cxxi; for a
    slightly diverging view, see George Kennedy, *The Art of Persuasion in Greece*
    (Princeton, N.J.: Princeton University Press, 1963), pp. 58–61.
5. For slightly different versions of this story, see Jebb, *The Attic Orators*,
    p. cxxii, and Kennedy, *The Art of Persuasion in Greece*, p. 59.
6. Jebb, *The Attic Orators*, pp. cxiv–cxvi; Harold Barrett, *The Sophists* (Novato,
    Calif.: Chandler and Sharp Publishers, 1987), pp. 9–14.
7. Barrett, *The Sophists*, pp. 21–22.
8. Kennedy, *The Art of Persuasion in Greece*, pp. 68–70; Barrett, *The Sophists*,
    pp. 23–25.
9. Kennedy, *Classical Rhetoric and Its Christian and Secular Tradition from
    Ancient to Modern Times*, pp. 31–35; James J. Murphy, "The Origins and
    Early Development of Rhetoric," in *A Synoptic History of Classical Rhetoric*,
    edited by James J. Murphy (Davis, Calif.: Hermagoras Press, 1983),
    pp. 12–15.
10. Isocrates, "Panegyricus," in *Isocrates*, 3 vols., translated by George Norlin
    (Cambridge: Harvard University Press, 1980), I: 164–165; Franklin D.
    Roosevelt, "First Inaugural Address," March 4, 1933, in *American Rhetoric
    from Roosevelt to Reagan: A Collection of Speeches and Critical Essays*, edited
    by Halford Ross Ryan (Prospect Heights, Ill.: Waveland Press, 1987), p. 4.
11. For a discussion of ghostwritten speeches, see Lois J. Einhorn, "The Ghosts
    Unmasked: A Review of Literature on Speech Writing," *Communication
    Quarterly* 30 (1981):41–47.
12. Kennedy, *The Art of Persuasion in Greece*, p. 128.
13. Kathleen Freeman, *The Murder of Herodes* (New York: W. W. Norton, 1963),
    p. 85.
14. Jebb, *The Attic Orators*, p. 159.
15. Freeman, *The Murder of Herodes*, p. 35.
16. Ibid., p. 53.

17. Ibid., pp. 37–38.

18. Plato, *Gorgias,* translated by W. C. Helmhold (Indianapolis: Bobbs-Merrill, 1952), pp. 11, 18, 15.

19. Ibid., pp. 25, 27.

20. Ibid., p. 79.

21. Ibid., pp. 79, 107.

22. Kennedy, *Classical Rhetoric,* p. 52.

23. Plato, *Phaedrus,* translated by W. C. Helmhold and W. G. Rabinowitz (Indianapolis: Bobbs-Merrill, 1956), p. 56.

24. Ibid., pp. 63–64, 72.

25. Kennedy, *Classical Rhetoric,* pp. 57–58.

26. See Kennedy, *The Art of Persuasion in Greece,* pp. 82–114; Kennedy, *Classical Rhetoric,* pp. 60–82. For a helpful topical outline and discussion of the treatise, see Forbes I. Hill, "The Rhetoric of Aristotle," in Murphy, *A Synoptic History of Classical Rhetoric,* pp. 19–76.

27. Aristotle, *Rhetoric,* translated by W. Rhys Roberts (New York: Modern Library, 1954), 1355b26. Hereafter citations to the *Rhetoric* will appear in brackets in the text.

28. "On the Execution Without Trial of Polemarchus," in Freeman, *The Murder of Herodes,* p. 62. This address, the only speech actually delivered by Lysias in a courtroom, was misquoted by Aristotle. Prosecuting Eratosthenes for the wrongful execution of Lysias's brother Polemarchus and the unlawful confiscation of his own property and money when the Thirty Tyrants— Eratosthenes was a member—briefly seized power in 404 B.C., Lysias actually said: "You have heard, you have seen, you have suffered, you wield the power. Deliver your verdict." Lysias demanded the death penalty, but it is doubtful that Eratosthenes was executed.

29. Kennedy, *The Art of Persuasion in Greece,* p. 86; Isocrates, *Helen* (Cambridge: Loeb Classical Library, 1945), III, 15; Aristotle, *Rhetoric,* 1358b10, 1358b16, 1368b1.

30. For a penetrating analysis, see *Cicero in Twenty Eight Volumes, I [Cicero] Rhetorica Ad Herennium,* translated by Harry Caplan (Cambridge: Harvard University Press, 1954), pp. vii–lviii. Hereafter, citations to this work— book, chapter, and section—will appear in brackets in the text.

31. Cicero, *De Optimo Genere Oratorum,* translated by H. M. Hubbell (Cambridge: Harvard University Press, 1976), I, 3, I, 12.

32. Quintilian, *Institutio Oratoria,* 4 vols., translated by H. E. Butler (Cambridge: Harvard University Press, 1979). Hereafter, citations to the book, chapter, and paragraph of this work will appear in brackets in the text.

Additional Readings

A student wishing to conduct further reading or research on classical rhetoric needs to start somewhere.

George Kennedy has written two books, which are arguably the best ones from a rhetorical point of view, on classical speakers, speeches, and theories. A perusal of Kennedy's footnotes and bibliography would greatly repay a student's research efforts.

Kennedy, George. *The Art of Persuasion in Greece.* Princeton, N.J.: Princeton University Press, 1963.

———. *The Art of Rhetoric in the Roman World.* Princeton, N.J.: Princeton University Press, 1972.

James J. Murphy edited a book containing six essays on the major figures and theorists in classical rhetoric. One will find especially helpful his Appendix B, which lists the basic bibliographical sources for Greek and Roman rhetoric.

A Synoptic History of Classical Rhetoric. Edited by James J. Murphy. Davis, Calif.: Hermagoras Press, 1983.

So many scholarly articles exist on classical rhetoric that it is not expedient to list them here. The student should consult the following excellent reference source:

Matlon, Ronald J. *Index to Journals in Communication Studies Through 1979.* Falls Church, Va.: Speech Communication Association, 1980.

Those who might enjoy reading a debate on whether one should or could use Aristotle as a basis for a textbook should see:

Brinton, Alan. "The Outmoded Psychology of Aristotle's Rhetoric." *Western Journal of Speech Communication* 54 (1990): 204–218.

Cronkhite, Gary. "Aristotle's Rhetoric as an Historical Artifact, Being a Response to the Suggestion It be Used as a Texbook." *Communication Education* 36 (1987): 286–289.

CHAPTER 2

Inventing the Speech

Aristotle (394–322 B.C.). A student of Plato, Aristotle taught in the Lyceum and wrote the *Rhetoric*, which identified logical, emotional, and ethical appeals in persuasive speaking.

From classical times to the present, the problems of what to say and how to say it have always vexed speakers. Whether invited to speak a few words at a meeting or assigned a speech to deliver in class, speakers have faced a triad of challenges: deciding what stance to take on the topic, composing and practicing the speech, and delivering the completed address before a live audience.

This chapter is about persuasion and supporting your speech with persuasive proofs. (These important subjects will be treated from a different perspective in Chapter 3.) In the first section of this chapter we shall discuss the relationship between the audience, the speech, and the speaker as they relate to persuasion. In the second section we shall discuss persuasive proof as it pertains to the speaker, the speech, and the audience.

PERSUASION

The Audience

We can start with the audience because persuasion is part of the philosophical strand of rhetoric that concentrates on what the audience ought to do. This section is audience centered: The focus is on moving the audience to a more truthful, just, and ethical position. Through the speech, the speaker conveys to the audience an urgent sense of moral duty.

Persuasion means to change an audience's values, attitudes, beliefs. Audiences have traditionally been divided into partisans, neutrals, and opponents. Of course, all the audience members may be partisan, neutral, or opponent on any given topic, but chances are that all three groups will be represented in most ordinary audiences. Let's talk about persuasion with each of these audience groups.

In the definition of persuasion, the infinitive *to change* is important. If you delivered an anti–death penalty speech to partisans, you could have three effects: (1) You might intensify their stand against the death penalty; (2) you might leave them about the way you found them; or (3) you might have the adverse effect of weakening their stand against the death penalty, or, in the worse case making them believe in it. With respect to change, you would have successfully persuaded in the first instance; in the second instance, you could claim some small success by maintaining that if they did not turn toward your position, at least they did not turn away from it; but in the third instance you would have failed.

If you gave the same speech to neutrals, you would have succeeded if you moved them, however slightly, toward your position; you could claim some success if they remained more-or-less neutral; but you would have failed if they decided to believe in the death penalty.

If you gave the same speech to opponents, you would have succeeded beyond your wildest imaginings if you moved even a few listeners even a little bit away from their old beliefs toward your position; you could optimistically claim some success if the opponents at least did not change their views; but you would have failed to persuade those who became even more in favor of the death penalty.

Persuasion also means to change an audience's behavior. By intensifying a proponent's commitment to the cause, for example, you could motivate an otherwise passive person to sign a petition. Speakers can measure their success in this area by how many listeners sign a protest letter against some policy, or consent to donate to the blood drive, or vote in a meeting for a proposal that you have advocated, or signed an organ donor card.

When choosing a topic and deciding how to persuade on that topic, the speaker must give attention to a thoughtful analysis of the audience. The speaker should at least attempt to determine how many of the potential audience members are partisans, neutrals, and opponents.

Whether in beliefs or actions, persuasion results when some change occurs. It may be that you did not change the audience's beliefs as much as you wanted to, but change them you did. As for those who neither changed to your position nor moved to a counter position, you could claim success if you perceive the proverbial glass of water to be half full, hence success, rather than to be half empty, hence failure.

It would be even better to understand something about these people and why they hold their positions. Ideally, the speaker will know a great deal about the audience.

In the *Phaedrus*, Plato wisely required a speaker to understand the audience, its attitudes, beliefs, and values. Nowadays, the usual advice is to rely on audience demographics, including geographical area, urban versus rural location, religious affiliation, socioeconomic status, and political preference. But unless the speaker is privy to highly accurate demographic information, he or she runs a grave risk of stereotyping people on one or more of the above criteria.

Indeed, a serious pragmatic and philosophical problem immediately arises when stereotyping college audiences in the guise of **audience analysis.** Although it is unlikely in most college classrooms, assume anyway that you will address a highly homogenous audience. But an audience of nursing students, for example, will not necessarily favor euthanasia, be against abortion, or even want to hear speeches on those subjects. And would-be engineers will not necessarily want to hear only speeches on the tensile strengths of various kinds of steel, and education majors may not be uninterested in the economy of the country. "Liberals" might be conservative on a given issue, and vice versa.

Although you should be aware of the ethical ramifications of stereotyping listeners on the basis of demographic audience analysis, you can study the audience. As the term progresses and you hear other's speeches, you can begin to draw some inferences about their value systems. As you listen to comments from the class, you can start to contour the beliefs of the audience. As you listen to reactions to your speeches, you can attempt to assess in a meaningful manner why members of the audience responded in the way they did.

The following method is not scientific, but it is nevertheless a viable way for you to begin to learn how to analyze an audience. Assume you want to address a controversial issue. You might ask your classmates to fill in a short questionnaire stating their attitudes on the topic, why they held those beliefs, how committed they were to them, and what kind of reasons might help them to change their minds. For instance, if you wanted to propose a flat-rate federal income tax system, you might find that members of your audience had reservations about the rich getting off too lightly, the poor paying too heavily, and the middle class paying the bulk; many might worry about fairness; and some might want to know what the flat-rate would have to be to raise the same amount as the present system. Armed with this kind of audience analysis, you could then decide how to appeal to the various members of your class.

In the classroom one can assess success of the speech by having the instructor ask how many changed their minds toward the speaker's position, how many stayed about the same, and how many actually changed their minds in the opposite direction from that intended by the speaker. In addition to a showing of hands, you can ask students to fill in a shift-of-opinion ballot that indicates their opinions before and after the speech. Students can also state briefly why they were persuaded or why not and, perhaps, what kind of appeals might make them change their minds. Class discussions after a speech often reveal degrees of persuasion, and individual students may be honest enough to say why they changed their opinion (one way or the other) or remained the same.

When examining how the audience is moved, we turn to the speech itself, which exemplifies the technical strand of rhetoric.

The Speech

From Corax to Cicero and Quintilian, the ancients realized that a speech usually had to appeal to a diverse audience. They adapted to this heterogeneity in most audiences by recommending an arguments section and a refutation in the classical organizational pattern. They fashioned these two sections to meet the persuasive needs of the audience.

The confirmation supported the persuasive thesis. To extend the above discussion of the anti–capital punishment speech, the speaker creates arguments that should reinforce partisans, lure neutrals, and at least make opponents stop and think. In terms of audience analysis, the speaker could poll the class to get a sense of the proponents, neutrals, and opponents.

A speaker should conduct research and find several arguments against capital punishment. Perhaps some of these will be suggested by polling the class. The reasons might include: (1) Innocent people have been executed; (2) males and blacks seem to be executed disproportionately to their numbers; (3) executions do not deter murderers; and (4) executions debase the society that they were meant to cleanse. Proponents probably believe most or all of these four arguments. Neutrals, as well as opponents, might be changed to your position if you could support your arguments with evidence. Research will demonstrate cases where guilty parties have confessed after an innocent person was executed; statistics will provide the facts for the second argument; the third argument might be proven by comparing the murder rates of contiguous states with and without capital punishment; and one can quote religious and political figures to back up the fourth assertion.

The refutation section in the speech is aimed at the neutrals and the opponents. Perhaps opponents mentioned some reasons that you had not thought of—this is another help in studying your audience. On the basis of what you learned from your informal inquiry, you could try to shame the audience by demonstrating that countries such as the Soviet Union, South Africa, and the Arab countries still have capital punishment, while the western European countries have banned executions, and asking in which league the United States wishes to stand. It might appeal to those whose bottom line is the dollar to demonstrate that because of the long appeals process and expensive lawyer's fees, life imprisonment may actually be cheaper than execution.

The pro–capital punishment speaker can also appeal to the three segments in the audience. One can argue that revenge on cold-blooded murderers is a catharsis for society; that death is the ultimate punishment; and that executed criminals will never commit another murder or assassination. In the refutation, such a speaker might claim that the number of innocent persons executed is not enough to balance the good of executing heinous criminals; that society can afford the extra cost of executions, and that statistics can be made to prove anything.

The point is that the speech should be tailored to the audience for the desired effect. It is unrealistic to think that your analysis and study of the audience will reveal every facet of every member's beliefs, but mapping your listener's values is better than flying blind. We turn now to the person who makes those rhetorical adaptations to the audience—the speaker.

The Speaker

The speaker is the driving force behind the speech. In Aristotelian terms the speaker persuades by revealing good sense, good moral character, and goodwill. This means that the speaker must marshall the best evidence that he or she can discover; find the most moving examples to stir the audience's emotions; and present him- or herself as a speaker as a reasonable and "good" person. The speaker who is trained in the technical strand of rhetoric determines how the speech will move the audience through audience analysis and rhetorical proof.

Purpose   In a sense, it is too simplistic to assert that a speaker has a purpose. In reality, a speaker has at least three purposes that are related to the three factions in a given audience. Let's take a purpose: to persuade against the death penalty. In making a speech against capital punishment the speaker actually has three persuasive purposes. Although related, the purposes are distinct: (1) to intensify or reinforce partisans; (2) to move neutrals toward the speaker's position, or at least constrain them from joining the opposition; and (3) to entice opponents to join the cause. Thus, we are reminded of Plato's observation that the speaker should invent arguments to appeal to the diverse minds in the audience.

Ethics   There is a problem with rhetoric that Plato understood very well. It represents the tension between technical rhetoric aimed at success and philosophical rhetoric that has a moral purpose. At times these two strands of rhetoric can be at loggerheads. Should the speaker tell the audience what they want to hear even if it will have bad consequences? A man won the presidency twice in the 1980s by telling the people what they wanted to hear, but now most citizens are paying the price. (If Plato were here, he would say, "I told you so.")

Should the speaker avoid discussing topics that are unpopular or disagreeable to the audience? In such instances, meaningful persuasion can occur, but it is certainly hard work. Take the early women speakers who addressed Americans on women's rights. Female speakers like Lucretia Mott, Elizabeth Cady Stanton, and Sojourner Truth had the dual tasks of persuading their audiences—both men and women—not only that women should have the full constitutional rights of citizenship granted to males but also that women could and should speak out in public about the question. They delivered their speeches under the most trying conditions, yet they persevered. Some of America's greatest speakers—Eugene Debs, a socialist who spoke for social and economic rights for workers in the early twentieth century; the Reverend Harry Emerson Fosdick, who against heavy conservative odds helped shape modern Christianity; and the Reverend Martin Luther King, Jr., who encountered much hostility in his drive to give black American people the right to vote and to end racial discrimination—delivered disagreeable messages to a sizeable portion of the population. Debs was imprisoned for his rhetoric and Martin Luther King, Jr., paid the ultimate price. Yet, their willingness to discuss disagreeable topics and take unpopular stands is in the best tradition of philosophical rhetoric.

The speaker also has an ethical obligation to the audience to reveal the sources of the argumentation. Interestingly enough, giving an oral citation of the sources that one has researched increases one's credibility. Continuing our example of the anti–capital punishment speech, most people would be more persuaded by statistics and testimony from articles in legal journals than by unsubstantiated assertions. Saying something like, "Prof. Knowalot, writing in the XYZ *Legal Journal* in 1986, stated that . . . ," not only supports the persuasive claim with evidence, but also demonstrates the speaker's trustworthiness. It further shows that the speaker had the good sense to do some research on the topic and communicates the speaker's good will toward the audience by exhibiting that he or she has in mind the best intellectual interests of the listeners.

Giving oral citations of one's researched evidence can be accomplished smoothly and convincingly. "According to yesterday's *Washington Post* . . . ," "In an article on taxation in the April 1987 *National Review*, we learned that . . . ," "If you doubt this point, listen to what the authors of the economics textbook used on this campus have to say . . . ," and "To give you a sense of the problem, let me quote some startling facts from *Facts on File*. . . . "

As the speaker should articulate truth to the audience, the listener should require truth from the persuader. Wise listeners should require from a speaker some citations of research conducted before they give credence to the speaker's persuasive stance. If the speaker lacks reasons and evidence for his or her position, the astute listener would rightly question that deficiency. A listener might also reasonably assume that the speaker does not possess the requisite credibility for one to assent to his or her persuasive intent.

Persuasive Proof   It is difficult to determine beforehand whether a persuasive proof will actually convince a listener. One can make some educated guesses and make some reasonable assumptions about what would persuade people, but the outcome is always open to question. This fact is nowhere better illustrated than in political campaigns. There, with the best polling devices, advisers, and speech writers that money can buy, presidential candidates float trial balloons, try out different appeals, and generally waffle on issues until public opinion reacts favorably or unfavorably to their appeals. The successful appeals are retained, and the unsuccessful ones are dropped. Doubtless this abuse of audience analysis is one of the factors that continually turns voters off in elections. But the point is that persuasion is an art, and one cannot guarantee that any particular appeal will work.

Yet, within the liberal arts context of the college classroom, it is possible to theorize in general about what will convince the audience. Within the context of educated and thoughtful persons, the rational or reasonable audience paradigm assumes that prudent listeners want to hear proofs rather than assertions; that arguments supported by sound sources are usually more compelling than those from questionable or highly biased origins; that listeners are willing to suspend judgment on highly controversial topics until they have heard a presentation; and that the audience respects the speaker's right to address them with the understanding that judicious people can agree to disagree.

PERSUASION AND PROOF

The immediate impetus for giving a speech in class will be an assignment. It is impossible to foresee here all of the kinds of assignments that can be made, for they vary from school to school and from teacher to teacher. Nevertheless, in choosing a topic to fulfill an assignment, students should remember that persuasion is created by the confluence of the speaker's purpose and the speech's proof.

Choosing a Topic

In his "Cotton States Exposition Address," in Atlanta in 1895, Booker T. Washington urged Southern blacks to "Cast down your buckets where you are." This metaphor is still serviceable to the student speaker. If you cast down your bucket where you are, you will often find speech topics that interest you, that you already know something about, and about which you would like to persuade others.

You might consider issues from subjects in your major or minor courses of study, such as whether the U.S. should have a progressive income tax or a flat-rate tax. Experiences from your summer employment may lead you to argue for or against labor unions, an increased minimum wage, or more work-related or real-world courses in college. An editorial that you read recently may spur you to speak for or against it, or a book that engaged you could be the departure point for a persuasive speech.

Perhaps you would like to discuss a topic that you do not know so much about, but about which you would profit from learning and the class from hearing. Are there campus issues or local, state, national, and international problems that need persuasive solutions? What are the persuasive roles of televised presidential campaign debates? Along these lines, brainstorming with a few friends may help you discover some interesting subjects. In any event, you would do well to write down several tentative topics and then seek the advice of your professor on their relative merits.

"There are no bad speech topics," an old saw says, "just bad speeches." If there is any truth to that aphorism, it surely lies in how one adapts a speech to one's audience.

After you have several topics in mind, you next need to consider the speech assignment more closely. Two factors may help you narrow your list of topics: (1) the nature of the assignment and (2) the availability of research materials.

The nature of the assignment may eliminate some of your ideas. If, for instance, the assignment was a speech to sell, your interest in how bereaved individuals are manipulated by funeral directors should be saved for a later speech. On the other hand, your hobby of photography may help you sell a camera to the class. If you are assigned a problem-solution speech, your work in a regional conservation club may help you with a speech on preventing acid rain.

The availability of materials and sources for research may also constrain your choice of topics. As a "good person speaking well," you will want to present facts, statistics, information, specific examples, and opinions from knowledgeable experts as evidence for your claims. The materials that you research will function as logical appeals, but they will also increase your credibility with the audience.

As you sort through your list of ideas, you may find that the library has more books or articles on some topics than on others. A good place to get a sense of the materials available on your subject matter is to consult some standard reference sources. The *Reader's Guide to Periodical Literature* will help you locate sources in news magazines and other periodical publications. The *Index to the New York Times* is particularly helpful for conducting background research. The *Congressional Digest* contains pro and con information on debatable topics. And of course you can easily search the subject headings in the library's card or on-line catalog. Do not overlook the reference librarian, who is there to help you.

Adapting the Speech to the Audience's Knowledge

Most speech assignments have some parameters of length that must be observed. Usually the speeches are shorter in the beginning of the course and longer toward the end of the term. Obviously, you should select a topic that can be covered in an appropriate manner in the assigned time. But how do you do that?

One of the major difficulties speakers encounter is the problem of limiting the topic. In this instance audience analysis is more concerned with what the speaker thinks the audience does or does not know, than what the audience's politics might be. The analogy of the microscope helps explain the problem. If you use a ten power microscope, you see more in the field of vision, but you do not see much detail. The higher the power of magnification, the more you see in detail but the less you see in the field of vision. In selecting a speech topic, you want to obtain the optimal mix of scope and focus to adapt your speech to the audience.

Assume you had ten minutes to address the class, and assume two potential topics, such as (1) President John F. Kennedy was assassinated by two riflemen rather than just by Lee Harvey Oswald; and (2) the federal government covered up the savings and loan (S&L) scandal. You could reasonably assume that your audience has at least a passing knowledge (scope) of the S&L scandal, so you could develop the topic in more detail and depth (focus). This would entail giving specific examples of government officials who were guilty of mis- or malfeasance. For the JFK topic, however, you might have to allot more time to the background data of the Warren Commission, which investigated Kennedy's death. This would enable the audience to understand the focus of your speech, which is to illustrate that two shots could hardly have been fired so rapidly by one man. In general, when the audience already has a broad knowledge of the subject, you can focus more narrowly on details of the topic. But when the audience is probably unfamiliar with the topic, it is probably best to keep the scope wide and the focus less detailed.

Suppose you decide to use your persuasive credibility, which you established in a summer job, to instruct the class on how banks process checks. You cannot assume that the class knows the technical terms that you had to learn on your job but that you now take for granted. Rather, focus on the details of the process as much as you can, but make sure you define and illustrate any unusual terms so that the audience understands the scope of your topic. Similarly, you can demonstrate your competence to sell a camera by discussing film speeds, aperture openings, shutter speeds, and zoom lenses. But make certain that the audience understands (would visual aids help here?) what film speeds, shutter speeds, and so on are. Only then can you make them understand the intricacies of the camera you want to sell and that it is the best buy.

Increasing the Value of the Class   If you give it some thought, you will probably listen to more speeches during this term than you have heard in your lifetime. If everyone gives five speeches, and there are about twenty students in the class, you will hear one hundred speeches (you also have to listen to yourself). With that fact in mind you can contribute a great deal to the educational and philosophical value of the class.

The point can be illustrated with a few examples. These examples also illustrate how to adapt the subject to the audience. You want to speak about acid rain. Would the class be more interested in the effects of acid rain nationwide or on the plants and buildings in the campus environment? You are concerned about date rape. The statistics are chilling enough, but would the class benefit more from learning what your campus is or is not doing about the problem and what measures an individual can take to be part of the solution rather than the problem? Toxic waste always seems to be in somebody else's backyard; is it also in yours? Do people in the class *really* understand how radar works or how it helped win the Battle of Britain in World War II? And how do honeybees, who often range over miles in search of flowers, know how to get back to the hive and communicate to other bees where the succulent flowers are? Should senators and representatives be limited to two terms as the president is? The more probing, provocative, and pressing the topics that you select, research, and deliver the more stimulating and rewarding the class will be for everyone involved.

Selecting the topic is probably the hardest part in a modern course on public speaking. In classical times, students debated *controversiae* (controversies) that were given them by the master. Students could select whether they wished to prosecute or defend on such issues as: "If a guest dies of overeating, is the host responsible?" "If one urged a friend to travel by ship, and the friend drowned when the ship sunk, is the person responsible for the death?" Modern pedagogical methods allow students the freedom to choose a persuasive topic, a chore that was not required of students in ancient times. But with that freedom to choose your persuasive stance comes the opportunity to discuss topics that are meaningful to you, that can be cast into a persuasive speech, and that can have some effect on your audience. Once you have a topic, and have conducted your own original research on it, you are ready to go to the next chapter on how to write the speech.

CHAPTER 3

Arranging the Speech

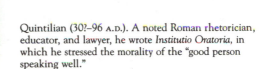

Quintilian (30?–96 A.D.). A noted Roman rhetorician, educator, and lawyer, he wrote *Institutio Oratoria*, in which he stressed the morality of the "good person speaking well."

According to the ancients, the organization of a speech mattered greatly. As we have seen, clarity was important because if the audience did not understand the speech, it could not be persuaded. Therefore, the purpose of this chapter is to enable you to write a working draft that conforms to the organizational patterns of persuasive speaking.

A BASIC ORGANIZATIONAL STRATEGY

The simplest way to organize a speech is to divide it into three parts. These parts are the introduction, the body or discussion, and the conclusion. This tripartite arrangement is useful for instructing listeners because it organizes the speech in a straightforward fashion.

The Introduction

When you first meet someone, you tend to size up the person quickly and then decide whether you like that individual. Your initial estimation might change, but first impressions have a strong effect. An audience similarly assesses a speaker. It appraises rapidly what it hears and what it sees. So you want to make the strongest possible initial impression on the audience. The purposes of the speech introduction, as suggested by Cicero, are to gain the audience's attention, to make it receptive to the message, and to obtain its goodwill. The introduction is also a good place for the speaker to begin demonstrating to the audience his or her good sense, goodwill, and good moral character, the factors in Aristotle's conception of ethos.

The following techniques can be used to introduce the speech. As you consider them, you need to reflect which technique would best fit the needs of the speaking situation. In prefacing the speech, you can use one of, or some workable combination of, the following methods:

Refer to the Previous Speaker "In the last speech round, Cindy talked about campaigns, especially the need for campaign financing reform. Taking her concern one step forward, I would like to look at three ways that experts believe would improve political campaign debates." When referring to the previous speaker, you are able to tap the goodwill that the audience had for that person and transfer it to you and your message. You might also be able to build on the information that the previous speaker already gave the audience, and thus delve deeper into the focus of the speech.

Refer to the Occasion "Most of you here today probably don't know the significance of the eleventh hour of the eleventh day of the eleventh month, but all Americans used to know the meaning of that phrase." The occasion often offers opportunities for you to increase audience receptivity. In marking the occasion, the speaker can appeal to shared expectations and common reasons for the audience's assembling to mark the event.

Refer to the Purpose In 1969 Spiro Agnew, vice president under President Richard Nixon, opened his famous attack on the news media by immediately broaching the topic: "Tonight I want to discuss the importance of the television news media to the American people." Here Agnew adroitly fused the speaker, the speech, and the audience. As vice president, he probably already had his audience's attention because of his ethos from the office. He skillfully alluded to the news media, which was blamed at the time for President Nixon's bad press on the Vietnam War, in order to make certain people receptive to the speech. As Americans, the audience would be desirous to listen to a speech on such an important topic from such an important public figure.

Compliment the Audience A reporter once monitored all the speeches of a U.S. senatorial candidate and determined that the candidate told every audience he faced that of all the audiences he had been looking forward to addressing, this audience was his most memorable and favorite one. Most people conceive themselves as the best and the brightest, so they rarely object if the speaker lays on compliments with a trowel.

Use Humor Carefully It's not necessarily a good idea to "start with a joke." If you do decide to use humor in your introduction, make sure it is (1) funny, (2) acceptable to the audience (in good taste), and (3) relevant to your topic.

Refer to the Place   Although a classroom is not Faneuil Hall, the U.S. Senate, or Gettysburg Cemetery, occasionally an opportunity will arise in which you can refer to your physical surroundings, their historical significance, or their symbolic importance to you or the audience in a way that will associate with the topic. For instance, General Douglas MacArthur addressed a joint session of Congress in 1951, to defend himself against his firing by President Truman. MacArthur referred to the place, and also trowelled on the compliments to his Congressional audience:

I stand on this rostrum with a sense of deep humility and great pride— humility in the wake of those great American architects of our history who have stood here before me, pride in the reflection that this home of legislative debate represents human liberty in the purest form yet devised.

Use a Quotation   With the source in hand, you can arrest attention by quoting from a poem, play, speech, book, song lyric, or aphorism that is germane to your speech. If the quotation is commonplace, you can trade on the audience's receptivity to the familiar by mentioning the person who made the statement and then quote the statement. But another way to do it —and this is especially useful if the quotation is not well known—is to recite the quotation first and then, after a brief pause that can excite the audience's interest, give the attribution. This is a good method to gain the audience's attention because it has to listen to determine who originally made the statement.

Use a Rhetorical Question   A **rhetorical question** is defined as a question so phrased that the audience supplies the obvious answer to itself. The rhetorical question is an excellent example of Aristotle's idea of the enthymeme. For instance, Senator Huey Long, speaking during the Depression for his Share the Wealth Society, began his "Every Man a King" radio speech with a rhetorical question. He analyzed the anger that his audience felt about the Depression, and he tapped that anger thus: "Is that a right of life, when the young children of this country are being reared into a sphere which is more owned by 12 men than it is by 120,000,000 people?" Huey knew the radio audience would answer "No!" and would therefore listen in order to learn how to soak the rich. Consider how the rhetorical question displayed Long's apparent good sense that the U.S should not be owned by twelve men; his goodwill toward everybody but the twelve men; and his good moral character in championing the many poor against the few rich.

However, it is generally not a good idea to ask an open-ended question in the introduction, because it is difficult to determine how the audience members will respond. When a student introduced a speech by asking how many classmates saw a recent movie, and only a small number raised their hands, the effect of the question was spoiled. Because so few could relate to the movie, it was immediately apparent to the audience that they would have trouble relating to the student's point. Moreover, it was an example of poor audience analysis. Another problem with the open-ended "raise your hand" question is that if the question is controversial most people will be reluctant to raise their hands without knowing the speaker's position. Will they be made fun of, or would they rather keep their views private? In any case, the effect falls flat and calls into question the speaker's good sense in beginning in such a maladroit fashion.

Maintain a Mystery Sometimes the introduction can be constructed to pique an audience's attention by involving it in solving an enigma, making it wait expectantly for the resolution of a mystery. For instance, one student slyly began an informative speech this way: "We all want it. But most of us can't get enough of it. It's intrinsically worth nothing. Yet you can go to jail for making it. It's the only thing that even though its value decreases, it remains the same. Only half of it is green, and it's not printed on paper. It is [slight pause to stir expectation] the almighty dollar."

Obviously, one or more of these techniques could be combined to introduce your address. A humorous quotation, a mystery surrounding the occasion or place, or any other workable combination could be used for a forceful introduction.

Adjusting Language

After you have secured the audience's attention and good will in the initial phase of the introduction, you need to adjust the audience to your speech and your speech to the audience.

The function of this adjustment is to orient the audience to your main points, to preview the structure of the address, to adjust the organization to the listener. This adjusting language helps the audience be receptive to your message because it forecasts for the audience the order of your speech. The adjusting process is comprised of language that acclimates and adapts the audience to the structure of the address. The following examples illustrate adjustment language that might be used with the sample introductions quoted above under "Refer to the previous speaker" and "Refer to the occasion."

Most experts agree that political campaign debates can be strengthened. They advocate removing the press, (slight vocal pause to let it sink in), letting the candidates control the issues (another slight pause), and having longer speeches. Those are the three topics I'll be talking about today, and I'll begin by examining the role of the media as an impediment to the debating process.

Well, all of those elevens that I just asked you about mean 11:00 A.M., November 11, 1918, which was Armistice Day for World War I. What Armistice Day was (slight vocal pause) and why we no longer celebrate it (slight pause) are the two topics that concern us this afternoon. Let's first examine what Armistice Day was.

Vice President Agnew adjusted his speech attacking the media to the audience and the audience to his speech by using two rhetorical questions that cued his main heads. "The question is, Are we demanding enough of our television new presentations? And are the men of this medium demanding enough of themselves?" Notice how the rhetorical questions were strategically stated so as to elicit an answer of "No" even before the audience heard the speech. This speech had the desired effect of making the press more docile toward President Nixon's policy in Vietnam.

After you have garnered the audience's attention and adjusted it to the address, you move to the body of your speech.

The Body

The body contains the main discussion or major part of the speech. It traditionally comprises the speech's principal points or ideas, which are termed the *main heads* of the address. These main heads serve two purposes:

1. They help you organize the address.
2. They help the audience understand your speech as it is spoken.

The main heads flow directly from the adjusting language that foretold what the main ideas would be. In assisting the audience to grasp the main heads of the speech, organizational patterns help make the main ideas clear and understandable. The topical, space, and time patterns are straightforward ways to present the main heads in a persuasive speech.

The Topical Pattern   The topical pattern is useful when a subject can be subdivided easily into its constituent parts. Speeches about things, processes, concepts, theories, mechanisms, philosophies, and so forth are normally presented topically.

A speech about diamonds could be topically organized around the 4 Cs: color, cutting, clarity, and carat weight. Each main idea would be devoted to one of the Cs: the color of a diamond, ranging from the absence of color to a yellow tint; the cutting of a diamond, which needs exact proportions; the clarity of a diamond, which ranges from no imperfections when viewed under a microscope to those that can be seen by the naked eye; and the carat weight, which determines the size of the jewel.

The Space Pattern   Sometimes an address is more efficaciously presented when spatial relationships are the controlling factors. For example, what makes it increasingly difficult to drive in New York City, Boston, and Washington, D.C., is perhaps not so much the volume of the traffic or the nature of the drivers as how their respective streets were originally and historically planned. A speech about how the different parts of a university campus are integrated into a working institution would use the space pattern, as would a talk on the architectural functions of the parts of a cathedral.

Speeches about sea, air, and land battles often employ the spatial pattern to clarify for the audience what happened where. For instance, in discussing the Battle of Jutland during World War I, you could use the topical pattern to discuss the ship and armaments of the British and German fleets. But if you wanted to demonstrate how the British battleships obtained their tactical advantage over the German fleet, you would use the spatial pattern. Keep in mind that visual aids are useful in a speech using the spatial pattern.

The Time Pattern   If you were interested in tracing how some people come to say "neither," as in *eye*, rather than "neither" as in *key*, you would organize your speech according to how and why people changed the pronunciation over time.

Choosing a Pattern   Any of the three patterns can be used for a speech on any topic. For example, a speech on what happens as a tooth decays could use the topical pattern if you wanted to detail chemical interactions; the spatial pattern if you wanted to focus on the parts of the tooth that decay; or the time pattern if you wanted to indicate the relative time that it takes for the various stages of the tooth to decompose.

The pattern you select for your topic can help you control your scope and focus. You could use one main head in the topical pattern to treat the scope of the national AIDS crisis, and then focus deeper, in the two or three remaining main heads, on its prevalence in your community. You could use the spatial pattern to discuss in very general terms the universe, or narrow it considerably to discuss the major stars in the Big Dipper. And you could use the time pattern to compare early feminist speakers, who used arguments from justice (it was a woman's right as an American citizen to vote), to later feminists, who often used arguments from expediency (give women the right to vote and they will use it to join with men to press for prohibition of alcohol).

Outlining the Body of the Speech   Once you have decided what pattern you will use, you need to invent the main heads of your speech. A topical speech would require the appropriate constituent parts. A spatial speech would be divided according to the geography employed. And a time speech would probably be organized around some chronology. As a sample talk, let's continue building the speech about political campaign debate reform. As an outline, the speech could take this form for the main heads:

I.   The media interferes with the debating format.
    A.   The journalists ask the questions and set the agenda.
    B.   Journalists are "soft" and "hard" on candidates.
II. The candidates should control the debatable issues.
    A.   They are running for office, not the media.

    B. There would be more direct clash on the real issues.

    C. For self-interest, candidates could not "duck" issues.

  III. The candidates need to give longer statements and responses.

    A. Short speeches oversimplify pressing problems.

    B. Longer responses are needed to answer complex questions.

The topic need not be divided into three main ideas; it could just as easily be two or four. The major consideration is how many main heads, plus supporting points, you can fit into the assigned time period.

After you develop the main heads, you need to go back and expand them. This is the point at which you support your arguments with your research:

    I.   The media interferes with the debating format.

      A. The journalists ask the questions and set the agenda.

        1. Mr. X, writing in the *New York Times*, October 10, 1989, stated: "...."

        2. For example, some of the questions reflect the journalist's interests rather than the people's concerns. Take the following quoted examples from the second debate....

Notice how the speaker communicated ethos in this main head: the credibility is enhanced by citing the researched sources that reinforce the speaker's thesis. The quotations may also reinforce partisans and sway the neutrals and opponents in the audience.

      B. Journalists are "soft" and "hard" on candidates.

        1. This fact is easily grasped. Listen to the soft questions that were addressed to presidential candidate X: .... Compare these to the difficult questions that were put to Y: .... The implications are that, depending on what journalist a candidate gets, the candidate can get off easily or be made to appear uninformed, unimaginative, or ignorant. This view is also supported by Mr. Z, political commentator for the *Washington Post*, who wrote: "...."

Here the speaker demonstrates good sense in using specific quoted examples from the debates to bolster the point and clinching the argument with another credible source. The speaker also demonstrated a good moral character by appealing to the values of fair play and equality, which the audience supports but which were not practiced in the debate to the detriment of one of the candidates.

To help the audience progress from one main head to the next you need a transition. This is another aspect of the oral or conversational style that helps adjust the audience to the address.

A transitional device can be an internal summary or a preview. An internal summary for the first main head in the speech we are developing could be: "To recapitulate, journalists set the debate's agenda and you saw that hard and soft questions were unfairly asked." A preview might be: "Let's now focus our attention on my second complaint, which is that the candidates should debate their own issues."

You would continue through each of the main heads, supplying supporting points and the transitional devices to take the listeners through the body of the speech until you reach the conclusion. In terms of scope and focus, most speeches should not exceed four or five main heads.

The Conclusion

If you have ever heard a speech in which the speaker suddenly stopped talking without warning, you understand the importance of concluding the speech. That speaker did not follow Aristotle's advice to make the audience disposed toward the speaker and to refresh the audience's memory. Whereas a strong introduction achieves the primacy effect (the strong impression made by first arguments), a good conclusion achieves the recency effect (the lasting impression of recent arguments). The impression that a speaker makes at the end of the speech will linger in the minds of the listeners; hence, the more potent the conclusion, the more compelling the rhetorical result.

Several techniques can strengthen the recency effect of your speech:

Challenge the Audience Having presented the speech, a wise speaker can invite the audience to change its mind or to take some action. Thus challenged, the audience is more likely to do as the speaker asks; unchallenged, the audience is likely to do nothing. For instance, in concluding his "My Side of the Story" speech in 1952, Senator Richard Nixon challenged the audience to wire and write the Republican National Committee asking it to retain him on the ticket. Senator Huey Long, who championed the poor during the Depression, requested that his radio audience enroll in the Share the Wealth societies that he was organizing throughout the nation. If the audience does take the requested action, this is an overt sign of a successful persuasive address.

Use a Quotation As in the case of the introduction, you could end your talk with a quotation from the same, or a different but similar, source. Beginning and ending your speech with a quotation gives it an artistic unity.

Summarize the Speech The simplest way to conclude a speech is merely to summarize the main heads in the body. Thus, the recapitulation repeats the main ideas once again in the hope that the audience will remember most of them. For the speech on reforming political campaign debates, a summary could be: "In conclusion, I would like to restate my major points: that the media intrudes in the debate, that the candidates alone should state the debatable issues, and that the candidates need to give longer speeches."

Round Out the Speech When using this technique, the speaker uses a few short sentences to end the speech quickly. The impact comes from the terseness and vigor of the words, when the audience might have expected a longer conclusion. One of the best uses of rounding out the speech was in a speech meant to induce the audience to quit smoking. Instead of the emotional appeals that you might expect, the speaker dramatically concluded: "This evening I have told you that you should stop smoking. I did. I hope you will, too." The brevity had a positive force because there was quiet, rather than the usual background noise, in the audience for a few seconds after the speaker stopped talking.

Oral signposts can also help the audience to discern that the speech is being concluded. You could say "In conclusion," "In summation," "Looking back," "To reiterate what I was saying," and "In closing." You could pause briefly just long enough to get most eyes fixed on you—the audience might wonder if you forgot your speech or what is happening—and, having garnered the audience's attention, you could conclude. Or you could raise or lower your voice, speak slower or faster, or use a combination of these techniques.

You could also intensify the verbal conclusion by combining it with a nonverbal signal. For instance, you could move to the right or left of the lectern to signal your conclusion. You could step backward from the lectern to draw the audience to you, or lean forward slightly over the speaker's stand to confront the audience. Or you could make some gesture, like folding your glasses and putting them away, gathering your notes, closing the book you quoted from, or buttoning your jacket or coat.

Timing and Checking the Parts of the Speech

In terms of allocating time for the introduction, body, and conclusion, certain guidelines are appropriate. These are merely suggestions, not fixed rules. Assume a six-minute speech. If you take a minute or so for the introduction and about the same time for the conclusion, you'll have about four minutes for the body, which is the major part of the speech. For a longer speech, you would merely scale up the proportions.

At a reasonable rate of speaking, a double-spaced typewritten page equals about one and one-half minutes of speaking time. When in doubt about time limits as you compose the speech, read aloud what you have written and time it: That is the surest way to know whether you have written enough to fill your time.

As you check over your rough draft, make certain you have fulfilled the organizational requirements of the basic persuasive speech. Verify the following requirements:

Your introduction contains one or more of the techniques to gain attention, and it has adjusting language.

Your main heads are clearly and cogently organized according to one of the speech patterns.

You have used transitional language (a summary or preview) between each main head.

Your speech ends with one of the concluding devices discussed above.

CLASSICAL ORGANIZATIONAL STRATEGIES

The organizational patterns, like the one developed by Corax and amended by Aristotle and Cicero, are rhetorical blueprints. They give the speech not only a particular form but also indicate to the speaker the kinds of materials that should be used in the different sections of the speech. Baldly stated, these patterns indicate what to say and where to say it.

The patterns that will be discussed in this section are the **classical pattern,** the **method of residues,** the **Burkeian pattern,** the **problem solution pattern,** and the **Monroe motivated sequence.** Of these patterns, only the classical pattern was developed by the ancients to organize an entire speech. Intended primarily for forensic speaking, the classical pattern is readily adaptable to all the persuasive speeches that a student may deliver. The method of residues, although not developed expressly by the ancients as a speech pattern, can nevertheless be traced to classical logic and rhetoric. The Burkeian pattern, although never intended by its modern author to be used as a speech pattern, has nevertheless been used for persuasive purposes. The problem solution pattern and the Monroe motivated sequence, although modern patterns, should not be rejected on the grounds of their newness.

The Classical Pattern

Corax invented the classical pattern. It had five parts:

Introduction
Narrative
Arguments
Refutation
Conclusion

You will remember that the author of the *Rhetorica ad Herennium* added the division after the narrative, and that Cicero added the digression after the refutation. You will also remember that Cicero was not keen on the digression because it cluttered the speech. The division is useful, but the author believes that it is overly mechanical and seems to get in the way of a smoothly flowing speech.

The classical pattern indicates the nature of the language for each section.

Introduction   Cicero held that a convincing introduction would make the audience well disposed, attentive, and teachable. Unlike an introduction for a basic persuasive speech, the classical exordium does not include any adjusting or previewing language. Such adjusting or previewing language would ruin the efficacy of the pattern by divulging its organizational strategy.

In the sample speeches in the appendix speakers introduced their persuasions with a variety of methods. Patrick Henry complimented the previous speaker, although Henry disagreed with him, and quickly turned the audience's attention to Henry's purpose. The Reverend Harry Emerson Fosdick, speaking during the high point of U.S. isolationism during the 1930s, referred to his purpose by pointing out the irony of Christians who celebrated the Unknown Soldier and sparked the audience's interest by daring them not to listen to him. Senator Richard Nixon, in his 1952 fund speech, referred immediately to the charges against himself, paid himself the indirect compliment that he would not ignore them as other candidates usually did, and then restated the charge against himself. President Jimmy Carter introduced his speech on the Panama Canal Treaties by praising American work and ingenuity with a brief historical overview, which was subtly slanted to make the U.S. appear imperialistic and to set the stage for the president's reasons why the U.S. Senate should ratify his treaties.

Narrative   In legal oratory, the purpose of the narrative was to tell about the crime, to relate the motives of the accused and defendant, to render the scene, and to dispose the listeners toward the speaker. However, the narrative form is easily transferrable to other kinds of speeches. The narrative is a rhetorical story that the speaker constructs so that the audience perceives reality, not necessarily as it was or is, but as the speaker wants it to be. A plaintiff would narrate the crime from his perspective while portraying the defendant in the most unfavorable light. The defendant would talk about the scene from his viewpoint while taking care to malign his adversary as much as possible.

Narratives should be real. A story about an actual event can be documented. Conjectural narratives run the risk of being too removed from reality and apparently made up. Narratives should be constructed to portray the speaker or the cause in the most advantageous light. An exception to this general procedure can be found in Jimmy Carter's Panama Canal Treaties speeches in which he endeavored to paint the actions of the United States government in a negative light. On the other hand, Senator Nixon narrated the background information about his alleged secret slush fund in such a manner as to make himself look entirely innocent of any wrongdoing.

Arguments   In the arguments section you marshal the evidence in favor of your proposal. Depending on your time limits, you can generally select three or four proofs to advocate your thesis. Then you develop the arguments as main heads with reasoning and analysis, quotations, and transitional materials to get the audience from main head to main head (e.g., "The major reason for tax incentives is . . . ," "Another ground is . . . ," "And the last justification is as follows . . . .").

Patrick Henry examined the past diplomatic relations with Great Britain by considering petitions that were rejected, supplications that were spurned, and the presence of the British fleet, which was meant to subdue the colonists; he concluded that the king and Parliament meant to conquer the colonies. Senator

Nixon developed four arguments in his apologia: why he had to have the fund, how he paid for necessary expenses, that he had legal proof for his assertions, and that he had taken no sums in cash. President Carter organized the proofs in his "Panama Canal Treaties" speech around two assertions: (1) that the treaties would not violate the security interests of the United States, and (2) that former U.S. presidents, secretaries of state, general officers, and leaders of Latin American countries strongly endorsed the treaties.

When beginning to write your speech, you will probably have some arguments that you want to present. As you research your topic, you might find additional or better arguments to support your thesis. When you have completed your research, you need to use the arguments, backed by the strongest evidence you could discover, that will best persuade the audience.

Refutation   After the speaker has presented all of the proofs for the case, he or she then turns the audience's attention to the refutation section. As with the proof, three or four refutations should suffice for most student speeches. Henry introduced his refutation with: "They tell us that we are weak." Senator Nixon began his counterattack in this manner: "But I want to say some things before I conclude that I think most of you will agree on." The transitional device that President Carter used to move from the proof to the refutation was: "Let me answer specifically the most common questions about the treaties."

The refutation can serve two functions, which can be combined if you desire:

1. You can use the refutation to refute objections that the audience probably has against the proposal or thesis. Here is where you target neutrals and especially opponents. As you conduct the research for your speech, with the primary emphasis on securing evidence for your proposal, you often come across opinions that reflect opponent's arguments against your stance. These positions can form some of the basis for your refutation as you seek additional reasons and evidence to rebut the opposition's views.

2. You can use the refutation to attack your opponent or the opposition. You should be forewarned that some speakers misuse the refutation to attack adversaries personally. This is called *argumentum ad personam,* because the speaker attacks the opponent personally rather than the opponent's reasoning and analysis. The idea is that if you can discredit your antagonists, you denigrate their arguments as well. This was the basic thrust of Senator Nixon's refutation section, in which he mounted an attack against the Democrats' vice presidential and presidential candidates, the liberal media, and even President Harry Truman. Patrick Henry maligned the characters of those who opposed him by questioning their logic, manliness, Godliness, and timidity with a series of vigorous rhetorical questions.

The refutation can also be misused in another fashion. Some speakers combine an attack on opposing arguments with an attack on the opponents. For example in the 1988 televised presidential campaign debates, George Bush used this kind of refutation against Michael Dukakis. Bush attacked Dukakis's ideas as too liberal and then assailed Dukakis himself as soft on crime and communism, as inexperienced, and, by implication, as presidentially incompetent.

Conclusion   Rather than a straight summary, the conclusion functions better as an appeal to action or a charge that the audience change its beliefs. It strives for a heightened impression to make an outstanding effect.

How not to do it is exemplified in President Carter's summation for his "Panama Treaties" speech. There, he contended that President Theodore Roosevelt would favor endorsing the treaties. But what Americans generally know about Roosevelt's virile presidency, bully nature, and talk-softly-and-carry-a-big-stick attitude in foreign policy strongly suggests that Roosevelt would not favor the treaties. Therefore Carter's conclusion was not compelling.

Other speakers have concluded their addresses much better. Senator Nixon asked the audience to wire and write the Republican National Committee. Patrick Henry vigorously concluded his speech with short but emotional exclamations, terse and impatient rhetorical questions, and the unforgettable mock gesture of plunging a letter opener into his heart when he uttered the final word of "I know not what course others may take, but as for me, give me liberty or give me death."

Adapting the Classical Pattern to the Speech   When considering the connection between the audience and the speech, the following guidelines for audience analysis should be kept in mind. The classical pattern is tailor-made for some requirements. If you believe you need to deal with reservations that the audience might have against your proposal, or if you believe you need to refute opponents' objections to your plan, the classical pattern is extremely useful. For instance, you could argue that legislation for controlling handguns is not necessarily unconstitutional. Realizing that opponents in the audience might subscribe to the dictum, "Guns don't kill people, people kill people," you could rebut by showing that while rifles can be used for hunting, handguns have no other purpose than to shoot human beings.

The classical pattern can be adapted to fit the requirements of eliminating competing solutions. This persuasive task can be accomplished in the arguments section, where the speaker gives reasons for the proposition, and the refutation section, where the speaker dispatches other proposals. Remember, however, that assigned time constraints for the speech may limit the number of proposals you can consider and the depth of analysis that you can apply to each possibility. For example, Patrick Henry used the classical pattern in the overall structure of his speech. But in the arguments section, he used the method of residues (discussed below) to contend that there was no chance for conciliation with the Crown, and in the refutation section he again used the method of residues to rebuke fears that the colonies were weak militarily. However, he dealt rather cursorily with objections that the colonies could not realistically fight Great Britain, a major world power.

Do not forget the fine advice that Aristotle gave concerning how to adapt the classical pattern to the persuasive purpose. If you analyze your audience and determine that their objections pose the greatest obstacle to your thesis, then by all means go to the refutation immediately after the narration. After rebutting, move to the arguments section and state your side of the case. As the author of the *Rhetorica ad Herennium* observed, the highest practice of the art is to know when to break the rules.

The Method of Residues

A speaker often faces the necessity of eliminating rival solutions to a pressing problem. This usually involves a rhetorical situation in which the listeners generally agree with the speaker about the nature of a problem but are undecided about how best to solve it. For instance, it is a fact that the U.S. has a negative balance of trade, but people disagree about whether the federal government should do nothing, introduce import quotas, or raise tariffs.

The method of residues is an organizational pattern in which the speaker systematically eliminates all the competing solutions until only the speaker's proposal is left. The persuasive power of the method of residues resides in the logic of the affirmative **disjunctive syllogism.** The affirmative disjunctive syllogism posits either A, B, C, or D (or however many choices there are); it then demonstrates not A, not B, not C, therefore D. Aristotle alluded to the method of residues [1399a6–27], Cicero discussed this form of reasoning in *Topica* [53–55] and *De Inventione* [I, 45], and Quintilian treated it in *Institutio Oratoria* [V, 10, 65–68] by noting that it functioned well in confirming or confuting.

Patrick Henry employed the method of residues twice in the substructure of his address: He used it first in the argument section to eliminate all the vain hopes that members of the audience might have for reconciliation with England and he used it later in the refutation section to confute the audience's reservations about whether the colonies were strong enough to fight the British.

To be logically compelling, a speaker who employs the method of residues must be certain to eliminate all the reasonable alternatives or disjuncts. President Richard Nixon used the method in his famous speech about Cambodia on April 31, 1970, which sparked the campus riots against the Vietnam war, which culminated in the killing of students by National Guardsmen at Kent State University in Ohio. Nixon claimed he had three choices to respond to Communist aggression and infiltration in Cambodia: to do nothing, which would accomplish nothing; to give military aid to the Cambodian Army, which was only marginally effective; or to go to the heart of the trouble, which was to bomb enemy sanctuaries and invade Cambodia. But there was a fourth disjunct—immediately to pull out of the Vietnam war entirely—which was the choice college students advocated at the time. Nixon's speech was not logically compelling because he buried that disjunct much later in the address and failed to treat it in a forthright or extensive manner.

Thus, in addition to considering all the competing proposals, you must present enough evidence and reasoning to negate each of them. If the audience perceives that you have failed to demolish one or more of the disjuncts, the logical force of the method will not be compelling and the audience will not accept the residue.

To illustrate how the method of residues works, let us build a hypothetical speech that advocates direct election of the president of the United States.

In the introduction, you use one or some combination of the techniques to gain attention and goodwill that have already been discussed. For instance, you could demonstrate to the audience how some popularly elected presidents have not been chosen by the electoral college, and how electors do not have to vote for the candidate who won in their state. As in the classical pattern, you do not include any adjusting or previewing language because that would ruin the power of the pattern. For instance, you will find that neither Richard Nixon nor Patrick Henry, who both used the method of residues within the overall structure of the classical pattern, used any adjusting or previewing language in their speeches.

You devote the body of the speech to a discussion of the disjuncts. Naturally you save the disjunct you advocate for the final consideration. The first disjunct for the electoral reform speech might be to do nothing; but, as Nixon argued for Cambodia, doing nothing is just that, and the potential harm continues. (You depend on the enthymeme that the president should be chosen by a popular majority.) The second disjunct could be to force electors to vote as their states voted; but the mathematics still indicate that a popularly elected president could lose in the electoral college. A third disjunct might be to allocate the votes in the electoral college on a proportional basis for each state; but that still allows for candidates to concentrate on big states at the expense of smaller ones. A fourth disjunct, the one advocated in the sample speech, could be to abolish the electoral college and to substitute a direct election of the president of the United States based solely on popular votes.

Now that you have in mind an overview of the body of the speech, let us focus more closely on how to handle the language for each disjunct. When examining every alternative, it is wise to acknowledge that each choice has some merits. This appeals to all factions in the audience, for it demonstrates your goodwill toward their position and your good sense in recognizing why they hold their position. But don't make the choice appear too good, or else there will seem to be insufficient reason to reject it! For instance, you could allow that to do nothing about the electoral college would maintain the tradition envisioned by the Founding Fathers. But immediately on the heels of giving some positive aspect of the disjunct, you focus the audience's attention on one or more overriding negative features of the alternative. The important idea is to give the audience sufficient evidence for rejecting the disjunct. This strategy relies on the efficacy of two-sided argumentation.

Two-sided argumentation entails giving both sides, positive and negative, of an issue. Since most solutions have some merits, audience members, especially those neutrals and opponents who might favor the disjunct that you are rejecting, should appreciate your honesty in recognizing those qualities and therefore be more receptive to your evidence for rejecting the disjunct.

Two-sided argumentation works best when you address a mixed audience of partisans, neutrals, and opponents. Even opponents should appreciate your even-handed analysis, and neutrals and partisans will rate your trustworthiness even higher. If you addressed a highly partisan audience, however, you might consider it unnecessary to use two-sided argumentation. At their respective national conventions, Democrats and Republicans are usually at pains to see nothing but evil in the opposition and nothing but good in themselves. An interesting exception to this rule is Congresswoman Barbara Jordan's keynote address to the Democratic National Convention in 1976, in which she skillfully blamed the Democratic Party for not keeping political faith with its traditional constituents.[1]

You use two-sided argumentation to discuss each disjunct discussed in its turn. Transitional devices, such as "Let's now look at the next option," "Some people favor another plan that we need to look at," or "My opponents say we should adopt their plan, so let's see what it is," should introduce each disjunct.

The author of the *Rhetorica ad Herennium* gave some good advice that can be employed in the method of residues. Remember that the author advised beginning and ending both the arguments and refutation sections with strong arguments.

Applying that analysis to the disjuncts, there might be some psychological advantage in beginning the body of the speech with a disjunct that is easily dispatched. Hence your strongest argument is in refuting the weakest competition. You then treat in turn the more difficult ones to surmount. President Nixon used that strategy in his Cambodia address by dispatching the easy pickings (to do nothing) first.

Special attention needs to be given to the disjunct you advocate. In order not to cue the audience too quickly that this is the proposal you are advocating, continue the two-sided argumentation you used for the rejected disjuncts.

When introducing your policy, mention a positive aspect in a proportion similar to your treatment of the previous alternatives. So far the audience should not perceive that this is your proposal. Next you can mention some negative factor, but not an overwhelming one, or else you will irreparably damage your choice. Still the audience is not aware that you are arguing for your disjunct, although the light may be beginning to dawn. Finally you state additional reasons and evidence for the viability of your proposal. By this time the audience will surely perceive your persuasive intent. But if you have been careful to refute logically the other disjuncts and have offered compelling arguments for your plan, the audience should be impelled logically to accept your proposal.

To conclude the speech you use one, or some combination, of the techniques presented earlier for closing a speech.

Schematically, the method of residues is developed as follows:

The Burkeian Pattern

This pattern is credited to Kenneth Burke, who perceived the motivational strategies inherent in some types of persuasive communications. Burke identified a recurring psychological pattern in generic rhetorical transactions. In his *Permanence and Change*, Burke conceived four compelling steps that moved the audience: guilt → victimage → redemption → salvation.[2]

For instance, traditional Christian preaching has stressed man's guilt from original sin, and how man can only obtain redemption and salvation through faith in Jesus Christ. The same motivational psychology was operative in Adolph Hitler's speeches. Hitler stirred German's anger and directed it at the Jews who he said were responsible for Germany's defeat and the Versailles Treaty. Hitler told his audiences that they had been victimized by the Jews and promised to redeem their country by eliminating the Jews, who were the cause of all Germany's troubles. Once the Jews were eliminated, Hitler offered the salvation of the Third Reich. The Burkeian pattern is particularly prevalent in demagogic discourse, as in the speeches of Senator Huey Long.[3]

Maria Stewart and Frances Harper, two famous black women speakers who spoke against slavery and for black women's rights in the nineteenth century, also used the Burkeian pattern. Maria Stewart's "African Rights and Liberty" and Frances Harper's "Liberty for Slaves" are excellent examples of how these women used the motivational strategy observed by Burke.[4] These black women instilled anger in their audiences by demonstrating how free black men and women lived at the sufferance of whites in nineteenth-century America and how slaves were abused under the peculiar institution (guilt). They blamed white people, who had the power, for not enfranchising free black women and for not freeing the black slaves of both sexes (victimage). They challenged their audiences, which often included white abolitionists, to work (redemption) to remove the legal obstacles that disenfranchised and enslaved blacks (salvation).

As mentioned earlier, Burke did not intend his finding to be used as an organizational pattern. The two women mentioned above were not aware that they were using his pattern, because they spoke long before Burke published his findings. Burke's genius was in discerning a motivational pattern historically used in many speeches. Therefore, it would not be disrespectful to Burke or inappropriate to teach this pattern. But it can be streamlined and clarified by stating it in the following three steps: anger → victimage/scapegoat → salvation.

The main heads of the Burkeian pattern are difficult to delineate. If it helps, the anger step can be conceived as the introduction, the scapegoating step as the body, and the salvation step as the conclusion. With this overview in mind, let us examine each of the three stages in detail.

The Anger Step   Burke used the term *guilt*, but the word *anger* better expresses the crux of this first step. Although it is true that preachers try to make their listeners feel guilty, wise political communicators steer clear of guilt. In the late 1970s, President Jimmy Carter made several energy speeches in which he quite correctly stated that the American people were guilty of wasting energy. The strategy backfired because the people were not prepared to accept this secular guilt. In fact, one of candidate Ronald Reagan's compelling messages in 1980 was that nothing was wrong with America, except for the gloom-and-doom Democrats. The basic message was "I'm okay and you're okay, but Carter is not okay."

Speakers can also tap the other emotions that complement the core emotion of anger, such as frustration, outrage, hatred, jealousy, and indignation. For instance, in his 1980 campaign Ronald Reagan traded on the anger and frustration inherent in inflation, high taxes, a weak America, the Iranian hostage crisis, and welfare queens who drove Cadillacs to pick up their food stamps (a veiled appeal to racism). In 1988, Vice President George Bush ran a "negative campaign" that focused on Willie Horton and the liberal agenda of high taxes and a weak military to tap emotions that made Americans angry at his opponent. Governor Dukakis focused on issues such as education, drugs, and health insurance in an attempt to make his constituents angry with the status quo. The basic idea in the anger step is to demonstrate a problem whose urgency makes the audience indignant that it has not been solved.

The Victim/Scapegoat Step   In this step the speaker asserts that the problem he or she is addressing has not been resolved because powerful forces have been unchecked. Adolph Hitler blamed the Jews, Franklin Roosevelt the economic royalists, Ronald Reagan the liberal Democrats, and Michael Dukakis the conservative Republicans. The speaker avers that these forces have wielded their great power to block actions toward reform or relief. As victims, the people either do not know how to restrict these forces or cannot restrain them. The important point, the speaker tells the audience, is that unless these forces can be mastered, the power figures will continue to dominate; hence, the anger and frustration felt by those who are harmed will continue unabated.

As the counterpart of the victim, the speaker identifies the group that has victimized the people. That group becomes the audience's scapegoat. (The term *scapegoat* derived originally from an ancient Jewish ritual in which the people cleansed themselves of their sins by symbolically placing their sins on a goat's head and then driving the goat into the wilderness.) Only by driving away the scapegoat, the speaker tells the audience, can the problem be solved.

The list of contemporary scapegoats used by persuasive advocates is a long one. It includes liberals and conservatives, Democrats and Republicans, secular humanists and fundamentalists, hawks and doves, intellectuals and middle-Americans, and the poor and the rich. Depending on your political perspective, other handy targets are pencil-headed professors, the leftist press, and the military-industrial complex.

The Salvation Step   In this step the speaker states that only the speaker and the speaker's solution can provide salvation to the audience. If the audience could do it for themselves, the speaker says, they would have done it already. The salvation step includes the speaker's plan for safeguarding the audience from evil victimizers. Thus, Hitler promised the German people a thousand-year reich, FDR introduced a New Deal, and a presidential candidate proposed Reaganomics.

The Problem Solution Pattern

A common speech assignment is to address a problem and propose a solution. In this rhetorical situation, the speaker can adapt the speech to the audience in a variety of ways. In one case the audience is unaware of the need and therefore uninformed about a workable solution. In this case you focus about equally on the problem and the solution. You start from scratch in terms of the classical status. You introduce the facts of the problem and solution, you define both of them, and you stress their qualities. For instance, some economists claim that a 100 per cent inheritance tax (fact) would better distribute income in the U.S. (definition) by limiting the concentration of accumulated wealth (quality).

In another case the audience recognizes the problem but is unsure what the best solution is. In this case you focus more on your course of action. In terms of classical status the audience agrees with the fact, but you need to convince them of your contention about its definition and quality. As an example, many citizens agree that the present presidential primary system has serious faults. Building on that consensus, you could define a national presidential primary held on one day and stress that it would bypass the relatively unimportant primaries and caucuses in unrepresentative states, such as New Hampshire and Iowa.

In a third case the audience realizes a problem exists and is aware of contending solutions, but you want to convince them your proposed solution is the best. In this case you focus the audience's attention on your suggestion. For instance, you propose a direct election of the president of the United States by abolishing the electoral college. In terms of the status theory, this could present a difficult rhetorical situation. Even if you focus only on your solution, the audience may define the solutions it knows about in a favorable manner. If you analyze your audience and determine that the audience will not forget about other strong competing solutions, you could consider using the method of residues in the solution part of your speech.

The problem solution pattern is a straightforward exposition of a need and a plan, but it lacks the artistic panache of some of the other patterns. None of the collected speeches in the Appendix illustrate the problem solution pattern, although in a strict sense all of them present a problem and a solution.

The Monroe Motivated Sequence

The Monroe motivated sequence was invented by Professor Alan H. Monroe. Like the classical pattern, it indicates the kind of language that should be spoken in each section. The Monroe motivated sequence is an excellent pattern to keep the audience's attention riveted on one problem and on one solution.

Monroe's pattern derives its psychological efficacy from its five steps. The speaker motivates the audience throughout the steps of the speech. At the conclusion the listener is motivated to accept the solution. The pattern has five steps:

Attention

Need

Satisfaction

Visualization

Action

To illustrate the pattern, we will sketch a pro and con speech on abortions.

The Attention Step   You introduce the speech by garnering the audience's attention and goodwill. Any of the devices discussed earlier can be used. The attention step leads the audience into the groove of the speech.

The pro-abortion speaker could research a heart-rending story about the victim of a rape or incest, or an example of a fetus that has Tays-Sachs disease. The anti-abortion speaker could offer a grisly picture of what happens to the fetus in the various kinds of abortive techniques. Both of these speakers would want to relate their positions to the women in the audience, who may confront the decision, and to the men, who will partake in the problem.

The Need Step   From the attention step, you move directly to the need step. You do not use adjusting language in the Monroe motivated sequence; however, you do use transitional devices as subtle hints of the step to come. "This tragedy is the core of a problem that you women in the audience may have to confront in your lives" could be the transition to the need step. Here, you identify a problem or need that the audience has.

The three cases concerning classic status that appeared in the discussion of the problem solution pattern are appropriate here. Depending on how the speaker analyzed the status of the audience in relation to the issue, the speaker would need to focus more on need, or about equally on need and satisfaction, or more on the satisfaction step.

The classical concept of status can illuminate the debate on abortions. The pro-abortion speaker argues the morality of abortions and the quality of life for the would-be mother. The anti-abortion speaker defines abortion as murder and focuses on the quality of life for the fetus. And both speakers argue jurisdiction:

the pro-abortion speaker to keep the status quo, and the anti-abortion speaker to change state or federal laws by a constitutional amendment.

You demonstrate your good sense and good moral character and build the urgency of the need you have identified by selecting language to illustrate it. You should marshal statistics, expert testimony from doctors, lawyers, and theologians, and specific examples to appeal to the audience's enthymemes. However, partisans and opponent's enthymemes on the subject of abortion are probably so hardened that the only reasonable target audience is one of neutrals. This particular controversy illustrates Aristotle's idea that not everyone can be persuaded [1355b13].

The Satisfaction Step   After developing the need, you logically introduce the step that would satisfy the need. Here the anti-abortion speaker might discuss a Constitutional amendment or advocate personal involvement by blocking the entrances to abortion clinics. The pro-abortion speaker might call for the faithful to counter the anti-abortionists' protests or ask the audience to join a letter-writing campaign against further restrictions on abortion.

In a strict sense, the need and satisfaction steps are the same as the problem and solution of the problem solution pattern. However, Professor Monroe demonstrated real genius in inventing the next step, which is not advocated in the traditional problem solution pattern.

The Visualization Step.   The visualization step is a motivational strategy. In the visualization step, the speaker imagines the future and paints a verbal picture of what will happen if the audience acts on the satisfaction step. The idea is to put the audience in the metaphorical driver's seat so that it can realize all of the advantages it will gain from accepting the satisfaction step. The speaker tries to make real for the audience, in the most glowing terms possible, what will occur when the satisfaction step is taken.

You can take three approaches in the visualization step.

1. If the old solution to a problem did not work, or the audience was unaware that the problem could be satisfied, you demonstrate to the audience how the need can now be better handled with your proposal. For instance, the anti-abortion speaker could visualize how unborn fetuses will no longer be murdered, how believers can make their morality into legality. The pro-abortion speaker might visualize how women will no longer have to bear a child from rape or incest or bear the heartache of caring for hopelessly deformed and doomed babies.

2. You can use the visualization step to show how a totally new satisfaction step can be implemented advantageously. Although candidate George Bush did not use the Monroe motivated sequence in his 1988 campaign debates, he did employ elements of the visualization step. He spoke fervently of how he would not increase taxes, how he would continue the prosperity of the Reagan-Bush years, how he would continue to make Americans feel safe with a stronger

military, and how he would not "go back to malaise and misery index."[5] The voters bought Bush's visualization over Dukakis's.

The visualization step is perhaps one of the most important steps in the sequence. If the audience can be made to see how beneficial, helpful, and expeditious your proposal is, then the more likely they will be persuaded. But all of this will not happen, Prof. Monroe wisely understood, unless the speaker moves to the last step.

The Action Step.   In the final step, which is the conclusion of the speech, Monroe advised the speaker to make direct and obvious appeals to the audience to change its mind, to buy the product, to adopt the solution, to be persuaded. The action step is the final and logical step in the sequence because nothing will happen if the audience does not take some action.

Our abortion speakers could appeal to their constituents to vote for them, to march, to write letters, to protest, to act. The important thing is for the speaker to challenge the audience to act because all will come to naught if they do not behave as the speaker insists.

The Motivated Sequence in Contemporary Life   The Monroe motivated sequence is used in contemporary society as a persuasive organizational pattern. If you make allowances for their short duration, television commercials often follow this pattern. The car salesman often employs the pattern. In the attention step, the salesman greets you and has some catchy thing to say. You are quickly steered to the need step in terms of how you probably need a new car, judging by the junk heap you just drove in. The satisfaction step entails taking a sleek car for a test drive. The visualization step can occur either in the car, when the salesman goes along for the ride and gives you a continuous stream of sales pitches, or in the office, where the salesman waits until you arrive back to begin visualizing your delight when you buy the car. The action step is the direct appeal to buy the car today.

CLASSICAL INFLUENCES ON THE PERSUASIVE SPEECH

The Greeks and Romans realized that the speaker wanted to create a persuasive speech, but that the speech was inextricably linked to the likes and dislikes of a human audience. The primary focus of this chapter was the relationship between the speech and the audience that the speaker created through organizational strategies.

Aristotle, Cicero, and Quintilian all advised that a speech had to be clear and cogent so that the audience could understand it. The time, topical, and spatial patterns denote a straightforward way to structure the main heads in a speech. These patterns indicate the nature of the language, appeals, and evidence that the speaker needs to invent for the parts of the respective patterns.

Persuasive speaking was the ancient's forte. Of the patterns discussed, only the classical pattern was strictly theirs. But the classical pattern made major contributions to argumentative theory. Corax perceived that an audience is likely to be composed of some persons who will favor the speaker's thesis, some who will oppose it, and some who are undecided. This fact of life doubtless led Corax to conceive of the arguments and refutation sections. The speaker used the arguments to reinforce the committed, to sway neutrals, and, hopefully, to move opponents. Likewise, in the refutation the speaker reinforced partisans, who were glad to see their beliefs vindicated; demonstrated to the neutrals the weaknesses of the opposition's position; and at least discomforted opponents, if not persuading them, by challenging their arguments. The wisdom of this approach was validated by Plato, Aristotle, the author of the *Rhetorica ad Herennium*, Cicero, and Quintilian. Further realizing that the speech needed to be adapted to the audience, Aristotle and the author of the *Rhetorica ad Herennium* reminded the speaker to switch the order of the arguments and refutation sections if that was warranted.

Taking the process of persuading people one step further, the classical authors all cautioned that the speech could not convince an audience through organizational pattern alone. It had to have substance. The speaker's research could be guided by the dictates of the pattern, but the persuasive case had to rest on solid evidence and reasoning.

The method of residues, Burkeian, problem solution, and Monroe motivated sequence paradigms are not classical patterns, although the method of residues can be discerned in Cicero's *Topica*. They are, nevertheless, modern affirmations of the relationship between the speech and the audience.

The efficacy of the method of residues rests on the classical idea that the audience is likely to know various solutions, and that one must present arguments and refutations for and against those choices. The only substantive difference (excepting the narration) between the classical pattern and the method of residues is that in the former the speaker refutes the other choices before affirming his or her solution. The efficacy of the Burkeian pattern lies in channeling the audience's deep-seated perceptions that stronger forces than itself have control over its destiny toward the conviction that the only way to conquer those forces is to adopt the speaker's policies. Although rather pedestrian, the problem solution pattern produces a clear and compelling communication, which facilitates the audience's reception of the speech. The Monroe motivated sequence is grounded in Cicero's idea of making the audience well disposed, attentive, and teachable.

These persuasive paradigms have served communicators well for the past 2300 years. They can all (except for the problem solution pattern) be discerned in the speeches printed in the Appendix.

So, having cast your address in the appropriate rhetorical mold, you are now ready to file the rough edges and polish it into final form. That is the subject of Chapter 4.

Notes

1. For an overview of Jordan's speaking career and bibliographical materials, see David Henry, "Barbara Jordan," in *American Orators of the Twentieth Century: Critical Studies and Sources,* edited by Bernard K. Duffy and Halford R. Ryan (Westport, Conn.: Greenwood Press, 1987), pp. 233–238.

2. Kenneth Burke, *Permanence and Change,* 2d. ed. (Indianapolis: Bobbs-Merrill, 1965), pp. 274–294.

3. See Paul C. Gaske, "The Analysis of Demagogic Discourse: Huey Long's 'Everyman A King' Address," in *American Rhetoric from Roosevelt to Reagan,* edited by Halford R. Ryan (2d ed.; Prospect Heights Ill.: Waveland Press, 1987), pp. 50–68.

4. For texts of these two speeches, see Judith Anderson, *Outspoken Women: Speeches by American Women Reformers 1635–1935* (Dubuque, Iowa: Kendall/Hunt Publishing, 1984), pp. 80–82, 169–173.

5. For a discussion of the presidential debates, see the author's article "The 1988 Bush-Dukakis Presidential Debates," in *Rhetorical Studies of National Political Debates,* edited by Robert V. Friedenberg (New York: Praeger, 1990) pp. 145–166.

CHAPTER 4

Styling the Speech

Cicero (106–43 B.C.). A famous Roman orator, lawyer, and senator, Cicero wrote six major works on persuasion and advocated speaking with an ornamented style.

The third classical canon was *elocutio,* or style. When the Roman theorists used the word *elocutio,* they meant spoken, oral, verbal, or word style. Thus style was the manner of selecting words; expressing ideas; and combining words into phrases, sentences, and the entire speech. In this chapter, we will stick as much as possible to the strict definition of *style* as word choice.

This chapter is divided into two main parts. The first part will treat how the speaker should select language that contributes to an oral style. This part owes its rationales to Aristotle's idea of clarity and appropriateness [1404b3]; to Cicero's *De Oratore,* in which he codified the four virtues of style: correctness, clarity, ornamentation, and propriety [III, 37]; and to Quintilian's three virtues of style: correctness, lucidity, and elegance. Quintilian included appropriateness under elegance [I, 5, 1]. This part is devoted to clarity and appropriateness, for it is assumed that you already write and speak in correct English.

The second part deals with ornamentation. It is an explication of the classical devices that enable a speaker to deliver a polished speech in a distinctive oral style. Contemporary communicators and their communications, such as the Reverend Jesse Jackson's "Rainbow Coalition" address, the Reverend Martin Luther King, Jr.'s "I Have a Dream" speech, and President John F. Kennedy's inaugural address, owe a debt to the classical tradition. Their speeches are distinguished from other pedestrian political persuasions because of their, or their speech writers', reliance on classical stylistic techniques. These devices have remained unchanged for over two millennia.

Both parts focus on how to adapt the speech to the audience. For, as Aristotle observed, it is not enough to know what to say; one must know how it ought to be stated [1403b15].

THE ORAL STYLE

A fact of life in public speaking is that you write a speech before you say it, and there the trouble begins. The problem is to compose the speech in an oral style. Most people do not write as they speak or speak as they write. To test this premise, take a speech in the Appendix and read a small segment aloud. You might find yourself not wanting to pause where the commas and periods are and uncomfortable with some of the word choices and the sentence lengths. The problem is that the style is the speaker's, not yours.

In managing your own oral style, you might have used different words, reordered the sentences, added new materials, expanded some thoughts, and deleted others. Additionally, and this is admittedly encroaching on the canon of delivery, you might have wanted to phrase the sentences differently than the commas and periods indicated.

So the primary problem is to write a speech as it should sound, not as an essay should read. Writing a speech for the ear, rather than the eye, necessitates forming new habits. But, like the newly foaled colt who stumbles briefly at birth, you will soon compose speeches in a sure-footed manner.

The oral style gives each member of the audience the feeling that the speaker is talking directly to him or her. You try to convey through word choice that you are carrying on an enlarged conversation with the audience. It is direct and personal, more informal than formal. To be sure, it is generally a one-sided conversation, but the idea is to convey the impression of talking to rather than at the audience, of talking with rather than over the people. There are a variety of ways to achieve the oral style.

Use Personal Pronouns

In attaining an oral style, you should compose your speech for the audience's ear. First of all, as in everyday conversation, use personal pronouns such as *we, us, our, you,* and *I.* The formal *one,* which you might use in an English theme, sounds stilted in speaking. *I,* which is generally inappropriate for scholarly writing, sounds normal in public speaking. Can you imagine 1988 presidential candidate George Bush saying: "Read one's lips"? Indeed, a perusal of the speeches in the Appendix will reveal that their authors used personal pronouns profusely throughout their speeches. They did this to identify with their listeners. They gave their audiences the perception that each member was being addressed in a personal manner by the speaker, that each listener was a direct party to the discussion.

Use Contractions

Although contractions might be red-lined in a theme or essay, they lend an air of informality that is another hallmark of the oral style. Contractions like *I've, you've, don't,* and *couldn't* subtly suggest an animated dialogue between speaker and audience. Don't be afraid to write contractions into your speech, otherwise your style may sound stiff and starchy. Senator Nixon's and President Carter's speeches in the Appendix illustrate how appropriate use of contractions can contribute to a good oral style.

Use Active Verbs

Consider the following sentence: It is to be hoped that active verbs will be employed in the oral style. Although the sentence is grammatically correct and sounds scholarly, because it is in the passive voice, it sounds stilted and lacks vigor. Unless you really want to sound stilted, the active voice serves best in most cases. We use the basic subject, verb, object structure of the English language in everyday conversation, you should carry this style over to the speech. For instance, consider Senator Richard Nixon's style in the conclusion of his Checkers's speech, where he made an appeal to the audience to help save his political career. He might have said:

> It is for them, the Republican National Committee, to decide whether
> my position on the ticket will help or hurt. One asks the audience to
> help them decide. It is to be desired that the audience members will wire
> and write the Republican National Committee whether one thinks one
> should stay on or whether one should get off.

Compare that with what he actually said. Note the personal pronouns, the active voice, and the impelling use of imperative verbs:

> Let them decide whether my position on the ticket will help or hurt.
> And I am going to ask you to help them decide. Wire and write the
> Republican National Committee whether you think I should stay on or
> whether I should get off.

That kind of direct and vigorous oral style was a contributing factor to Nixon's overall success with the American television and radio audiences in 1952.

The active voice also communicates an air of dynamism. Passive verbs and the convoluted sentence structures of the passive voice get in the way of thoughts that should march directly to their goal. Sentence flow slows down, the speech seems weak, and you sound submissive.

Phrase the Speech Vocally

Generally speaking, thought units in a speech are shorter than those in writing. The reason is fairly simple. Most speakers do not have enough breath to say an inordinately long sentence, and most audiences cannot take in long thought units. In the passage from Nixon's conclusion quoted above, note how the short vocal units almost jabbed the audience into acting as Nixon wanted them to. From a literary perspective, Patrick Henry's style in his "Liberty or Death" speech might be termed choppy. Yet, the sudden bursts of charged eloquence had a telling effect on his listeners.

You have to make a conscious effort to write your speech in shorter sentences. As you begin to develop the habit of writing in the oral style, say aloud some of the sentences in the first draft of your speech. After some false starts, you will begin to hear in your mind how the speech should sound, and you can therefore pace it in a vocal, rather than in a written, style.

As a matter of fact, when you read your drafts aloud, your ear may tell you that you should recast sentence order, use different words, or otherwise edit your thoughts. Do not be afraid to experiment and make changes in diction. If revisions sound good to you—and you can only ascertain that if you read your drafts aloud—accept the changes for the better.

Plan for Delivery

As you compose your speech, keep in the back of your mind how delivery might help the audience comprehend your message. Although delivery will be discussed in the next chapter, some preliminary considerations are in order here.

Consider whether a finger gesture will help enumerate your points as you say "first," "second," and "third," for example. Consider moving slightly to the right or left to help cue a transition from one main head to another. Make little notes to yourself, such as "Say this slower and more deliberately," "Emphasize this point with loudness," "Pause slightly before saying this," and "Stress this concept with hand gestures" about points of delivery that may help the audience appreciate your talk. These devices should adjust the speech to the audience and the audience to the speech. The point is that thinking about how you will deliver the speech will help you incorporate the oral style into your composing process.

If you can, try to compose directly at the word processor, talking to yourself as you type; this will give you a closer approximation of the oral style. Take advantage of the word processor's capabilities to block and move paragraphs, and use the thesaurus and spell checker. The word processor also gives you the advantage of double- or triple-spacing your speech, which will help you revise it or make it legible if you decide to use the text at the lectern or speaker's stand. You can also take advantage of **bold**, <u>underlining</u>, and *italics* to highlight important words and phrases.

If you prefer, you can write out a complete draft of the speech and perhaps later transfer the draft to the computer. In any event you should double-space your writing so that you can edit your work. Quintilian observed that the speaker should use the eraser to correct the speech drafts. But he cautioned not to edit too much, for, he said, a speaker could be "like the doctors who use the knife even where the flesh is perfectly healthy" [X, 4, 3].

You may feel more comfortable with a written outline that is fairly detailed. Or you may write out parts of the speech and outline other parts. For instance, you could write the introduction and conclusion, but merely outline the body. The important goal is not a particular kind of draft but a draft in the form that works best for you.

THE ORNAMENTED STYLE

From a stylistic perspective, Presidents Franklin D. Roosevelt and John F. Kennedy are exemplars of an elevated style. They realized that the president is the *vox populi* (voice of the people). Not everyone can speak with distinction, but Roosevelt and Kennedy realized that voters appreciate a chief executive who can speak eloquently for them. As employers of stylistic devices, these two presidents were unexcelled in the twentieth century.

But how did their style, or that of Jesse Jackson or Dr. King, fit into the classical scheme of elocution? You will remember that the author of the *Rhetorica ad Herennium* devised three kinds of style, the grand, the middle, and the plain, and that Cicero argued that the speaker should use an *ornamented style*.

Let's first determine what an ornamented style is not. The ornamented style is not a classical **grand style**. The author of the *Rhetorica ad Herennium* gave a sample speech in the grand style, and it was indeed weighty and massive. Even Cicero cautioned speakers not to deliver a speech in a sustained grand style. The grand style was rarely used even in the worst stereotypical excesses of the nineteenth century. Senator Charles Sumner's invective against slavery and South Carolina in his "The Crime Against Kansas" speech (Washington, D.C., May 19–20, 1856) was a notable exception and Sumner was clubbed on the floor of the Senate by Congressman Preston Brooks, who resented Sumner's attack against his home state of South Carolina! The grand style is not used in public address today, nor is it the style advised in this textbook.

The ornamented style is not a plain style. Neither is the plain style recommended in this book. The **plain style** really was a diminished or lessened style, the most ordinary kind of speech in everyday talk. Interestingly enough, the author of the *Rhetorica ad Herennium* chose as an example of the plain style the encounter of two men in a bathhouse who had an argument over the one man's being beaten up by the other's slave boys.

The ornamented style approximates the **middle style**. In Latin, *mediocris* means middle, moderate, middling, ordinary, average. Cicero believed the middle style was robust, and was amenable to ornamentation. The middle style was also recommended by Aristotle, who said the speaker should avoid both meanness and undue elevation [1404b4].

The stylistic devices that are presented here are not easy to achieve, but they are accessible to the student speaker. The ancients termed these stylistic devices *figures of speech*, but their definitions of them are less than crystal clear. The author of the *Rhetorica ad Herennium* divided figures of speech into figures of diction and figures of thought [IV, 18]. Quintilian helped some when he made the distinction between figures from the form of language and figures from the arrangement of words, and he noted that both were rhetorical [IX, 3, 2].

Translated into something more understandable, figures of speech may be divided into the **figures of sound**—like the Rev. Jesse Jackson's alliteration of "My constituency is the damned, disinherited, disrespected, and the despised" from his "Rainbow Coalition" speech at the Democratic National Convention in 1984—and **figures of thought**—like President John Kennedy's famous chiasmus of "Let us never negotiate out of fear. But let us never fear to negotiate" from his inaugural address.

Figures of Sound

Anaphora   Anaphora is defined as beginning phrases, clauses, or sentences with the same or very similar words. The rhetorical efficacy of anaphora comes from the fact that the speaker reiterates the same thought (as well as the same sound) repeatedly so that it is dinned into the minds of the listeners. The repetition of similar sounds gives the speech an air of artistic elegance, but the practical function is to tread the thought into a listener's mind.

Perhaps the best known use of anaphora is the famous "I Have a Dream" speech by Dr. Martin Luther King, Jr. Dr. King used anaphora of "One hundred years later" (repeated three times), "Now is the time" (four times), "We cannot be satisfied" (five times in slightly different ways), "I have a dream" (eight times), and "Let freedom ring" (six times). To weigh the function of this oral style with a live audience, it is interesting to calculate how long it took the audience to respond to King's anaphora. Usually King had to repeat the phrase three or four times before the crowd understood the technique and began to clap and cheer. Thus, the audience reacted as much to the sound of the anaphora and the way that King delivered it as to the subject matter of those parallel thoughts.

Another example of anaphora is in President Franklin D. Roosevelt's "War Message" of December 8, 1941. FDR heightened Japanese perfidy by accumulating their infamous acts. He ticked them off in anaphora:

> Last night Japanese forces attacked Hongkong.
> Last night Japanese forces attacked Guam.
> Last night Japanese forces attacked the Philippine Islands.
> Last night Japanese forces attacked Wake Island.

Thus FDR hammered home four times the fact that the dastardly deed was done at night (by U.S. time) and by the Japanese.

President John F. Kennedy used anaphora in his inaugural address. Referring to the U.S. and the Soviet Union, he used four times the anaphora of "Let both sides" to indicate the kind of cooperation he envisioned. And six times he prefaced major foreign policy announcements with the anaphora of "To those."

Epistrophe   Epistrophe is similar to anaphora. Epistrophe is the ending of phrases, clauses, or sentences with the same or similar words.

President John Kennedy used epistrophe in his "Arms Quarantine" speech on the Cuban missile crisis in 1962. He first quoted the Soviet government, and then Soviet Foreign Minister Gromyko, ending the first quotation with "That statement was false," and the second with "That statement was also false." JFK's epistrophe orally stressed the Soviet lies.

In a clever use of epistrophe, FDR climaxed the anaphora of "I see millions" (repeated four times) in his second inaugural address with epistrophe: "I see one-third of a nation ill-housed, ill-clad, ill-nourished." The various "ills" became the focus of his indictment of the Depression.

Dr. Martin Luther King actually used epistrophe twice when rendering his famous anaphora of "I have a dream." That is, he began his sentences with "I have a dream" and ended two of them by repeating "I have a dream." The printed text does not communicate the epistrophe, but a recording or a video tape easily demonstrates his superb vocal phrasing of it.

Father Coughlin, the radio priest, used a sophisticated epistrophe in his "A Third Party" speech in June 19, 1936. Treating in four paragraphs how he believed President Roosevelt had double-crossed the nation, Coughlin took a famous phrase from FDR's first inaugural address—that he would drive the money-changers (the bankers on Wall Street) from the temple (the American banking institution)—and turned it against the president. At the end of each of the four paragraphs Coughlin asked the rhetorical question, "Is that driving the money changers from the temple?" After hearing Coughlin's searing arraignment, the audience would naturally answer "No."

Within one sentence, Martin Luther King constructed a memorable epistrophe that stressed the idea of togetherness: "With this faith we will be able to work together, to pray together, to struggle together, to go to jail together, to stand up for freedom together, knowing that we will be free one day."

Alliteration   Used in small quantities throughout a speech, **alliteration** can distinguish the address. Alliteration is using successive words with the same initial sound. Father Coughlin, in the speech mentioned above, took an alliterative rhetorical side swipe at FDR: "Roosevelt or ruin [is now] Roosevelt and ruin." In his attack on the media in 1969, Vice President Agnew used alliteration in "Normality has become the nemesis of the network news." Dr. King sprinkled alliteration throughout his speech, as when he spoke of "marvelous new militancy" and "molehill of Mississippi."

Alliteration is relatively easy to invent, especially if you can use the thesaurus function on your computer program. It is well to remember, however, that a little alliteration goes a long way.

Rhythmical Phrasing   In writing your communication, you might invent an opportunity to create some rhythmical cadences. These would give grace and elan to your speech. Here are some examples.

Consider how you might vocally phrase the following line from Abraham Lincoln's second inaugural address. (Although we do not know how Lincoln actually phrased this sentence, it sounds best when cadenced as indicated by the slashes; a double slash indicates a slightly longer pause.) "Fondly do we hope / fervently do we pray // that this mighty scourge of war / may speedily pass away." When FDR delivered his verbal assault on Mussolini, he delivered the lines in iambic vocal stress: "The <u>hand</u> that <u>held</u> the <u>dagger</u> // has <u>struck</u> it / into the <u>back</u> / of its <u>neighbor</u>." (The underlined words indicate the vocal beat, the slashes his actual vocal phrasing.)

Figures of Thought

The Rhetorical Question   The rhetorical question has already been defined and illustrated as a question so phrased that it elicits the desired response from the audience. For instance, when Congresswoman Shirley Chisholm advocated the Equal Rights Amendment [ERA] on the floor of the House of Representatives on August 10, 1970, she phrased her question so that the audience would answer "Nothing!" to itself: "No one would condone exploitation. But what does sex have to do with it?"[1] So do not overlook the rhetorical question's ability to improve your style.

Apophasis   Apophasis is an exceedingly subtle stylistic form that is downright fun to use. Apophasis is affirmation by denial. By ostensibly denying a point, you actually affirm it. Apophasis was one of Richard Nixon's knacks. To discredit Senator John Sparkman, who had questioned Nixon's slush fund, Nixon pointed out that Sparkman had his wife on the government payroll and that Senator Nixon did not have Pat Nixon on his payroll. Nixon concluded this counterattack thus: "Now just let me say this. That's his business and I'm not critical of him for doing that." Well, of course, Nixon intended to disparage Sparkman, or he would not have mentioned it; he affirmed his criticism by ostensibly denying it. Nixon did the same thing against Democratic presidential candidate Adlai Stevenson: "I don't condemn Mr. Stevenson for what he did." Sure.

Senator Edward Kennedy employed apophasis in his 1969 apologia for Chappaquiddick. "Although my doctors informed me," the senator said, "that I suffered a cerebral concussion as well as shock, I do not seek to escape responsibility for my actions by placing blame either on the physical, emotional trauma brought on by the accident or on anyone else." Then why mention the concussion and shock at all?

Lucretia Mott, one of the earliest feminist speakers in the United States, used apophasis in her "Discourse on Women" speech in 1849. Mott was invited to give a refutation against a speech by a Professor Dana, who ridiculed women's efforts to gain their civil and political rights. When she said "I have not come here with a view of answering any particular parts of the lecture alluded to," it was apophasis because that is exactly what she did, and exceedingly well, too! She even used an apophasis as a transitional device to introduce her argument section late in the speech: "It is with reluctance that I make the demand for the political rights of woman." But she proceeded to make it![2]

And in the 1988 presidential debate between George Bush and Michael Dukakis, the vice president sallied forth with a magnificent apophasis. After attacking Dukakis for his association with the American Civil Liberties Union, which Bush claimed favored x-rated movies for ten-year-olds, taking away the Catholic church's tax exemption, having kiddie pornography laws repealed, and taking God off the currency, Bush coyly said "And I hope people don't think I'm questioning his patriotism."

Apostrophe   **Apostrophe** is a rhetorical device whereby the speaker feigns to turn away from the audience to address a person or thing that need not necessarily be present. In terms of delivery, this is often accomplished by a slight twisting of the body to give the hint of addressing somebody or something else. President Ronald Reagan was very effective in using apostrophe. He would look off to stage right or stage left to address the ubiquitous liberal, pessimist, or Democrat who attacked Reaganomics.

Maria Stewart and Frances Harper, two of the earliest black women speakers, also used apostrophe. "O ye sons of Africa," Stewart implored blacks, who were not present in the audience, exhorting them to raise their voices for black rights. Frances Harper addressed the absent South, telling the audience to "Ask Maryland. . . . Ask Virginia. . . . Ask the farther South" why they traded in black people. She then answered for the absent states that the reason was money profit.[3]

Two recent speeches illustrate apostrophe. In his "The Fight Against Terrorism," President Ronald Reagan addressed two groups. To his critics, who were against his policy of bombing Colonel Qaddafi, Reagan responded in apostrophe: "When our citizens are abused or attacked anywhere in the world, on the direct orders of a hostile regime, we will respond, so long as I'm in this Oval Office." Later in his speech, Reagan indirectly addressed Qaddafi: "Despite our repeated warnings, Qaddafi continued his reckless policy of intimidation, his relentless pursuit of terror. He counted on America to be passive. He counted wrong."

In a classical application of apostrophe, Governor Mario Cuomo addressed President Ronald Reagan, who was understandably absent from the 1988 Democratic National Convention:

> There is despair, Mr. President, in faces you never see, in the places you never visit in your shining city. In fact, Mr. President, this nation is more a "Tale of Two Cities" than it is a "Shining City on a Hill." Maybe if you visited more places, Mr. President, you'd understand. . . . Maybe, Mr. President.

Chiasmus   **Chiasmus,** which comes from the Greek letter *chi*, which is written χ, means an inversion of terms in the sentence order. Cicero's observation that eloquence came before theory was stated in chiasmus: "it is not eloquence from theory but theory from eloquence born." Stated graphically, this is the scheme of chiasmus:

eloquence from theory

theory from eloquence

Chiasmus is not one of the easier stylistic expressions to invent, but if you have some samples before you, perhaps you can try your hand at achieving some memorable phrase. Examples of chiasmus are as follows. Jesus asked whether the Mosaic law was made for man or man for the law. At the Scopes trial in Dayton, Tennessee, William Jennings Bryan, a fundamentalist who was against Darwinism, asserted that he was more interested in the Rock of Ages than the ages of rock. The Reverend Harry Emerson Fosdick claimed that mankind will end war, or war will end mankind. Perhaps the most famous chiasmus with which you are familiar is in President John F. Kennedy's inaugural address: "Ask not what your country can do for you, ask what you can do for your country."

Metaphor and Simile   "He is a lion in battle" is a **metaphor.** "He is like a lion in battle" is a **simile.** The difference between these two stylistic devices is that similes use words such as *like* and *as* to make the comparison, while a metaphor invites the listener to make the comparison without the verbal prodding of a *like* or *as*.

Metaphors and similes help adjust the speech to the audience and the audience to the speech. They bring the known to the unknown; they add color to the style; and, as Aristotle observed, they give "clearness, charm, and distinction" to the speech [1405a6].

Robert Green Ingersoll, one of America's greatest nineteenth-century speakers, eulogized his brother in 1879. If Ingersoll had been a man of simple words, he could have said at his brother's funeral something like the following: "My brother died in early middle-age, and that is sad." Instead, Ingersoll, a master of metaphor, spoke in almost poetical terms:

> The loved and loving brother, husband, father, friend died where manhood's morning almost touches noon, and while the shadows still were falling toward the west. He had not passed on life's highway the stone that marks the highest point, but being weary for the moment he laid down by the wayside and, using a burden for a pillow, fell into that dreamless sleep that kisses down his eyelids still. While yet in love with life and raptured with the world, he passed to silence and pathetic dust.

Ingersoll also defined life in a striking fashion: "Life is a narrow vale between the cold and barren peaks of two eternities. We strive in vain to look beyond the heights. We cry aloud, and the only answer is the echo of a wailing cry."

In a short radio address delivered on his ninetieth birthday (March 7, 1931), Supreme Court Justice Oliver Wendell Holmes based his entire talk on the metaphor of a horse race. He observed that even though the race was over, "There was a little finishing canter before coming to a standstill."

One of the most powerful metaphors ever employed in a national convention speech was William Jennings Bryan's at the Democratic convention in Chicago in 1896. A major issue of the time was the gold standard, which helped the rich to stay rich and the poor to stay poor. In fact the speech was quickly dubbed the "Cross of Gold" speech after the stunning metaphor at its climax: "You shall not press down upon the brow of labor this crown of thorns, you shall not crucify mankind upon a cross of gold." As you might imagine, Bryan used his hands dramatically to pull down over his brow a make-believe crown in the first clause, and extended his arms as if on a cross when he uttered the second.

Thirty-six years later, in the same city, to another Democratic national convention, Franklin Delano Roosevelt offered the American people another metaphor: the New Deal. It was a metaphor that Father Charles Coughlin considered inapt. But rather than boldly asserting that President Franklin D. Roosevelt had lied to the American people about solving the Depression, Father Charles Coughlin invented a masterful metaphor to indict what he argued were FDR's sham activities: "Your erstwhile saviour, whose golden promises ring upon the counter of performance with the cheapness of tin." The comparison of tin with gold aptly revealed Coughlin's feelings about the president's failure to redress the imbalance of work and wealth in the U.S. during the 1930s.

FDR wanted to assail Mussolini for attacking France in 1940 but was constrained from doing so because of the Italian-American sentiment at the time. So Roosevelt inserted a memorable metaphor into a commencement speech that he delivered at the University of Virginia in 1940. The address became known as the dagger speech, and FDR did not have to name Il Duce directly: "The hand that held the dagger has plunged it into the back of its neighbor."

A tenet of the Republican party has long been that income tax cuts for the rich will spur investment, which will in turn eventually produce new industries and increase employment. The Democrats long ago attacked this theory with the marvelous metaphor of the trickle-down theory, which invited the poor to realize that the rich received money abundantly while the poor received it meagerly. To blunt this image, spokesmen for the Reagan administration invented a metaphor to counterattack the negative image of the trickle-down theory. Speakers for Reaganomics claimed that when the tide comes in, everybody's boat goes up, thus everybody benefits from Reaganomics. Jesse Jackson counterattacked with a metaphor of his own in the famous "Rainbow Coalition" address at the 1984 Democratic convention: "Rising tides don't lift all boats, particularly those stuck on the bottom."

The 1988 presidential campaign debates produced two carefully crafted metaphors. Senator Lloyd Bentsen invited the American audience to draw innumerable negative associations when he turned to Senator Dan Quayle and said, "Senator, you are no Jack Kennedy." Vice President George Bush scored a one-liner on Governor Michael Dukakis when Bush averred that Dukakis's answer on how to reduce the deficit was about as clear as Boston Harbor.

Consider how these two metaphors acted as enthymemes. Bentsen implied that Quayle possessed few if any of JFK's political experiences, and the voter completed the argument by inferring that Quayle was not vice presidential or presidential timber. Bush scored against Dukakis, who claimed to champion the environment, by alleging that a body of water in Dukakis's own state was a mess. Listeners completed the argument thus: If Dukakis cannot clean up Boston Harbor, how can he possibly clean up the country?

Antithesis   Antithesis is the contrasting or opposing of ideas in clauses or sentences. In juxtaposing ideas, antithesis piques interest by comparing in a novel fashion relationships not hitherto perceived. Antithesis was used throughout President John Kennedy's inaugural speech, and he set the mood in the first sentence: "We observe today not a victory of party but a celebration of freedom—symbolizing an end as well as a beginning—signifying renewal as well as change." Kennedy stylistically asked his audience to consider how an end could be a beginning, how renewal could be change.

Francis Wright, one of the very first women speakers to address American audiences, was an extremely capable stylist. In the following example, taken from a speech she delivered in 1828, she used antithesis to convey the harms of not giving women their legal and civil rights. Her genius was to group her sentences in pairs and to use antithesis within the pairs. Also observe how she began her balanced clauses with anaphora:

> Are they cultivated?—so is society polished and enlightened. Are they ignorant?—so is it gross and insipid. Are they wise?—so is the human condition prosperous. Are they foolish?—so is it unstable and unpromising. Are they free?—so is the human character elevated. Are they enslaved?—so is the whole race degraded.[4]

Maria Stewart also constructed a compelling antithesis to starkly contrast black slaves with their white owners. In her 1833 speech, notice also that her anaphora helped enforce the antithesis of "we" versus "they":

> We have pursued the shadow, they have obtained the substance; we have performed the labor, they have received the profits; we have planted the vines, they have eaten the fruits of them.[5]

If you are a close reader, you have noted that Stewart also polished her style by beginning the verb in each of the "we" clauses with the letter *p*, a subtle hint of alliteration. No wonder that Judith Anderson wrote that Stewart, despite having been an orphan without the opportunity of attending public schools, "managed to learn to read and write at a fairly sophisticated level for black females of her time period."[6]

Irony   Irony generally implies unexpected meanings in words or phrases. Irony occurs when words are spoken in opposition to their general meanings, when the words are not expected, or when they appear at first glance to be inappropriate.

JFK spoke ironically when he said: "For man holds in his mortal hands the power to abolish all forms of human poverty and all forms of human life." He jarred the audience with his comparison of man's ability to work for good—abolishing poverty—or to work for evil—to destroy the world with atomic bombs. Kennedy also used irony, this time expressed in antithesis, to express the MAD doctrine [Mutually Assured Destruction]. The MAD doctrine invigorated the missile race: "For only when our arms are sufficient beyond doubt can we be certain beyond doubt that they will never be employed." And so the Soviets and the Americans built ICBMs for thirty years on an ironic doctrine that was indeed mad.

President Abraham Lincoln also expressed a poignant irony in his second inaugural address:

> Both read the same Bible and pray to the same God, and each invokes His aid against the other. It may seem strange that any man should dare to ask a just God's assistance in wringing their bread from the sweat of other men's faces, but let us judge not, that we be not judged. The prayers of both could not be answered. That of neither has been answered fully.

Sarcasm   A little **sarcasm** goes a long way, but it has its rhetorical effectiveness in ridiculing some person or thing. Father Charles Coughlin, in his "Third Party" speech, in 1936 took a rhetorical sideswipe at FDR: "For God's command of 'increase and multiply,' spoken to our first parents, the satanic principles of 'decrease and devastate' has been substituted." Only a dyed-in-the-wool Democrat could fail to understand Coughlin's equation of FDR and satan.

Senator Nixon also used sarcasm against Stevenson and Truman in a classical fashion:

> You've read about the mess in Washington. Mr. Stevenson can't clean it up because he was picked by the man, Truman, under whose administration the mess was made. You wouldn't trust a man who made the mess to clean it up—that's Truman. And by the same token you can't trust the man who was picked by the man that made the mess to clean it up—and that's Stevenson.

Asyndeton   **Asyndeton** is leaving out the conjunctions or connectives between coordinate elements in a sentence. Perhaps an illustration or two would make asyndeton clearer. Angelina Grimke, a South Carolinian who joined the ranks of the northern abolitionists, gave a short speech in New York City in 1863. She began her address with asyndeton: "I came here with no desire to speak; but my heart is full, my country is bleeding, my people are perishing around me." (Did you spot a possible apophasis—that she really did intend to speak—and the anaphora of "my" repeated three times?) Here is her introduction without the asyndeton: "I came here with no desire to speak; but my heart is full, my country is bleeding, and my people are perishing around me." So what is the effect in leaving out the "and"? You will appreciate the essence of asyndeton if you read aloud the two versions above. If you pause after each clause in the quoted sample that

Grimke actually delivered, you will hear the impact of asyndeton. The rhetorical effect of asyndeton is to jab the point with a short pause or vocal stop. The connective "and" invites the speaker to continue talking without a pause, and hence the force of the thought is lost in the jumble of sentence elements.

President Franklin D. Roosevelt personally penned the most famous line from his second inaugural address. He wrote it in asyndeton and delivered it in that manner: "I see one-third of a nation ill-housed, [pause] ill-clad, [pause] ill-nourished." His verbal artistry with the anaphora of "ill" should be apparent, and this famous line was the rhetorical climax of four sentences that began with the famous anaphora of "I see millions" concerning people who were ravaged by the Depression.

Using Stylistic Devices

Assuming that you have invented alliteration, chiasmus, anaphora, epistrophe, and other stylistic techniques, you will want to make certain that you deliver these devices as you conceived them. To deliver a sarcastic comment or an alliterative phrase or a striking metaphor, you will have to practice and deliver these inventions as you designed them. Here are some helpful ways to ensure that your hard work will not have been in vain as you prepare to practice your speech for final delivery.

Leave nothing to chance; write out or type the stylistic inventions. That way, you will be certain to say what you mean, mean what you say, and say it in exactly the manner you intended. First, select the form of the memory aid. Decide whether 4×6-inch file cards or sheets of paper best fulfill your needs. The file cards have the advantage of containing only one thought or device on each one of them, but have the disadvantage that you have to rearrange them as you use them (numbering each one on the upper right-hand corner helps keep them in order). Sheets of paper allow more information on a page, but they are easily rustled as you shuffle them.

Second, decide how much of the stylistic device you need to include on your file cards or sheets of paper. If the technique is fairly involved, then you should probably write it out in its entirety. Triple-spacing on the computer makes it easier to read. If you can trust your memory, then short abbreviations might be enough to help you deliver an anaphora or epistrophe.

Deciding How Much Ornament to Use

But, you might ask, how much ornamentation is appropriate to a beginning student of public speaking? To what degree may I reasonably be expected to ornament my speech? Indeed, in the back of your mind you might be thinking what Quintilian thought when he remarked that figures of speech were a real ornament to style, but that they could be perfectly silly when used overmuch [IX, 3, 100].

You should realize that most professional speech writers would feel pleased if they could invent copious instances of these stylistic techniques. Remember that the ornamented passages quoted here are only small parts of the speech from which they are taken. In most cases the entire speech is not replete with the figures of speech. Many of the stylistic devices are illustrated in President John Kennedy's inaugural address, but you must recall that he had some of the best available logographers to draft that speech. So, when contemplating how much ornamentation to use, be guided by Aristotle's metaphor. He complained that a particular speaker's ornamentation was tasteless because he did not use ornaments "as the seasoning of the meat, but as the meat itself" [1406a19].

Down through the ages, critics from the Asian-Attic controversy to the present day have scorned what they thought were excesses of verbal ornamentation. Cicero was the whipping boy in antiquity. True enough, his speeches did range toward the grand style. But even Cicero advised an ornamented middle style. The other Greek and Roman theorists also favored an ornamented middle style. In the nineteenth century, a few speakers extended the idea of an ornamented style to the extreme, but this was never advocated by any classical authority.

Another facet of the how-much-is-too-much question is our contemporary understanding of what the ancients actually meant by the three kinds of style. Indeed, the ancients seemed to be clearer on what style was not than what it was. This problem is compounded by the difficulty of translating their Latin and Greek into English. The so-called grand style is too easily associated with verbal ornamentation when it really meant a heavy, grave, and ponderous style. The terms *plain style* gives the wrong connotation, especially when it is juxtaposed to the grand style. Perhaps the word *simple* would be a better translation. Avoiding the excesses of either kind of expression, the ancients used the middle style to denote the ideal *elocutio*. But they clearly understood that the middle style could and should be ornamented, although not excessively so.

Part of our contemporary difficulty with the ornamented style is that we tend to associate it with a flamboyant fist-brandishing delivery. This association truly existed in some nineteenth-century speakers; it was often discerned in Southern demagogues. But this association is not borne out in the best of historical and contemporary speaking practices. The speeches quoted above reveal an ornamented middle style that is neither heavy (grand) nor simple (plain).

Notes

1. Shirley Chisholm, "For the Equal Rights Amendment," in *American Rhetoric from Roosevelt to Reagan*, 2d ed., edited by Halford Ross Ryan (Prospect Heights, Ill.: Waveland Press, 1987), p. 222.
2. See *Man Cannot Speak for Her*, 2 vols., compiled by Karlyn Kohrs Campbell (New York: Praeger Publishers, 1989), II: 75, 89.

3. See Maria Stewart, "African Rights and Liberty," Boston, February 27, 1833, and Frances Harper, "Liberty for Slaves," New York City, May 13, 1857, in *Outspoken Women: Speeches by American Women Reformers 1635–1935*, edited by Judith Anderson (Dubuque, Iowa: Kendall/Hunt Publishing, 1984), pp. 169–173, 80–82.

4. Frances Wright, "Of Free Enquiry," in *Outspoken Women*, p. 253.

5. Stewart, "African Rights and Liberty," in *Outspoken Women*, p. 171.

6. Stewart, "African Rights and Liberty," in *Outspoken Women*, pp. 171, 169.

CHAPTER 5

Delivering the Speech

Lysias (459–380 B.C.). A Greek speech writer for courtroom cases, he was most noted for his art of concealing the art of oratory.

When asked what were the three most important functions in persuasive speaking, Demosthenes is reported to have said, "delivery, delivery, delivery." Quintilian opined: "For my own part I would not hesitate to assert that a mediocre speech supported by all the power of delivery will be more impressive than the best speech unaccompanied by such power" [XI, 3, 5]. Consider the following cases.

On October 30, 1938, Orson Welles delivered the "War of the Worlds" radio broadcast that scared millions of Americans into believing that Martians had invaded the earth. Welles achieved lasting fame by joining a carefully crafted script with a moving radio voice. President Franklin Roosevelt had an exceptional voice for reaching voters over the radio, and the movie newsreels carried his visual delivery to the motion picture audiences. In the 1960 presidential debate between Senators John Kennedy and Richard Nixon, Kennedy's delivery gave him a definite advantage over Nixon. In the 1988 vice-presidential debates, Senator Bentsen appeared more confident and comfortable than Senator Quayle. In the late twentieth century, a movie and television actor became known as the Great Communicator.

The great speakers of this century, including Franklin D. Roosevelt, Adolph Hitler, Father Charles Coughlin, Winston Churchill, General Douglas MacArthur, John F. Kennedy, Martin Luther King, Jr., and Jesse Jackson, have in common at least one characteristic: a dramatic dynamism in their delivery.

The ancients divided delivery into categories that are still used today. Aristotle led the way with the variables of the voice, which he stated were its volume, pitch, and rate—although he did not elaborate on these variables—and he hinted at bodily movement [1403b30]. The author of the *Rhetorica ad Herennium*, which was the first complete treatment of delivery, emulated Aristotle's lead by suggesting voice quality and physical movement [III, 20]. Cicero followed in those footsteps, but added the important factor of eye contact with the audience. Quintilian used the factors of voice and gesture [XI, 3, 14].

The ancient's basic conception of how to deliver a speech is remarkably serviceable today. To be sure, twentieth-century speakers do not slap their thighs, which, for some unknown reason, the Romans believed expressed extreme emotion. But we should not discard the insights of the ancients just because they wore togas and drove chariots. When it comes to human nature, most of their observations still apply because people were the same then as they are now. They were patriotic, they liked good food and fine wine, they liked a good show at the Coliseum, and they reacted to speakers in much the same way we react today. For instance, Quintilian noted that Romans dreaded monotones, disliked singsong speakers, did not appreciate being sprayed with the speaker's saliva, objected to speakers that inhaled loudly, and complained about overly nasal voices [XI, 3, 52–58]. He was also annoyed by speakers who sawed the air with their hands, rubbed their noses, walked up and down when delivering the speech, and shifted their weight from foot to foot [XI, 3, 119–129]. Presumably these behaviors in a speaker also bother you.

When their students came to them for instruction, the Greek sophists and Roman teachers such as Quintilian had two goals in mind when treating delivery. The overarching goal was to teach the students new habits of delivery. To acquire these new customs, the teachers had to teach new methods. Of course, while student speakers were mastering these new ways of delivering a speech, their delivery would be wooden. But as they progressively mastered vocal production, gestures, and eye contact, the persuasive effect would become more natural. Indeed, the author of the *Rhetorica ad Herennium* observed that the goal of a good delivery is to ensure that the speech comes from the heart [III, 25, 27]. Ideally the habits of good vocal production, gestures, and eye contact would become internalized, and the student would apply the skills in delivery to all speaking situations.

Classical teachers clearly understood that delivery was not some kind of an overlay that one applied to language. At its best, delivery corresponded to the language itself. The most effective delivery is really a wholeness or oneness with the speaker and the speech. The delivery is fused to the language so that it is a part of the living speaker.

The ancients also understood that the effect of delivery was rhetorical: It helped to make the speech more believable. They realized that the persuasive effects of delivery were obtained by teaching students new habits in emphasis and variety. You would not want to listen to a speaker who delivered the speech at the same volume, at the same rate and pitch, and without any gestures.

Modern rhetorical theorists have coined a word to describe the effects of delivery. *Dynamism* is the contemporary term that denotes a strong, vivacious, and compelling delivery. Dynamism comprises the power that the speaker has over the audience, how well the speaker knows the speech, the physical presence in the speaking situation, and the energy in giving the address. Other variables being equal, the more dynamic the delivery, the more persuasive the speaker and the communication.

This chapter is divided into the three classical variables that speakers have manipulated from ancient to modern times in order to fashion a compelling delivery. These major factors are the voice, eye contact, and gestures.

THE VOICE

Although the modern public address system no longer requires a speaker to project the voice to the far reaches of an auditorium, and television has tempered the shrill voice and frenetic gesticulations of a Coughlin or Hitler, throughout history all noteworthy speakers have used to the best of their abilities the voices they had. These speakers learned to modulate their voices by manipulating the loudness or **volume** at which they spoke, their **rate** or words per minute (wpm), and the **pitch** or musical tone of their voices.

Volume

Before the advent of amplified sound, it behooved a speaker to possess a stentorian voice that projected to all listeners, whether in a large hall or in the open air. Although it is hard to believe, the eighteenth-century evangelist George Whitefield is reputed to have spoken in open fields to 10,000 people without (of course) the aid of electronic amplification. If you wonder how he did it, you might want to know that the audience cooperated with him fully, for Benjamin Franklin noted that Whitefield's listeners maintained the strictest silence. Such a voice as Whitefield's could emphasize prominent points and charm the audience with verbal fortissimos and pianissimos.

Most speeches today are delivered in much smaller assembly halls. Depending on the situation you may also expect amplified sound. Yet, under the best of circumstances, you have probably been subjected to speakers that you had to strain to hear or have been annoyed by their misuse of a microphone. Even in the acoustics of a classroom, you will have to project your voice. Your first obligation is to make sure your voice can be heard by all members of the audience.

Have you ever been in an audience when the following happened? The speaker timidly asks if everyone can hear and then asks those who cannot hear to please raise their hands. The speaker evidently never reasoned that audience members who cannot hear will not hear the question and thus cannot answer by raising their hands! Such a faux pas is a sign of an ill-prepared speaker.

If you do need to speak louder, find out *before* your speech. The surest way to test whether you are speaking loudly enough is to ask a friend to sit in the back of the empty classroom while you speak. If your friend has even the slightest difficulty hearing you, you will have to speak louder, because when the audience fills the classroom they will actually absorb some of the sound. Coughs and other background noises will also interfere with the clear reception of your voice. Make certain that you practice your speech with greater volume so that you will project, as practiced, on the day that you give your speech.

If you will use a microphone, you must also prepare well. As a precaution try to get a sense of what your voice sounds like with the microphone. Do this well before you give the speech. Many people are surprised by the sound of their voices when they first use a microphone. You want to be accustomed to the sound of your amplified voice.

Test your loudness with the microphone. You or a friend can adjust the volume control as necessary. If you speak in an audible voice, the sound system will usually project your voice to everyone in the room.

Try to get a feel for how you will interact with the microphone. The microphone was made for the speaker, not the speaker for the microphone. If possible, raise or lower the microphone to your height, and adjust it toward or away from you. You want to stand up straight behind the speaking stand and place the microphone about a foot or so from your mouth. There is nothing more pathetic than a short person straining to reach an obstinately tall microphone, or a tall person hunching down to meet a short one.

Once you have established how loudly you will have to speak in the classroom, you need to consider how to manage your volume for rhetorical effect. With regard to the Asian-Attic controversy over the so-called grand style, it is interesting to note the connection between those who used a grand style and those who also spoke in bombastic voices. The culprits were the Asianists, for they also delivered their speeches in loud, obtrusive voices.

The ancients recommended the conversational tone. The author of the *Rhetorica ad Herennium* observed that the speaker should use the tone of conversation, which was the closest to the volume of everyday speech [III, 13, 23]. Of course, you might have to increase your volume somewhat in larger rooms, but the basic idea is to talk with the audience in a tone that approximates everyday conversation. Some political analysts have claimed that one of the reasons Governor Al Smith of New York lost the presidential election in 1928 to Herbert Hoover was that Smith boomed his words into the radio microphone like a stevedore. Added to his heavy New York accent this delivery made Smith sound like a burly gangster. Admittedly the volume of the voice has assumed a subsidiary role in radio and televised speaking, but it is still an important variable for the classroom speaker.

In conversing with the audience, you need to consider where you should be relatively louder or marginally softer. Here is a situation where you can make the written draft work for you. Do not be afraid to mark your manuscript with cues to yourself, such as "louder here," or "softer here," or "get gradually louder" and so forth. In general, rising emotion requires an increase in loudness; important words or phrases can be stressed by increased volume; and quotations, facts, and figures can be stressed with resonance. Conversely, secondary ideas, subdued emotionalism, and subsidiary points can be delivered in a more normal volume.

Wendell Phillips, an abolitionist speaker before the Civil War, turned volume to his advantage. Once, when confronted with a jeering crowd that was determined to shout him down, Phillips calmly left the rostrum and walked down to the front of the auditorium where members of the press were. Newspaper reporters were trained in shorthand, so Phillips started dictating his speech to the reporters. He reasoned that at least the newspaper subscribers would read his speech even if the audience would not hear it. After the audience perceived his ploy, it quieted down enough that Phillips could remount the rostrum and give his speech.

You want to make a strong initial impression on the audience and that usually can be accomplished by speaking in a fairly forceful voice at the beginning of your speech. You thus command the audience's attention. Likewise, a stronger voice may be appropriate when concluding your speech. However, these suggestions should not be taken as rules. You can set a contemplative mood, if you want to, by speaking the introductory words in a subdued fashion; likewise, you can communicate irony, paradox, sorrow, and similar emotions in a softer voice.

The author of the *Rhetorica ad Herennium* advised the speaker to use a conversational tone in the introduction and the conclusion of the speech and to use the full voice for the arguments and refutation sections. The rationale was that a strong voice at the beginning of a speech would harm the voice because of overexertion, the voice might be too fatigued to use a full voice in the conclusion. Perhaps you have heard a speaker's voice become raspy and hoarse by the end of the speech. At any rate, the author suggested that the conversational tone in the introduction and conclusion would be more agreeable to the tastes of the audience [III, 11, 21–22].

In beginning to think about how you might deliver your speech, consider giving yourself some cues on your manuscript. Although you probably will not use a full manuscript to deliver your speech, you can make it work for you in these preliminary stages. For instance, you could write in the margins instructions such as "speak softer here," "begin to get louder here," "stress this phrase with increased loudness," and "get very soft here." These cues can help you deliver your speech by reminding you how to emphasize orally your major points and ideas.

Rate

The **rate** of speaking, usually expressed in words per minute (wpm), is the speed at which you talk. A conversational speaking rate is 125–175 wpm. President Franklin D. Roosevelt spoke at about 120 wpm on the radio and at about 100 wpm, which is very slow by modern standards, to live audiences. Intercollegiate debaters have been clocked at 200-plus wpm, a rate that is intelligible only to the cognoscenti of that arcane art. Unless you are a nervous Northeasterner in a roomful of soporific Southerners, or vice versa, you will probably speak at a rate that is acceptable to your classmates.

When exploiting the full effects of rate, vocal pacing is the paramount object. Vocal pacing, sometimes called phrasing, gives variety and emphasis. Here too it helps mightily to make a written draft of the speech. You will probably notice that as you practice your speech you do not necessarily want to pause where you have commas or periods. You may speak in shorter or longer phrases than you have written, because it sounds better or more natural. You might even recast some sentences as you speak them, invert the order of words, or choose new and better words at the moment of utterance. Within reason, these adjustments are appropriate and welcome because they facilitate the oral style.

PAUSES WHERE NATURAL

In general, your rate should be slightly slower in the beginning of your speech. Adolph Hitler, for example, spoke at a measured pace in the beginning of his speeches to warm his audiences for the torrents to come. An audience is like a rock. To move a large mass, it is better to apply pressure gradually than to lunge at it.

Although not a fast rule, one way to conclude your speech is to slow down the pace. This not only cues the audience that you are concluding your speech but also gives the conclusion dignity and propriety. A well-known exception to this practice is found in Martin Luther King's "I Have a Dream" speech in 1963. King delivered his peroration at a driving rate that gave the impression of an unstoppable steam locomotive. Indeed, that was the image that he wished to project: The civil rights movement was picking up steam, and, once under way, it could not be stopped.

There are other situations in which common sense tells you to decrease your speaking rate. If your speech contains unfamiliar terms, words, or concepts, you want to pronounce these words more slowly so that the audience can comprehend them. When delivering poetry, important quotations, and vital statistics that you want the audience to understand, help the audience grasp these ideas by slowing down slightly.

You can master the manipulation of rate by experimenting. As you did with volume, mark your manuscript to remind yourself to vary the rate. Whenever you need to shorten or to lengthen phrases, use a slash [/] to mark how long the phrasing should be. Try your hand with the following examples. First, read the line without pausing:

> Unless you students volunteer to help and the Red Cross needs your help the campuswide blood drive will not succeed.

If you delivered the line without phrasing, it probably sounded more awkward than compelling. You may also have noticed that the line was so long that it exhausted your breath supply. Go back and insert some slashes where you think you should pause for emphasis. Take into account where you need to pause for a breath. These vocal pauses are not long, just short cessations of sound, rather like very short rests in music. Try phrasing the line another time, this time pausing slightly where the slash marks indicate a pause:

> Unless you students volunteer to help / and the Red Cross needs your help / the campuswide blood drive will not succeed.

Maybe the line could be spoken even better. Consider the following vocal pacing:

> Unless you students / [to emphasize students] volunteer / [to heighten *volunteer*] to help / and the Red Cross / [as juxtaposed to other agencies] needs / [to stress the real need] your help / the campuswide blood drive [not some other kind of activity] will / not / succeed [to heighten each word].

See what you can do with President Roosevelt's peroration for his 1932 Democratic convention acceptance speech, otherwise known as the New Deal speech:

> We are fighting fighting to save a great and precious form of government for ourselves and for the world I join with you I am enlisted for the duration of the war.

This is how he actually delivered it:

> We are fighting / fighting to save / a great / and precious / form of government for ourselves and for the world / I join with you / I am enlisted / for the duration / of the war.

Can you improve on his pacing?

In addition to very short pauses, longer pauses can be employed for effect. Such a pause is called a rhetorical pause and is a planned pause that lasts just long enough to draw attention to itself. For example, in the vice presidential debates of 1988, Senator Lloyd Bentsen used vocal pacing to craft a measured reply to Senator Dan Quayle. Responding to Quayle's claim that he had as much experience in Congress as John Kennedy did when he ran for president, Bensten replied: "Senator, I served with Jack Kennedy, [pause] I knew Jack Kennedy [pause], Jack Kennedy was a friend of mine. [pause] Senator, you are no Jack Kennedy."[1]

Experiment with rhetorical pauses in the following line. How long do you think the pauses should be? Could one or more rhetorical pauses, varied slightly in duration, better communicate the thought?

> AIDS / is a disease that strikes fear / in the federal government / and in college-age students. / Yet / the government has done too little / too late / and students / do not take the disease seriously enough.

When an orator speaks louder, the rate usually tends to increase, and vice versa. Perhaps you have heard an intercollegiate debater practically frothing at the mouth while delivering a rebuttal at an ear-piercing decibel level. You can gain variety and emphasis by slowing down while speaking relatively softly. This technique confounds normal expectations. That is exactly what President Roosevelt did in the conclusion of his famous Victory Dinner Address in 1937, in which he excoriated the Supreme Court for voiding much of the New Deal. Roosevelt implored the people to support his "court-packing" scheme by concluding his radio address with eight lines that combined anaphora and epistrophe:

> Here is one-third of a Nation ill-nourished, ill-clad, ill-housed —NOW!
> Here are thousands upon thousands of farmers wondering whether next year's prices will meet their mortgage interest —NOW!
> Here are thousands upon thousands of men and women laboring for long hours in factories for inadequate pay—NOW!
> Here are thousands upon thousands of children who should be at school, working in mines and mills—NOW!
> Here are strikes more far-reaching than we have ever known, costing millions of dollars—NOW!
> Here are Spring floods threatening to roll again down our river valleys—NOW!
> Here is the Dust Bowl beginning to blow again—NOW!
> If we would keep faith with those who had faith in us, if we would make democracy succeed, I say we must act—NOW![2]

Normally, a speaker would have delivered the lines increasingly louder on each successive line. However, FDR wisely tempered that tendency by alternating a loud and soft voice to deliver each line.

Pitch

General Douglas MacArthur could combine pacing, volume, and pitch quite effectively in his emotionally charged cadences. In a speech entitled "Don't Scuttle the Pacific," delivered to Congress in 1951, after President Truman had fired him for insubordination, the general complained:

> Why [downward inflection and slight pause], my soldiers asked of me [started on a higher pitch and inflected downward, and slight pause], surrender military advantages to an enemy in the field? [rhetorical pause] I could not answer [a slight stressing of each word, delivered in a downward inflection, with a voice that got softer on each successive word].

His emotional rendition, of which this is only one example, stimulated great Congressional applause and helped the American people forget about his insubordination.

Of the variables of the voice, pitch is perhaps the most difficult to describe. Pitch means the musical tone at which you speak. In normal conversation, you vary the pitch of your voice without thinking. Likewise, when you deliver a speech, you need to modulate your voice for emphasis and variety.

CHANGING INFLECTION
HELPS MOOD

Inflections are the means by which your pitch communicates meaning. Inflections are the fluctuations (rising or falling) of the pitch on words, phrases, and sentences. Try changing the pitch of your voice on FDR's peroration:

> We are fighting / fighting to save / a great / and precious / form of government for ourselves and for the world / I join with you / I am enlisted / for the duration / of the war.

The pitch of the voice is particularly adept at communicating subtle shades of meaning and emotions. Anger, frustration, sarcasm, indignation, and so forth can be communicated and heightened by subtle inflections in pitch. As you compose your speech, and later practice it, consider how you can strengthen your words by using inflections to augment your meanings.

Combining the Variables of the Voice

The variables of the voice—rate, loudness, and pitch—act in tandem and not separately. The well-modulated voice sometimes emphasizes rate over loudness and pitch, sometimes pitch over rate, and so forth. Although different variables have the central role at different junctures throughout the speech, they all play an integral part in delivering your words. In practicing your speech, be open to different ways to manipulate your voice, and finally select the one that seems best to fit the end and to sound the most persuasive to you. With careful practice, this process will become almost second nature to you.

EYE CONTACT

Of all the variables of delivery, **eye contact** with the audience is probably the most important to master. Political speakers recognize this fact and try to give their audiences at least the appearance of having good eye contact. The teleprompter ensures this deception. The teleprompter is a machine that projects the text of a speech onto a piece of clear glass, which is placed at an angle, so that the speaker can read the text while apparently looking out at the audience. The glass lets the audience see the speaker but not the text of the address. Presidential persuaders appear to have good eye contact with their live audiences, but the giveaway is a tiresome and repetitive left-to-right and right-to-left sweep of the eyes and turn of the head as they read from the right- and left-hand teleprompters that are placed at both sides of the rostrum. Since you will not have a teleprompter, let alone two, you will have to make do with real eye contact. The point is that considerable effort is invested to ensure that speakers, news broadcasters, and even many actors (who no longer bother to memorize lines) have ample eye contact.

Eye contact means that the orator looks directly at the eyes of all the members of the audience. Audiences expect speakers to look at them, not to be evasive, not to give sideways glances, not to look at the floor or ceiling, and not to read the speech. Just as you look at people when you converse with them so you look at the audience when making a speech to them. And remember that eye contact does not mean looking at an imaginary point at the back of the room, a few inches over the heads of people, or at people's shirts or blouses. It means looking directly into the audience's eyes.

The importance of eye contact was recognized in ancient times. Cicero believed that it was the most important factor in persuasion because the eyes express emotion, and everybody can read a speaker's eyes. Cicero hit on the idea of empathy, although he did not use that modern term.

Empathy is the ability of the audience to share the speaker's passions and fervor. Some of this empathy comes from the language of the speech and some of it comes from the delivery. Usually, the more eye contact, the greater the empathy the audience has with the orator. People have been trained from childhood to look at other people when they speak, and to "read" each other's eyes. If the orator does not look the audience in the eye, the listeners can not easily identify with the speaker. The eye is the window to the soul, and the speaker who does not look at the audience shutters his or her eyes. Empathy relies on the eyes, for Cicero observed that no one can produce emotion in the listener with the eyes shut [III, 220–222]!

Two important rhetorical phenomena occur when the speaker has good eye contact with the audience: (1) empathy and (2) feedback. Feedback consists of those responses that the audience broadcasts back to the speaker about the speech.

If the ancients understood feedback, they did not write about it. They surely were aware of how an audience responded to a speaker because they advised the speaker to gaze at the audience. We also know that the ancients advised the speaker to react to the audience by rearranging parts of the classical organizational pattern. But this adaptation was to take place before the speech was begun. The ancients apparently did not routinely adapt to the audience's feedback. In other words, once under way the speaker probably delivered the speech as planned and did not veer from the established course.

With regard to the concept of feedback modern rhetorical theory has made an advancement over classical practice. Feedback is useful to the speaker attempting to adapt to the audience. At the highest level, it can be used to adapt to the audience on the spot. People in an audience react in much the same way as they do in everyday conversation. They nod their heads in agreement or disagreement. They look puzzled when they do not understand something. Their faces register approval or dislike with regard to what they see and hear. They shift uncomfortably in their seats when a point is pressed home. And they look away when bored.

These kinds of reactions are helpful resources. If the audience is giving favorable feedback, you can assume that they agree with your speech, appreciate your points, and are impressed with your delivery; in short, they are with you. Conversely, if audience members are shaking their heads in disagreement, it is time to reiterate your point more forcefully or bring additional reasoning or evidence to bear. If the audience appears bored, try increasing your dynamism with greater emphasis and variety in the rate, loudness, and pitch. Feedback is a continuous audience response that a wise speaker wants to monitor. And this requires constant eye contact with the audience.

The goal of eye contact is to look at every person in the audience. Most classroom audiences contain from fifteen to twenty-five people, and you can easily establish eye contact with that many people. As the size of the room increases, especially in depth, it becomes harder to maintain eye contact with people in the back of the room, mainly because it is difficult to see them clearly. Nevertheless, you should make every effort to glance occasionally to the outer reaches of such an audience in an attempt to include everyone in your gaze and make them feel that even though they are in the back of the room you value their presence.

You have doubtless listened to speakers with poor eye contact. To varying degrees, they probably read most of the speech, seemed to drone on forever, and only occasionally looked up to ascertain if the audience was still there before reinserting their noses into their notes. In fine, theirs was not a scintillating performance.

Exceptional eye contact entails looking at the audience most of the time. There are, however, times when you might make exceptions to this rule. When reading a long quotation, rendering a poem, and reciting statistics and figures, it might be just as persuasive to pick up the book or other original material and read from it. In these instances, having the actual materials in hand increases your credibility. Otherwise you need to establish copious eye contact with your auditors.

The modus operandi in optimal eye contact is to sweep the entire audience. The sweep should be slow enough to look all the people in the eye, that is, not so fast that you appear to be the proverbial busy fellow who says hello and goodbye in one breath as he rushes past you. On the other hand, unless you want to stare down some miscreant in the audience, you should not hold any person's gaze too long, because it will make him or her feel uncomfortable. The sweep should be from right-to-left, left-to-right, and you should alternate that pattern with one that sweeps from the front rows to the back, and from the back rows to the front. The more you can vary these formats, the more natural and less mechanical your eye contact will be.

You need to practice your eye contact. Unlike sex appeal, good eye contact is something you can learn. In order to do so, you might take a hint from Demosthenes, who, according to Quintilian, practiced his speeches before a mirror to gauge the effect of his delivery [XI, 3, 68]. Adolph Hitler also practiced his speeches before a mirror. Practicing your speech before a mirror gives you excellent feedback. You can see how well you know your speech; if you are looking down at your notes too much, you do not know your speech well enough, and you will have to practice more. You can also assess the effectiveness of your gestures (the subject of the next section). When you *can* establish direct eye contact with yourself in a mirror, you will have demonstrated to yourself that you know your speech very well, and you will have attained the goal of good eye contact.

When rehearsing your speech, imagine that people are sitting in the audience. As you deliver the speech to yourself in a mirror, force yourself to look to the right and to the left in random patterns. This will help you check that you are establishing eye contact with all the members of the audience.

After you have practiced your speech before a mirror, you might try a few practice sessions in the classroom where you will actually deliver the speech. If that is not possible, perhaps you can secure a room about the size of your classroom. The idea is to get out of your dorm room, sorority or fraternity house, or apartment and practice delivering the speech in an environment that more closely approximates the classroom. Once you are accustomed to sweeping the imaginary audience in random patterns, you will be able to translate your practiced habit to the real audience.

GESTURES

Since classical times gestures have been subdivided into three categories: hand and arm gestures, head gestures, and body gestures. These kinds of gestures are separated only for purposes of discussion, because in reality all parts of the body work together to produce the gesturing speaker, who matches the gestures with modulations of the voice, which in turn correspond with the words of the speech. As with the canon of style, the ancients treated delivery in considerable depth. Unfortunately, the ancient's writings on delivery tended to be very rule oriented with a lot of do's and don'ts.

Have you ever wondered why hitchhikers "thumb a ride?" It is a gesture that seems to be universally understood. Quintilian observed that the turned back thumb was used in his era to point a direction, yet he thought it unbecoming in a speaker [XI, 3, 104]. Quintilian even advised how a speaker should wear the toga, and recounted how Cicero arranged his toga to cover his varicose veins [XI, 3, 143]. Although Quintilian's observations concerning the cultural tastes of the Romans are instructive, and often humorous, many of his prescriptions are not relevant to contemporary society.

But the problem with gestures runs deeper than cultural differences. The ancients experienced difficulty in even discussing the canon of delivery. The author of the *Rhetorica ad Herennium* complained that it was a demanding task to describe bodily movement with words and to illustrate vocal tones with writing [III, 27–28]. The author realized that it is relatively easy to teach the stylistic device of anaphora, but it is almost impossible to write about how one should gesture with the arm. After discussing delivery at great length, Quintilian—one senses almost in exasperation—admitted that various methods would suit different speakers. He allowed that what really mattered was whether the delivery was becoming to the speaker [XI, 177].

Writing about bodily movement is no easier today. Yet we can see four common threads that seem to connect the various classical treatments of gestures:

1. Appropriateness. As with the canon of style, the author of the *Rhetorica ad Herennium* thought that gestures should be appropriate, which would mean that the speaker should not appear to be an actor or a day laborer [III, 26].

2. Variety. Quintilian recognized that diversity was important in delivery [XI, 51].

3. Emphasis. All the classical rules revolved around the speaker's need to communicate to the audience the speech's important points. Otherwise everything would seem to be equally significant in the speech, and that is clearly not the case.

4. Timing. To be optimally effective gestures must be timed to coincide with the words they stress. Suppose a labor leader is urging a crowd of workers, "You must organize now." If the speaker wishes to emphasize *now*, the gesture must come on that word, not a half second later or earlier. As you consider the kinds of gestures, reflect on their appropriateness and how they should be timed to accentuate your important thoughts.

The Body

The Reverend Henry Ward Beecher, who preached against slavery and for a liberalized religion and Darwinism, served the Plymouth Church in Brooklyn, New York, from 1847 to his death in 1887. The most famous preacher of the age, Beecher absolutely refused to speak from a pulpit. He preferred instead to range over a large platform, which was elevated above the congregation and jutted into it. Perhaps taking a cue from Beecher, many of the video vicars of the late twentieth century prefer to roam across a soundstage to battle sin.

Politicians, on the other hand, almost always seem to preach their Democratic and Republican doctrines from the podium. If you are the President of the United States, you even get the presidential seal attached to the lectern as a trapping of the office. Likewise, speakers at high school and college commencements, service clubs, public forums, and professional meetings, usually stand behind a lectern.

Classroom speaking situations vary. Some classrooms have a speaker's stand, which may be placed on a raised platform; sometimes the lectern is movable; sometimes a desk suffices. Whatever the case, and whatever your size, your deportment on the platform affects the audience's perception of you and your message.

You are on display from the time you rise from your seat until you begin to speak. Even before you open your mouth, the audience is evaluating you. Do you approach the audience with energy, or do you amble to your place? Are you poised and confident or insecure and uncomfortable? Are you erect and ready to assume the stature of authority, or does the burden of your unpracticed speech weigh you down? Do you look eager to confront the audience, or is this just another assignment to muddle through? Are you dressed neatly and appropriately, or do your clothes betray the fact that you just tumbled out of bed, having stayed up late to learn your speech? This is a time when actions speak louder than words, so take care what message your behaviors broadcast to the audience.

Your exit is also important. Do you leave the platform with an air of confidence or one of dejection? Do you establish fleeting eye contact with members of the audience as you leave, or do you look at the floor in disgrace or toward the ceiling for help from heaven to get back to your seat? Does your face communicate that you are pleased with your speech (even if you are not), or does it betray your displeasure with your performance? Remember that nothing so much punctuates your speech as your leaving of it.

If given the option, you should learn how to use a lectern and also how to deliver a speech without one. You would then have mastered both kinds of speaking situations that you will most likely encounter in later life. You may prefer to deliver your speeches from behind a lectern, to stand alone in front of the class, or to deliver some of the speech from the lectern and some away from it. In the classroom there are no fast rules for obtaining optimal bearing on the platform, except to select the way that seems to work best for you, or whatever your teacher assigns. Accordingly, the rest of this section on body gestures is divided into how to use the rostrum constructively and how to stand alone effectively.

Speaking With a Lectern   A fact of life for most speakers in the "real world," is that they deliver their speeches from behind a lectern. This is both a help and a hindrance. Rostrums give an air of formality to a speech, they tend to dignify the speaker, and they hold the manuscript pages of an ill-prepared speaker. On the other hand, a stand can limit freedom of movement on the platform. When the speaker is using a microphone, he or she is a virtual prisoner of the rostrum. Depending on its size, a speaker's stand can hide most of the body (which some speakers are thankful for), and it physically and psychologically separates the speaker from the audience.

When using a lectern, you want to assume a stance of stability or equilibrium behind it. This is the base from which you will sally forth to gesture and to which you will return. The normal speaking attitude is to stand erect in the military "at ease" position with your feet apart. Point your feet apart at about a forty-five-degree angle. If you stand with your feet too close together, you will tend to wobble from one foot to the other. If you stand with your feet placed comfortably and reasonably apart, you will have a firm base from which to deliver your speech. Stand up, right now, and try these and the following do's and don'ts to find a position that works for you.

The following technique helps channel nervous energy, which normally accompanies the beginning of the speech. Plant your feet firmly on the floor, in the position advocated above, and push them into the floor as you speak. The audience will not be able to see you do this, but the energy you expend in pushing your feet into the floor will help calm your tension and channel your nervous energy. This is much better than clicking a ball point pen, tapping a pencil, jiggling your pocket change, strumming your fingers on the lectern, cracking your knuckles, or fidgeting with your notes.

One of the more common body gestures behind the lectern is to turn to the right or left. In turning, most speakers pivot from the waist so that they do not actually move their feet. Turning to the left or right as you gaze in those directions helps emphasize the sweep of your eye contact. Turning also communicates contrast and juxtaposition. The verbal transition, "On the one hand," can be accompanied by a turn to one side; an apostrophe can be delivered by turning aside to address the absent person who is its object.

Another common movement is to lean slightly backward or forward. Leaning slightly backward tends to draw the audience toward you. Leaning toward the audience—the extreme is to lean over the lectern—confronts the audience in a direct and physical fashion. Hitler had a tendency to lean forward as he stood on his toes: This menaced the audience and gave him psychological mastery over his listeners.

Another interesting effect can be obtained with the body. Try standing about an arm's length away from the stand as you begin the speech. As you warm to your subject, approach the stand by degrees so that by the time you are heavily involved in your subject you are pressed against the lectern. This gives the audience the impression of a dynamism so potent that it would burst forth except for the constraint of the lectern. If you want to lessen this effect on the audience, move back from the speaker's stand. Whatever stance you take behind the lectern, do not dangle your arms over it, which looks awkward, or lean on it for physical support, which gives the impression that you cannot stand on your own two feet.

Of course, you do not have to stand behind the lectern for the whole of the speech. You may elect to stand at one side of the stand for some of your speech; move to the other side for your second main head; or deliver your conclusion in front of the stand. (You would be unable to move very far from the stand if you were using a microphone because you would move beyond its range.)

Consider these pitfalls. If you do relocate, move for some purpose that makes sense rhetorically. Stay in the new place for a reasonable length of time. Do not become the "professorial pacer," who treads relentlessly back and forth before the audience. Eschew the "drunken sailor" gesture of swaying on the balls of your feet or shifting your weight from foot to foot, as if on an unsteady ship; your audience could become seasick through empathy. Beware also of the "fig leaf" stance, which may be decorous for sacred paintings and sculpture, but is definitely unbecoming to a secular speaker.

Speaking Without a Lectern   If you elect, or are forced, to speak without a lectern there are more drawbacks but greater recompense. Whereas the speaker's stand may conceal some of your body, there is nothing now to hide small but unsightly practices, such as standing on one foot and then the other, standing on the side of one foot, standing with one foot partially on the other foot, and other such ungainly postures. Moreover, you had better know your speech very well because you will look silly holding a speech manuscript in your hands. On the other hand, your bearing is not attenuated by an intervening lectern; your physical presence is enhanced by all of you, not just part of you; and your freedom of platform movement for emphasis is unrestrained. Of course you can still tilt, turn, and lean the body for emphasis.

There are several general patterns of movement used when speaking without a lectern. A triangular movement can be particularly effective when you want to organize your speech around three major parts. If you conceive your base as front and center, you can think of this position as the apex of an equilateral triangle. The first movement is then a step or two diagonally to the left or right. As a transitional device to another main head, you move laterally to the right or left. The final movement, which cues your conclusion, is diagonally backward, which can be accomplished by turning slightly as you take a few steps, toward your base position. Stand up and practice this movement to get the feel of it.

There are other patterns of movement. If you want to make four points you can first move diagonally out to the right or left; then laterally with the audience; then backward at the same diagonal angle of your first movement; then laterally to the base position. (For those of you who know geometry, you will have traversed a rhombus). Another variation would be to move to the shape of a parallelogram. You can also negotiate a pentagon that corresponds to the five sections of the Classical pattern. These platform movements can also serve as mnemonic devices: Each position can represent a different section of your speech.

The Arms and Hands

What to do with the limbs, as the Victorians called them, has always vexed photographers and speakers. Photographers fret over hands that clutter the picture and arms that need to drape naturally, whereas speakers never quite seem to know what to do with their appendages. Military speakers solved the problem by clasping their hands behind them in the "at ease" position. But unless you want to look like a master sergeant giving a speech to a civilian audience, you have to master other mannerisms.

The Arms and Hands at the Rostrum   When deciding what to do with your hands and arms at a speaker's stand, remember the concept of homeostasis. The basic choices are to hold or not to hold the rostrum. Some speakers are comfortable grasping the stand with one hand, while others hold on with both hands, and others seem content to just place their hands somewhere on the lectern. Still others simply let their hands rest at their sides.

As when moving the body for emphasis and variety, you should consider how to vary what you do with your hands at the lectern. When you move your hands from your sides to the lectern or whatever, leave them in the new place for awhile to avoid extraneous movements that interfere with your speech. If you can, try out the lectern before you give your speech to find the most natural and comfortable position for you. As you practice your speech, consider where you might appropriately place your hands.

The Arms and Hands without a Rostrum If you will not use a lectern, the usual deportment is to let your hands rest at your sides. Unless you want to appear to have delusions of grandeur, avoid the "Napoleonic stance." If you have presidential aspirations, you could affect President John Kennedy's habit of putting his hands in and out of his suit coat's pockets. If you want to affect a casual air, you could put one hand in the pocket of your pants or skirt, but beware of rattling coins and keys as you talk. (To be safe, remove them from your pockets before the speech.)

The Arms and Hands with or without a Rostrum The actual gestures of the arms and hands do not depend on whether you use a lectern. Quintilian gave us two good guidelines concerning gestures:

1. The eyes should generally look toward the direction of the gesture [XI,3, 70]. Quintilian did not mean that you actually look at your gesture, but that you look out in the general direction of the gesture. This makes good sense. When turning your body slightly to the left, or when gesturing with your right hand, your eyes would naturally focus to the left or right, respectively.
2. The speaker should not raise the hands above the level of the eye or below the level of the chest [XI, 3, 117]. Gestures made too much below the chest will probably not be seen, especially if you stand behind a rostrum. Low gestures may also appear timid and abortive. As for gestures that are too tall, Quintilian was probably right when he opined that speakers who wave their hands and arms high in the air appear to be carrying something aloft. In modern parlance, such a movement is called the "waiter's gesture."

Within reason, Quintilian's two rules are worth remembering, but they do not need be strictly followed for there are times when they should be broken for special effect. For example, here is how FDR delivered the peroration of his New Deal speech. For most of this passage, his hand was extended above the level of his eyes, and the actual movement came from the wrist:

> We are fighting [hand down] fighting to save [hand down] a great [hand down] and precious [hand down] form of government [hand down] for ourselves and for the world [hand and entire arm swept upward]. And so I accept the commission you have tendered me. I join with you [hand swept up] I am enlisted [sharp hand-and-arm chop downward] for the duration [hand down] of the war [hand-and-arm swept down].

Try this passage yourself. As you gesture, notice how the gestures reinforce the vocal pacing, how increased loudness on key words is almost mandatory, and how the upward sweeps of the hand coincide with rising inflections whereas downward movements reinforce falling inflections.

The hands and arms can almost communicate a sign language by themselves. They certainly augment spoken language, as in the following examples.

Palms turned away from body—generally denotes rejection. Try stressing this passage: "We don't want the criminal element in this community."

Palms turned upward—generally communicates supplication, pleading, and exhortation. "When will students learn to do their homework?"

Hand chop—punctuates important words. "The student body will never give in to *that*."

Pointed finger—accuses, warns, or draws attention to. "The motto on some Revolutionary War flags was a coiled rattlesnake with the caption 'Don't tread on me.'" "Listen . . . or you won't be able to do the assignment."

Clenched fist—communicates bellicosity and termination. "We will gain the inevitable triumph so help us God."

Splayed fingers—signals stamina and resolve. "We will never be satisfied until the Communists are driven from the seats of power."

Arm and hand gestures are also useful for describing concepts. Try these examples. Show the audience how English foot soldiers drove spikes into the ground to stop French knights at the Battle of Agincourt by grasping an imaginary spike and shoving it into the ground at an angle. Illustrate how, during the Civil War, the cannon ports on the U.S.S. *Monitor* opened to fire and then closed as the turret rotated slowly around, while the crew reloaded for the next shot. This can be accomplished by placing your palms together, then opening them away from one another for the shot, and then putting them back together, all while transcribing a small arc in front of you. Demonstrate how the federal deficit has increased at a greater rate than the gross national product (GNP), by making one arm, which represents the deficit, progress upward at a steep angle while the other arm rises at a flatter angle.

You might be interested in trying two gestures of the hands and arms that Quintilian recommended:

1. Place your middle finger against your thumb and extend your remaining three fingers slightly outward. Extend your arm slightly out in front of your body and move your hand slowly and slightly up and down and from side to side. Quintilian recommended it for the exordium and the narration [XI, 3, 92].

2. Bring your first three fingers and thumb together at their tips while leaving the little finger in a relaxed position. As you begin the speech, the gesture begins in the area of the chest and moves with a downward arm movement that ends with your hand resting at your side. This gesture is supposed to convey modesty or humility. Supposedly, it is a gesture that both Demosthenes and Cicero used to begin the exordiums of some of their famous speeches. [XI, 3, 96–97].

The Head

The head is not an inconsequential means of gesturing. Mussolini always seemed to have his head thrown back in an imperious manner. Hitler's head seemed to thrust and parry with the audience. FDR tended to tilt his head back slightly and jut out his chin to express disdain first for the Depression and later for the Nazis. President Eisenhower punctuated important words with a sharp downward head movement, and President Reagan brought the amiable head nod to a high art. Indeed, the facial sullenness of President Jimmy Carter, which seemed to reinforce the misery index, juxtaposed with the twinkling eye, cheerful face, and happy-go-lucky bobbing head of Ronald Reagan, which said the best was yet to come, was an image to which the voters reacted.

President Reagan also perfected other facial gestures. Grim set lips, accompanied by a slight turn to address stage right (the audience's left, where one would naturally find leftists), communicated determination to fight the Evil Empire. His slight and wry tilt of the head to the right or left signalled a punch line to come. And Reagan sometimes shook his head when he was verbally affirming a point, and vice versa. Thus he left it up to the audience whether to read the verbal message or to react to the nonverbal cue.

To communicate dynamism, you should hold your head erect while speaking. Quintilian thought it inappropriate for a speaker to droop the head, because it showed too much humility, or to throw the head back, because it showed arrogance [XI, 3, 69]. He also counseled against tossing or bobbing the head until the hair flew free because it suggested fanaticism [XI, 3, 71]. Interestingly enough, Adolph Hitler's hair was usually unkempt by the end of his speeches.

ASSEMBLING DELIVERY SKILLS

Just as you can learn to arrange and style a persuasive speech, so you can learn how to deliver that speech. As you begin to compose an address for both the ear and the eye, this learning becomes internalized. The key to mastering skills in delivery is experience.

The goal is to practice the various skills in delivery so that they became second nature. At first you will have to remind yourself to sweep the audience for good eye contact, but eventually you will do it without thinking about it. After you become accustomed to vocal pacing, rhetorical pauses, and changes in rate, pitch, and volume for vocal variety and emphasis, you will begin to perform those rhetorical techniques less mechanically and more naturally. Gestures that at first must be planned in advance will become an integral part of your dynamic delivery.

But none of this will happen until you master the fifth classical canon of *memoria*. For in truth, the fifth and last canon enables the speaker to learn the speech. *Memoria* is the glue that holds the speech together, and it is the oil that lubricates a smooth delivery.

Notes

1. Warren D. Decker, "The 1988 Quayle-Bentsen Vice Presidential Debate," in *Rhetorical Studies of National Political Debates*, edited by Robert V. Friedenberg (New York: Praeger, 1990), p. 179.
2. *The Public Papers and Addresses of Franklin D. Roosevelt, 1937*, compiled by Samuel D. Rosenman (New York, Macmillan, 1941), p. 121.

CHAPTER 6

Learning the Speech

Demosthenes (384–322 B.C.). A Greek sophist and
speech writer, he delivered some of the most famous
orations in classical antiquity.

MEMORIA

Memoria is the least understood of the five classical canons, because we have little
information about how speakers employed the canon. We know that the ancients,
beginning with the Greeks, developed mnemonic devices to help the speaker
remember the speech. The clearest picture emerges from Quintilian, who suggested that the speaker might talk through the speech as one walked, in the
mind's eye, through the rooms of a house by associating the entryway with the
introduction, the living room with the narrative, the dining room with the arguments, and so on [XI, 2, 20]. The system was supposed to cue the speaker what to
say and when to say it. The ancients devoted considerable energy to memorizing
their speeches. Their audiences thought it was unseemly to speak with sheaves of
paper in hand. Even notes would be a dead giveaway that the speech was not practiced enough, plus it is hard to gesture with notes and eye contact would suffer
appreciably.

Modern Problems with Memoria

At first glance, *memoria* is not a relevant canon to the contemporary speaker.
Except for intercollegiate contest speaking in individual events, few speakers
bother to memorize their speeches, because today's audiences tolerate speakers
who rely on notes. But have you had to endure a speaker who merely read the
speech?

Another problem with the canon of memory arises if the contemporary speaker tries to apply *memoria* in the manner in which the ancients evidently used it. The issue is audience adaptation.

General Dwight D. Eisenhower is reputed to have said that a general should always plan seriously but never take the planning seriously. (His style combined chiasmus with irony.) He meant that a general should plan the battle carefully but should never be so wedded to the planning that he cannot adapt to unforeseen exigencies on the battlefield. General Eisenhower's observation is germane to how a speaker adapts the persuasive speech to the audience.

As we have seen, the ancient's method of delivering a speech seemed to be that once a speaker got under way, he stayed the course. This obviously violates General Eisenhower's useful dictum about adapting to unforeseen events. In ancient rhetoric there would have been few, if any, adaptations to the audience's feedback. First, the ancients invested considerable time and effort in memorizing their speeches, so it would be difficult (but not impossible) to leave out practiced portions and insert new materials on the spot. The second reason is that many of the speeches that the ancients gave were timed. Like us, they evidently did not like to listen to long-winded addresses, so they used water clocks to time speeches. Quintilian advised speakers not to waste the water—to waste time [XI, 3, 52]. Finally, the ancients often delivered set speeches that were not supposed to be adapted to the audience but were to be delivered as they had been invented, arranged, and styled.

Speakers today face some of the same constraints that the ancients confronted. Most speeches for the classroom are assigned a time limit. When one is invited to speak before a service club for fifteen minutes, for example, that time limit must be followed so that the club members can get back to work on time. In the House of Representatives, debate is often limited to a few minutes per member, and even in the windy Senate, cloture can be invoked to end a filibuster. Most speakers must deliver their speeches within some time constraints. That means the speech will have to be prepared to close parameters, like the ancient set speech.

So here is the problem: If you have to prepare and practice a timed speech, then how can you adapt to the audience? If you adapt too much to the audience, by inserting new language on the spot, you run the risk of exceeding the time limit; if you delete materials that do not seem to be working with the audience, the speech could be well under time. If your instructor is a stickler for time, you probably cannot significantly adapt for fear of exceeding or not meeting the time limit and seriously affecting your grade. Hence your speech becomes a set piece, much like the speeches delivered in collegiate speech tournaments. If your instructor is more tolerant, you can do some adapting on the spot.

Modern Solutions for Memoria

This chapter is a bridge between the ancient canon of memory and the needs of contemporary speakers. It deals with how to capitalize on the best aspects of the canon of memory while remaining relevant to current practices.

In short, there is room for adapting to the audience within the canon of memory. You may recall that the author of the *Rhetorica ad Herennium* suggested that a speaker might want to reverse the order of the confirmation and confutation on the spot, so there is even some precedent for audience adaptation within the classical framework.

So that the solutions do not become problems, let us understand what the canon is and is not.

1. *Memoria* does not mean the delivery of a lockstep, memorized speech. In fact, some U.S. presidents have made slight changes in diction right up to the time of delivering a presidential address. For instance, President Lyndon B. Johnson inserted in his own handwriting some last-minute changes in the text of his famous "The Right to Vote" address in 1965.

    Franklin D. Roosevelt was probably the most skilled presidential communicator in the twentieth century, if not in the history of the nation. One of the reasons for his success was that FDR had a hand in the composition, arrangement, and stylistic polishing of his addresses. As he worked his way through the developmental stages of his speeches, he also learned them. For radio addresses, he often marked the text off in five-minute intervals, which suggests that he read the text to ascertain its length. Although he did not try to memorize his addresses, he tended to master them as a byproduct of his constant revisions. A case in point is his second acceptance speech at the Democratic national convention in 1936. As he was about to go to the rostrum at Franklin Field, he saw an old friend. FDR extended his hand for a handshake, lost his balance on his leg braces, and fell. His speech manuscript dropped in disarray. The Secret Service men picked up Roosevelt, gathered his speech text together as best they could, and handed it to the president. Roosevelt went to the rostrum to begin his speech without time to rearrange his pages. He was able to deliver the opening lines from memory while he put the pages back in their numerical sequence. The process of learning your speech that is advocated in this chapter is similar to the one that President Roosevelt used.

2. The canon means that you will continually revise your speech in the practice situation until you deliver it. No matter how carefully you have researched your speech, cast it into one of the organizational patterns, and polished its style, when the time comes to learn your speech, you will probably have to make some additional refinements. These corrections are the kinds of rhetorical revisions that many famous speakers make as they prepare to deliver their addresses. You also have to keep in mind that you might need to adapt to the audience on the spot. It is a difficult tightrope that the speaker has to walk, but one that can be traversed with careful preparation and practice.

3. The canon of memory is not a veneer that the speaker applies to learning the speech. When you see one chapter on how to deliver the speech and then one on how to learn it, you might reasonably infer that the two processes are

distinct. But this division is made only to fit the format of a textbook. In reality, learning how to deliver the speech and learning the speech happen at the same time.

4. Learning the speech is an ongoing process. As you practice your speech, you may add some new or different gestures while deleting some that you had planned. You may decide to speak louder or softer in places that seem more natural after saying the speech a time or two. You may keep some gestures that you planned, delete ones that did not work out, and add new ones that seem becoming to the speech. You might try different vocal inflections and pauses as they occur to you. And you may recast parts of the speech so that your language is more appealing to the ear than to the eye.

Memoria and the Habit of Quality Control

The utility of this chapter rests on the metaphor of quality control. Borrowed from the manufacturing process, quality control means that the product is continually inspected from its inception to its finished state.

This chapter is the bridge between a speech draft and a spoken speech. At this point, you have the finished draft of your speech. You have given consideration to how it should be delivered. Yet, even as the speech is going down the final stages of the assembly line, you need to check it closely. As in the preceding chapter on delivery, the emphasis here is on acquiring new habits of practicing the speech to maintain quality control. The athlete practices jump shots so that in the game their shots will be accurate and second nature. You practice your speech to be able to deliver it correctly and naturally.

MEMORY MATERIALS

Before you begin to learn your speech, you need to exercise quality control on the materials that you will use as you deliver the speech. These materials fall into two broad categories: (1) materials that you will want to quote closely, and (2) memory aids for delivering the speech.

Quoting from Researched Materials

The logical appeals that you will use in your speech need to be delivered exactly as they appear in the original source. One method is to type or write legibly quotations, statistics, and similar factual information on three-by-five- or four-by-six-inch file cards. Place only one unit of information on each file card and number the cards in the upper right-hand corner so that you will not get them out of order as you use them.

Another method is to bring the actual documents to class. Mark the places to be quoted in a book, periodical, or journal with slips of paper. Having the actual sources in hand makes your speaking more persuasive, because the physical presence of the materials adds credibility to the logical appeals. If you will debate someone or will engage in a question-and-answer session after your speech, having the original sources may prove helpful. In response to a point raised by your opponent or to a question from the audience, you may have recourse to the document. You could use it to support a response or an answer with additional evidence that you remember reading but did not use in your speech.

When employing the file cards or the actual sources, arrange them on the stand before you begin your speech. When you are ready to quote, pick up the cards or books and hold them out in front of you. In this way the materials function as a gesture because they reinforce the message. Read the quotation or statistic, usually at a slower rate and in a slightly louder tone to drive home the importance of the materials. You may want to hang on to the book or card for just a few moments to execute an additional gesture: a chop or jab gesture with the card or book in hand to reiterate or drive home the point. When you are finished, place the cards or book back on the speaker's stand.

If you are not using a speaker's stand, adapt the process to the situation. Place books and periodicals on a nearby desk or chair, pick them up to read, and then put them down when finished. Generally speaking, it is not a good practice to hold a book or magazine throughout the speech because it will hinder effective hand gestures, and you will probably become needlessly tired holding it.

Note cards are somewhat easier to use when there is no lectern. But they also hold the risk of detracting from your delivery. To decrease this risk you can hold the cards in the palm of your left hand, which frees your right hand for gestures. Make certain you keep them in order. However, if you plan to use memory aids, you should probably use a speaker's stand.

Using Your Own Stylistic Devices

This category concerns the stylistic inventions that you have created. Techniques such as anaphora, epistrophe, chiasmus, and metaphor have to be delivered as you conceived them, or you run the risk of ruining your rhetoric. This means that they must be delivered almost verbatim. In order to assure that your hard work will not be in vain, write out these stylistic devices. You will find it helpful to use file cards, and write a unit per file card. However, *do not pick up cards with stylistic devices on them.* Instead take a fleeting glance at these cards, just to check your memory, so that it appears to the audience that you know these stylistic devices as a regular part of your speech. Of course, if you can deliver these devices without memory aids, so much the better!

Exercising Quality Control with Your Cards

Use reasonable judgment on how many cards to use. For instance, it may not be necessary to place short excerpts, easily remembered facts, or simple metaphors on cards. However, longer quotations, complex facts, and an involved chiasmus are prime candidates for inclusion on cards. The idea is not to take an unwieldy stack of cards to the rostrum for an eight-to-ten minute speech. Take only those cards that are absolutely necessary.

The best way to use the cards is to number them consecutively. When you have finished with each card, make certain that you place it on the bottom of the pile. Then, the next card is ready for use when you need it. You need to practice doing this so that it is unobtrusive.

Some speakers find that these cards can do double duty for them. These speakers use the cards both as memory aids and to help them progress through the speech. They often write a line or two at the bottom of the card, sometimes in a different color ink. This line or two is not part of the actual quotation or fact but a lead into the part of the speech that immediately follows the quotation. This practice may be sufficient to keep the speech moving.

Quality Control in Delivering Your Speech with Memory Aids

Whereas some materials have to be delivered more or less verbatim, these materials constitute a small percentage of your speech. The bulk of the speech will not be memorized.

A reasonable and attainable aim is to use one sheet of paper containing the organization of your speech. One sheet of paper has several advantages over several sheets. You will not shuffle pages, which is distracting, because there is only one page. You will not look down as much with only one page, for more pages seductively invite you to look more at them. With the bulk of your speech in your head, you will establish better eye contact with the audience. The one page gives you the security of an overview of your speech and frees you to use your note cards for materials that need to be delivered precisely.

Speakers find that a single sheet of paper (perhaps two) is a sufficient memory aid for the basic structure of the speech. For instance, you could block out on a single page an outline of the five parts of the Classical pattern with some words to jog your memory:

Introduction: quote statistics on the rise of hazing incidents on college campuses.

Narrative: tell graphic story of drinking hazing and of physical hazing at two universities, stress tragic death of both students.

Arguments:
1. Why hazing harms pledges and actives.
2. Why hazing harms image of fraternities, sororities, and the university.
3. Why hazing is sadistic, and should be stopped.

Refutation:
1. Why the vicious cycle of I-had-to-go-through-it-so-should-you attitude must be stopped.
2. How bonding can be accomplished with other activities.

Conclusion: Appeal to class to effect change in their living units by talking to friends and supporting the drive to end hazing on campus.

You could list skeletally the options to be negated by the method of residues:

Introduction: Discuss the increasing murder rate in the country and especially in urban areas. Quote statistics from *New York Times*.

Disjunct 1: The status quo does not work because of the revolving door principle of crime-prison-parole-crime-prison, etc. Quote from article in law review, and from *Washington Post*.

Disjunct 2: Capital punishment deters only the executed criminal, not others; has disadvantage of debasing society. Quote ethical considerations from two authors.

Disjunct 3 [your proposal]: Life sentence without parole is the answer: deters the murderer, stops revolving door policy, and does not debase society in punishing the criminal. Quote opinions from three note cards

Conclusion: appeal to the class to change mind, let reason rule over emotions, still punish criminals but not punish society that executes them.

You could itemize the steps in the Monroe motivated sequence:

Attention: Talk about how photographs are a part of every trip, vacation, holiday, and party.

Need: College students want a camera that is inexpensive, durable, and capable of adding features later. Discuss how cost is a consideration; fragile cameras not useful in most collegiate settings; do not want to be locked into a camera with no add-on capability.

Satisfaction: College students should consider buying Brand X because:
—it is cheaper than most cameras
—it is rated as practically foolproof
—it has a hard plastic case and lens protection
—you can add on different lens and a timer

Visualization:
—imagine taking crisp pictures on a trip
—how the flash takes good indoor shots
—how you can afford to buy film because the camera is less expensive
—how the add-on of a self-timer can put you in the picture
—how the add-on of a telephoto lens will enable you to capture distant shots

Action: Buy this camera at any discount store . . . but buy this camera NOW to start gaining all of its advantages in your collegiate life.

You can also streamline the Burkeian pattern on one page:

Guilt/Anger: reference to recent election
               voters angry

yet most politicians returned to their seats
voter apathy—low turn-out for election
Victim/Scapegoat: voters feel powerless
vote does not seem to count
political action committees [PACs] are controlled
by powerful special interests
people unable to check the abuses
Salvation: only way to solve is by limiting terms
discuss three terms for congressmen and two terms for
senators
—how they will be more responsive to voters than PACs
—government service a duty not a career
—appeal to class to support the speech and/or write
congressmen/senators to support such a bill

You can easily place the problem-solution organizational pattern on one page.

Introduction: cite statistics on U.S. trade imbalance, facts on Americans losing their jobs, and U.S. dependence on foreign companies.

Problem: nothing wrong with principle of free trade, just that free trade is a one-way street to disadvantage of U.S.A.:
—automobiles, computers, agricultural products
—unfair foreign barriers, quotas, tariffs
—soft U.S. stand means the problem will continue

Solution: tariffs on foreign imports until a true free trade market exists
—tariffs will motivate foreign countries to lower their restrictions
—tariffs will help restore American jobs and competitive edge
—tariffs will also bring money to federal treasury

Conclusion: until foreign countries truly engage in free trade, U.S. should retaliate with tariffs to protect U.S.A.

The goal toward which you should strive is to know your speech as well as possible. After you have mastered the steps in learning your speech, you may find that you will need few, if any, memory aids to deliver your speech.

HOW TO LEARN YOUR SPEECH

The fundamentals of speech communication course is a learning laboratory. You have to exercise the first five letters of the word *laboratory* before you can expect the last seven letters to emerge. The amount of labor you devote to the speech is generally related to the grade you will receive for your oratory, so the more work expended in practicing the speech, the higher the praise from your instructor.

The following process begins after you have composed your speech. It assumes that the speech draft is in a fairly finished form. During the takeoff of an airplane the pilot must decide at a certain point whether to continue the takeoff or to abort by reversing the engines and applying the brakes. Once past the commit line, the airplane will either fly or crash land at the end of the runway. Although a speaker faces less drastic consequences than the pilot, at some point you will have to commit yourself to go with the draft that you have. You will not have enough time to make major revisions in your speech and then expect to learn it. The earlier you start researching, writing, and learning your speech, the less need there will be to cram several day's work into the night before the speech is due. So, before you begin to learn your speech, you need to be reasonably satisfied with the basic text and to be committed to it.

Reading Aloud for Time

After you have written your speech, you need to read it aloud in order to time it. Try to go to the classroom where you will actually deliver the speech. Failing that, go to a room where you will not be bothered by friends, and where you can deliver your speech aloud without disturbing others.

Read the speech through in its entirety. Do not stop if some parts of the speech do not sound right—you will fix these problems later, so just mark them with a pen as you continue reading. Try to speak as closely as you can to the rate that you will use when delivering the speech. This rate should be the tempo you normally use in everyday conversation. So that you will know how much to write to approximate the time limit, a double-spaced typewritten page with normal margins generally takes about one and one-half minutes to deliver.

The point in this first reading is to ascertain how long the speech is, since most speeches have a time limit. Assume you have to deliver an eight-to-ten minute speech. The ideal time for such a speech might be around nine minutes (about six pages). This would allow you some room to adapt to the audience on the spot if necessary. If you add or delete some materials, you will still be within the time constraints. If the speech is the appropriate time, congratulate yourself! If the speech is too long, it will have to be reduced; if it is too short, materials will have to be added.

At this juncture, it may be appropriate to take your speech back to the drawing board to make the necessary changes. Prune or add material to get the speech into the parameters of the assignment. Now is also the time to fix those egregious errors that you marked with your pen while reading the text. You can smooth out the prose so that it sounds better to the ear. Make certain that your changes do not exceed or undershoot the time limit. Once you have a speech that fulfills the assigned time limit, you can move to the next section.

Practicing Your Speech

In this stage, you begin in earnest the process of learning your address. The basketball player must practice jump shots, the violinist must practice vibrato, the swimmer must practice flip turns, and the speaker must practice delivering the speech. How many times you have to practice your speech probably varies from person to person, and from speech to speech. In general, the longer the speech is, the more times you will have to practice it. Just keep in mind that practice pays the athlete with a better score, the musician with a better performance, and the speaker with a better grade.

The organizational pattern that you select will also help you master your speech. It is easy enough to remember that the Classical pattern has an introduction, narrative, arguments, refutation, and conclusion. The sections in the other speech patterns are equally easy to remember. Thus the organizational patterns themselves are mnemonic devices that can help you remember your speech. With the pattern in your mind's eye, you can monitor where you are in the speech, what the nature of the language is for each section, and the connection between each section and the entire speech. This synergy between the words and organizational format will enable you to remember and to deliver your speech as planned.

The process of learning your speech is simple but time consuming. Baldly stated, it means that you deliver your speech over and over until you know it cold. This has not changed since Quintilian's time when he freely admitted it was a difficult and timesome task [XI, 2, 28]. You have to expend the labor so that you will realize the oratory.

The goal in mastering your speech is not to memorize it in the traditional sense of memorizing a poem or a play. In those instances, the pieces have to be memorized word for word. In speaking, the goal is to deliver the speech more or less as you planned it. Do not be alarmed in the practice sessions if the order of some sentences gets inverted, as long as they make oral sense; if some sentences get rearranged, as long as your meaning is clear; or if you accidentally change the flow of paragraphs, as long as you communicate the gist of your speech. Even if all of these things occur, you should not worry too much. No one but you has the text of your speech, and therefore no one but you will detect these deviations.

The best place to practice your speech is the room where you will deliver it. As you read through your speech the first time or two in the practice situation, you will have to force yourself to look out to the imaginary audience. Try to say a few sentences without looking down at your text, and continue through the entire text in that manner. Do not worry if you find yourself recasting your language from the written style into the conversational style. Do not worry if you recast words, phrases, clauses, and even entire sentences—as long as they are intelligible—because you are appealing to the ear. These are the normal adjustments that a speaker makes when moving from a written text to a spoken speech. At first your delivery may be awkward, but it will improve with practice.

Each time you practice your speech, force yourself to rely less and less on your text. There are no short cuts to this task. If you do not compel yourself to depend less on your notes each time, you simply will not learn your speech. And if you do not learn your speech, your lack of preparation will be obvious to everyone in the audience. You will have poor eye contact and less dynamism, and you will probably utter those detestable vocalized "uhs," and "ums," that you may have occasionally endured as a member of the audience.

In the later stages of learning your speech, here are some challenging tips you might try. As already suggested, try delivering the speech to yourself in a mirror to see if you really know it and to gauge the effect of your delivery. If you have access to a tape recorder, or a video recorder, record your speech to get valuable feedback on how you are progressing. When you know your speech well, try delivering it to yourself as you walk to and from class. When you are satisfied with your progress, invite a friend to listen to you and give you some additional feedback.

At some point, after the fifth or fifteenth time, you will have mastered your speech. It will not be memorized verbatim, but you will know it cold. You will feel more confident and you will remember your speech better if you practice it several times a day for three or four days rather than nine times the night before it is due.

When you can demonstrate the following behaviors to yourself, you will know your speech. Can you deliver the speech in a "dress rehearsal" without notes or memory aids? Can you deliver your speech to yourself in a mirror? If you pass one or both of these tests, you will have demonstrated to yourself that you have mastered your speech. When you know your speech very well, you are ready to deliver it to the class.

It has been stressed repeatedly that practicing the speech so that you know it very well is not the same as memorizing it. The ancients evidently memorized their speeches word for word. Most contemporary speakers do not memorize for good reason. The hitch is that if you ever forget something in a memorized sequence, you probably won't remember where you are, where you have been, or where you are going in the piece. A break in the flow of a poem or a speech can be disastrous. Do not attempt to memorize a speech; it can be hazardous to your mental health.

This catastrophe will not happen when you have truly practiced your speech extensively. Because you have practiced the speech repeatedly, you know that you tend to deliver it slightly differently each time. But each time the essence is the same. Hence, you are accustomed to slight changes. If you have a momentary memory lapse, your one-page outline should help you get back on track. The one-page sheet will probably preclude even short lapses. But if such lapses should occur, you have a safety net.

You need to adapt the "speaker's poker face." The audience will never know you have faltered unless you communicate it to them. If you grimace, sigh, look upset, utter uhms or uhs, or stop dead in your tracks, you will most certainly reveal your memory lapse. On the other hand, if you move quickly to the next section, no one will be the wiser.

Let us assume that you inadvertently skip or forget a major section of your speech. As quickly as you detect the error you can make a transition back to the original intended flow. Transitional language, such as "Let me backtrack to another point I wanted to make," "Before going any further, let me mention another point," or even something as blatant as "I almost forgot to make this point, so I will make it now," can cut your losses to a minimum. You would be unable to make these on-the-spot adaptations if you memorized your speech, but you will be able to adapt only if you practice your speech enough.

Another asset accrues from knowing your speech well. You can adapt to audience feedback on the spot. If you see puzzled looks or shaking heads, you can quickly add some additional reasoning and evidence that you did not originally intend to use or perhaps some more forceful gestures to drive your point home. If you memorize your speech, you will probably not be able to adapt in that fashion, if at all.

It is not recorded how Demosthenes would have responded to the question of what are the three factors in a successful delivery. But surely he would have rejoined: "Practice, practice, and practice."

CONCLUSION

The Ongoing Study of Rhetoric

The study of public speaking originated over 2300 years ago. This makes rhetoric one of the oldest of the liberal arts. How and why a speaker can or cannot persuade an audience fascinated the ancients, and in that tradition theorists continue to study persuasive discourse today. In a real sense, the study of persuasion has both advanced and remained the same. For instance, the ancients considered persuasive speaking an art, and contemporary thinkers and their theories have been unable to achieve for rhetoric the status of a science. The ancients never claimed that their rules and formulations would guarantee success every time. Neither do contemporary communication consultants claim success always. Presidential candidates presumably have the best speech writers and media people that money can buy, but only one of them wins, and so it goes down the line from senators to representatives, governors, mayors, college class officers, and students in a speech class.

Some enduring constants remain from ancient to contemporary times. As an art, rhetoric is akin to medicine. A physician may not know why you are sick or what caused your illness, yet he or she can generally treat the symptoms with medicine that heals. Theorists might not know why or how an audience is convinced, but they can usually offer rhetorical prescriptions that persuade.

People, then and now, tend to be swayed by evidence and reasoning rather than by assumption and unsupported assertion. Aristotle developed the three modes of proof—logical, emotional, and ethical—as the core materials in inventing a speech. These are still functioning factors in persuasive discourse today, and will continue to be so into the future.

Organizational strategies also help persuade people. The ancients did not write the last word on how to structure a speech. But the Greek and Romans developed the classical pattern and the method of residues, which have served speakers well for over two millennia and will continue to do so.

The style or choice of language has a positive effect on listeners. In this regard, the author of the *Rhetorica ad Herennium* almost had the last word. The major stylistic devices, and many of the esoteric ones, are directly traceable to that source. Whether speakers acknowledge their debt, or even know they have one, eloquent speakers knowingly or unknowingly will continue to speak with a polished prose style that was developed long ago.

A dynamic delivery always makes an influential impression on the audience. Quintilian gave the most complete account of delivery, which was in turn based on Cicero and other Roman rhetoricians. His treatment remains remarkably practical today.

But of what the scientific mix of these classical canons is, contemporary theorists can offer no better predictions than their predecessors. Whether one canon is always, sometimes, or never more important than another one; whether a given speech, crafted by the best writers, will persuade; and whether one should dissemble for some greater good, are questions that continue to vex thinkers today.

As for persuasive scruples, rhetoricians from the ancients to their modern counterparts have always lamented the strengths and limitations of ethical discourse. Consider three examples:

1. The American Civil War may be said to have been caused by speakers. White and black abolitionists railed against the peculiar institution while Southern fire-eaters defended it. Each group thought it spoke the truth, each claimed the Constitution and the Bible were on its side. In the ensuing conflict did right make might, or might make right?

2. For a hundred years after the Civil War, white supremacists plied the country with racist rhetoric while black men and women raised their voices against the wrong. Ironically, it was a Southerner, President Lyndon B. Johnson, who championed the landmark civil rights laws of the 1960s through the Congress. Did elected U.S. officials lead the times or did the times lead them?

3. In the 1984 presidential election Walter Mondale admitted that he would raise taxes, and his honesty helped contribute to his defeat. Should he have remained silent, or told the people what they wanted to hear, which was the strategy of the other candidate?

Such problems have always existed, and they will continue to plague future speakers. However, it took women suffragists almost a hundred years of speaking to overcome the sham arguments that men used to deny women the vote, but vote they finally did in the 1920 presidential election. And in the late twentieth century, American citizens are finally recognizing and rejecting the bogus arguments (advanced by one political party, acquiesced in by the other party, championed by the president of the United States, and supported by both houses of the Congress) supporting the notion that a nation can live beyond its means. In a democratic country, truth does seem to win through in the long run.

Senator Albert Jeremiah Beveridge, one of those spread-eagled orators of the late nineteenth and early twentieth centuries, when discussing the issue of gold and silver coinage in the United States, said "The American people are tired of talking about money—they want to make it."[1] Lest you tire of reading about speaking, this conclusion hastens to an end so that you can begin speaking.

Notes

1. Albert Jeremiah Beveridge, "The March of the Flag," *Great American Speeches 1898–1963*, edited by John Graham (New York: Meredith Corporation, 1970), p. 19.

APPENDIX

Classical and Contemporary Communications

Seven speeches are collected here. They are Patrick Henry's "Give Me Liberty or Give Me Death," Frederick Douglass's "What to the Slave is the Fourth of July," Henry Ward Beecher's "Woman Suffrage Man's Right," Rev. Harry Emerson Fosdick's "My Account with the Unknown Soldier," Senator Richard Nixon's "My Side of the Story," President Jimmy Carter's "Panama Canal Treaties," and First Lady Barbara Bush's 1990 commencement address at Wellesley College "Choices and Change." These addresses were selected for the following reasons:

- First, this collection of speeches follows the classical practice of giving the student some sample speeches to emulate. These speeches exemplify the classical rhetorical techniques that have been discussed in this book.

- Second, these speeches illustrate the three strands of classical rhetorical theory. From a technical perspective, all of the speeches illustrate stylistic, argumentative, and organizational strategies that are classical in origin. Henry's, Fosdick's, Nixon's, and Carter's speeches all followed the classical pattern with applications of the method of residues, and Beecher adapted the classical pattern to his rhetorical situation. Bush's speech is a good example of how the speaker used rhetoric to turn an attack on her back onto the attacker. From the sophistic perspective, the speeches illustrate the kinds of materials that should persuade an audience. However, some observations will be made concerning deficiencies of proof in a few addresses. From the philosophical perspective, all of these speeches illustrate the moral necessity of an audience's changing its belief or action. But in Carter's case, the reasons why the audience ought to be persuaded were problematical, and in Nixon's case these reasons were downright unethical.

- Third, these collected speeches are exemplars of one or more of the classical canons of rhetoric. Arrangement, style, and delivery played an important role in Patrick Henry's success. Both Beecher and Fosdick invented arguments and refutations that were adapted to their respective audiences. Nixon's speech was successful because he fulfilled the requirements of all five canons, even with regard to *memoria* because he delivered his speech without the aid of a manuscript, notes, or a teleprompter.

- Fourth, the speeches illustrate, although rather loosely, Aristotle's three genres of speaking. Although none of the speeches are strictly forensic, which is defined as speaking in the courtroom, Nixon's famous "Checkers" speech certainly has forensic elements: He successfully defended his secret campaign fund in the court of public opinion. Bush's speech at the 1990 Wellesley commencement is clearly epideictic for it was delivered on a ceremonial occasion. As for deliberative oratory, Henry's "Liberty or Death" speech is the only one that is technically deliberative, because he made the speech before the Virginia convention in Richmond. Functionally, however, President Carter's "Panama Canal Treaties" address is deliberative because he addressed the nation in an attempt to convince the people to move the Senate to ratify the treaties.

One has the most difficulty in categorizing the speeches of Beecher and Fosdick, partly because religious rhetoric was not practiced in classical Greece. Beecher's "Woman's Suffrage Man's Right" seems to be epideictic, because it was a public lecture, but it also had deliberative overtones: It urged the lecture audience to favor the ballot for women. Fosdick's speech, delivered first before a secular audience and then as a sermon in the Riverside Church in New York City, defies classical compartmentalization. Arguably, it partook of all three genres: it blamed past wars and called them unjust, it excoriated the tendency toward war in the mid-1930s, and it asked its listeners to forsake future involvement in war.

Following each speech text is a rhetorical criticism of that speech. Each text represents a different nexus of speaker, speech, and audience. All of the speakers faced in their respective audiences proponents, neutrals, and opponents. Accordingly, each rhetorical criticism tries to highlight the salient interactions that are necessarily different from speech to speech. Yet, some common foci can be expected.

Rhetorical technique is front and center. The critiques will closely examine organizational patterns, sytlistic devices, and the forms of proof, which are the core of the classical scheme. As necessary, they will include an assessment of the ethics of the speech, for not all of the speakers and their speeches were good persons speaking well. One should not in every instance expect detailed information about the canons of delivery and memory; this data is often unobtainable, particularly for the older speeches about which little is known beyond the final text and delivery. Wherever possible, the critiques will explain the persuasive effect of the speech on the audience.

Patrick Henry's "Liberty or Death"

Patrick Henry (1736–1799). A lawyer and patriotic orator, he delivered the "Liberty or Death" speech that helped to instigate the American Revolution.

PREFACE

Patrick Henry was one of the foremost orators of the American Revolutionary War period. As a country lawyer he gained Virginia's attention in 1763 when he argued the compact theory of government in the Parsons' Cause. He persuaded a jury to award the clergy only one penny in damages. He debated vigorously in the Stamp Act Resolves in Virginia during May 1765. This debate concerned the first resistance adopted by a legislature against Great Britain. But Henry's most famous speech was his "Give Me Liberty or Give Me Death," delivered on March 23, 1775, at Richmond, Virginia.[1]

The speech was delivered in St. John's Church, Richmond, which served as the meeting place for the Virginia Convention. Henry used his speech to argue for a set of resolutions to arm the colony and prepare for defense. Ironically, Henry delivered his deliberative speech in an ecclesiastical setting.

The speaker and the speech represented the three strands of rhetoric. For the philosophical strand, Henry's purpose was to convince the delegates of their moral duty to begin the process of ending the colony's relationship with Great Britain. Henry himself was an exemplar of sophistic rhetoric. He was the ideal speaker to lead the state to greater attainments. And Henry also represented the technical strand of rhetoric, for he sought a change of attitude that would translate into positive action: rebellion against the King of England.

Unfortunately, the text of Henry's speech only approximates what he actually said. If Henry had notes or used a prepared speech text, which is a possibility, these materials have vanished. The text that is printed here was composed by William Wirt and published in 1817, some forty years after Henry actually spoke.

As one might imagine, scholars have debated over whether Wirt's text closely approximates what Henry actually said. Judy Hample held that Wirt composed the speech. Although Wirt relied on several excellent first-hand accounts, the most notable being St. George Tucker's recollections of the actual speech, Hample concluded that most of the speech is Wirt's invention.[2] To Wirt's credit, however, he did not present the speech as a text but as a report of what was said. On the other hand, David McCants believed, and offered other scholars' research to support his claim, that Wirt's report closely approximated what Henry actually said.[3]

Although what Henry actually said at St. John's Church may never be determined, one can nevertheless criticize the rhetorical text. The five canons will be the focal point of a rhetorical criticism of Henry's speech.

The Canon of *Inventio*

Since the textual authenticity of the speech is in question, it is difficult to say how Henry invented the speech. Nevertheless, some reasonable inferences can be made.

We know that the Richmond convention consisted of partisans, neutrals, and opponents. The Whigs tended to favor Henry's idea of government by compact, and hence they would be favorable to his resolutions. The Tories were staunch supporters of the King and royal rule, so they would not support Henry's call for treason. There were doubtless Whigs and Tories who were somewhat neutral in the debate.[4] It is also reasonable to assume that Henry adapted his arguments to these three groups. For his proponents, he used arguments that would reinforce his and their position that Virginia should fight; for his opponents, Henry probably realized that he should address their reservations on breaking with Great Britain; and hopefully those in the neutral camp would be swayed toward Henry's position by one or both of his pointed appeals.

The Canon of *Dispositio*

To accomplish his rhetorical aims, I believe that Henry used the classical organizational pattern. This is an example of how Quintilian held in the *Institutio Oratoria* that the canons of invention and arrangement were interrelated [I, Proemium, 22; III, 3, 2; VI, 5, 1]. The pattern enabled Henry to muster an arguments section for his partisans, and a refutation section for his opponents. Since I hold that the speech followed the classical organizational pattern, I should note that Hample observed that Wirt was "an accomplished rhetorician," that he could write such a speech, and that his eloquence almost matched Henry's.[5]

The Canons *Actio* and *Elocutio*

Fortunately, some eyewitnesses to Henry's remarkable speech left accounts of what they saw and heard. These will be cited in the criticism. Suffice it to say here that almost all observers stressed the difficulty of accounting for Henry's delivery, yet all agreed that it was extremely powerful and moving.

The Canon of *Memoria*

About this canon little is known. Henry's actual speech seems to have been delivered either extemporaneously or impromptu. My guess is that Henry probably delivered his speech extemporaneously.

The slight differences between extemporaneous and impromptu are worth noting. In general terms, an extemporaneous speech is one in which the speaker has some time to prepare the thoughts, to think about the nature of proofs, and to compose a skeletal outline in the mind. For instance, one can easily imagine Henry at his seat listening to the debate, and all the while mapping in his mind a speech that would marshall arguments for his measures and refute his opponent's reservations. In terms of delivering an extemporaneous speech, the speaker would probably not have time to write out a draft but would merely jot down an outline of words and phrases to help keep the speech marching to its conclusion. Here is where, for instance, the acquired habits of organizing and delivering the speech, which were stressed in chapters 3 and 5, would aid the speaker in adapting to a new situation.

The impromptu speech is defined as one that is delivered almost on the spur of the moment. Usually an impromptu speech is delivered with little or no preparation. Unless one is a highly trained speaker and accustomed to speaking in an impromptu fashion, impromptu speeches are usually rambling and not well organized; however, they can be charged with an expressive delivery as one becomes energized with the emotion of the moment.

The last observation concerns the nature of the printed text that follows. William Wirt originally presented the speech text with interpolations, such as "he said," "said he," and "continued Mr. Henry," because it was not a verbatim account but a close reconstruction of the speech. I have excised Wirt's interpolations. I also cast appropriate verbs into the present tense as Henry would have most likely delivered it; Wirt used the past tense. I have also taken the liberty of placing in brackets the five sections of the speech that correspond to the classical organizational pattern.

 ## "LIBERTY OR DEATH": THE SPEECH
Delivered at St. John's Church, Richmond, Virginia,
March 23, 1775.

[Introduction] No man thinks more highly than I do of the patriotism, as well as the abilities, of the very worthy gentleman who has just addressed the house. But different men often see the same subject in different lights. Therefore, I hope it would not be thought disrespectful to those gentlemen, if, entertaining opinions of a character very different to theirs, I should speak my sentiments freely, and without reserve.

This is no time for ceremony. The question before the house is one of awful moment to this country. For my own part, I consider it as nothing less than a question of freedom or slavery. And in proportion to the magnitude of the subject, ought to be freedom of debate. It is only in this way that we can hope to arrive at the truth, and fulfill the great responsibility which we have to God and our country. Should I keep back my opinions at such a time—through fear of giving offence—I should consider myself guilty of treason toward my country and of an act of disloyalty toward the Majesty of Heaven, which I revere above all earthly kings!

[Narrative] Mr. President. It is natural for men to indulge in illusions of hope. We are apt to shut our eyes against a painful truth, and listen to the song of that siren, till she transforms us into beasts. Is this the part of wise men, engaged in a great and arduous struggle for liberty? Were we disposed to be of the number of those who having eyes, see not? and having ears, hear not? the things which so dearly concern our temporal salvation? For my part, whatever the anguish of spirit it might cost, I am willing to know the whole truth! To know the worst and to provide for it! I have but one lamp by which my feet are guided, and this is the lamp of experience. I know of no way of judging the future but by the past.

[Arguments] And judging by the past, I wish to know what there has been in the conduct of the British ministry for the last ten years which justifies those hopes with which gentlemen have been pleased to solace themselves and this house? Is it that insidious smile with which our petition has been lately received? Trust it not, sir! It will prove a snare to your feet! Suffer not yourselves to be betrayed with a kiss! Ask yourselves how this gracious reception of our petition comports with those warlike preparations which cover our waters and darken our land! Are fleets and armies necessary to a work of love and reconciliation? Have we shown ourselves so unwilling to be reconciled that force must be called in to win back our love? Let us not deceive ourselves! These are the implements of war and subjugation—the last arguments to which kings resort. I ask what means this martial array, if its purposes be not to force us into submission? Can gentlemen assign any other motive for it? Has Great Britain any enemy in this quarter of the world to call for this accumulation of navies and armies? No, sir, she has none! They are meant for us! They can be meant for no other! They are sent over to bind and rivet upon us those chains which the British ministry has been so long forging.

And what have we to oppose them? Shall we try argument? We have been trying that for the last ten years. Have we anything new to offer upon the subject? Nothing. We have held the subject up in every light of which it is capable; but all has been in vain. Shall we resort to entreaty and humble supplication? What terms shall we find, which have not been already exhausted? Let us, not, I beseech you, deceive ourselves longer. We have done everything that could be done to avert the storm which is now coming on. We have petitioned —we have remonstrated—we have supplicated—we have prostrated ourselves before the throne, and have implored its interposition to arrest the tyrannical hands of the ministry and parliament. Our petitions have been slighted! Our remonstrances have produced additional violence and insult! Our supplications have been disregarded! We have been spurned, with contempt, from the foot of the throne! In vain, after these things, may we indulge the fond hope of peace and reconciliation? There is no longer any room for hope. If we wish to be free, if we wish to preserve inviolate those inestimable privileges for which we have so long been contending, if we mean not basely to abandon the noble struggle in which we have been so long engaged, and which we have pledged ourselves never to abandon until the glorious object of our contest be obtained, we must fight! I repeat it, sir, we must fight! An appeal to arms and to the God of Hosts is all that is left us!

[Refutation] They tell us that we are weak, unable to cope with so formidable an adversary. But when shall we be stronger? Will it be next week or next year? Will it be when we are totally disarmed, and when a British guard shall be stationed in every house? Shall we gather strength by irresolution and inaction? Shall we acquire the means of effectual resistance by lying supinely on our backs, and hugging the delusive phantom of hope, until our enemies shall have us bound hand and foot? Sir, we are not weak, if we make a proper use of those means which the God of nature has placed in our power. Three millions of people, armed in the holy cause of liberty, and in such a country as that which we possess, are invincible by any force which our enemy can send against us. Besides, sir, we shall not fight our battles alone. There is a just God who presides over the destinies of nations, and who will raise up friends to fight our battles for us. The battle is not to the strong alone; it is to the vigilant, the active, the brave. If we were base enough to desire it, it is now too late to retire from the contest. There is no retreat, but into submission and slavery! Our chains are forged! Their clanking may be heard on the plains of Boston! The war is inevitable—and let it come! I repeat! Let it come!

[Peroration] It is in vain to extenuate the matter. Gentlemen may cry, "Peace, peace," but there is no peace! The war is actually begun! The next gale that sweeps from the north will bring to our ears the clash of resounding arms! Our brethren are already in the field! Why stand we here idle? What is it that gentlemen wish? What would they have? Is life so dear, or peace so sweet, as to be purchased at the price of chains and slavery? Forbid it Almighty God! I know not what course others may take, but as for me, give me liberty or give me death!

ANALYSIS

Patrick Henry's famous "Liberty or Death" speech is an exemplar of rhetorical technique. In addition to the Classical pattern, Henry used several other devices to energize his speech. These techniques were the method of residues and the rhetorical question. The method of residues is an application of the disjunctive syllogism, in which the speaker presents A, B, C, and D and then negates A, B, and C, leaving D as the residue and only viable alternative. Henry used the method in the arguments and refutation sections. The rhetorical questions throughout the speech are so phrased as to elicit from the audience the desired response.

The Canon of *Dispositio:* The Classical Pattern

The Introduction   Perhaps following the advice of the *Rhetorica ad Herennium*, Cicero, and Quintilian to make the audience attentive, receptive, and disposed toward the speaker, Patrick Henry wanted to reveal his ethos as a member of the convention who had possessed goodwill, good sense, and good moral character. He achieved this goal by inventing two interdependent persuasive appeals that reinforced his ethos. He first introduced these appeals in his introduction, but they appear with some regularity throughout the speech.

HENRY'S GOODWILL   Henry's first goal in the introduction was to exhibit his goodwill toward the audience. For the partisans, he needed to appear belligerent enough to stand with that group; he needed to appease the neutrals by appearing to be moderate; and yet he could not seem too bellicose so as to turn off his opponents.

Henry garnered the audience's attention by referring to the previous speaker, who is unknown. Although this speaker (perhaps a Tory?) had evidently spoken against Henry's resolutions, Henry nevertheless complimented the man by praising his patriotism. This especially evinced Henry's goodwill toward his opponents. However, he quickly, yet respectfully, moved to the offensive by appealing to a value shared by all the members of the audience. Henry tapped his listener's commitment to freedom of speech by asserting that it was not "disrespectful" to speak one's "sentiments freely, and without reserve." Henry tried to seek assent from his audience that they could agree to disagree in legislative debate. But this was just an opening skirmish.

HENRY'S GOOD SENSE   To illustrate his good sense to all segments of the audience, Henry had to demonstrate why a member of the convention should advocate treason against King and Parliament, which was the effect of his resolutions to arm the Virginia state militia.

Henry displayed his good sense in the second paragraph of his address. Building on the goodwill that he established in the first paragraph, Henry extended that strategy. Claiming that it was not a time to stand on ceremonial niceties, Henry went to the pith of the argument. In an appeal that would have a profound impact on white men who owned black slaves, Henry stated a stark polarity. The audience faced "freedom or slavery." White masters well knew what black slavery meant, and they would be loath to allow themselves to become slaves of Great Britain. Henry adapted exceedingly well to his Virginia audience. The master/slave metaphor made preeminent good sense to the partisans, perhaps to the neutrals, and it certainly would have made even the opponents pause for reflection. Thus, the freedom/slavery choice was insinuated into the introduction, and it would recur throughout the speech.

HENRY'S GOOD MORAL CHARACTER   Henry needed to display his moral character. At least some would suspect his motives because he advocated military action against constituted authority. Henry had to establish the morality of his cause.

His opponents were just as patriotic as Henry was. They just happened to believe that they were loyal British subjects—and that Henry should be, too. Henry had to turn their misplaced loyalty toward a higher and more moral goal. In order to do this, he argued a subtle enthymeme concerning God versus King. Accurately reasoning that religious men in Virginia would ultimately obey God over the King if it came to that, Henry forced the issue. Building on the colonist's premise that "freedom of debate" was the only way to obtain "truth," Henry claimed that he had pure motives in speaking. He would, he assured his audience, be guilty of "treason toward my country" and of an act of "disloyalty toward the Majesty of Heaven, which I revere above all earthly kings" if he did not speak out. (Note the veiled stylistic slight of King George III, who was a mere earthly king, when compared to the Majesty of Heaven, which was God.) By implication, Henry asked his audience to complete the enthymeme that they, too, would be guilty of treason toward Virginia and God if they at least did not listen to Henry's speech. This religious reference was also telling because the delegates were meeting in a church. Perhaps Henry traded on the sense of place to imply that God was looking over the delegate's shoulders to make sure they took the correct course of action.

THE PERSUASIVE POWER OF HENRY'S INTRODUCTION   From a technical perspective, Henry's introduction was also effective. To his partisans, he indicated his allegiance to Virginia versus Great Britain, and they would have applauded that. One assumes they also would have assented to his appeals to the adversaries.

For the neutrals and opponents, Henry developed three compelling motifs. He gained an initial hearing by mentioning the tradition of debate inherent in the Virginia legislative assembly. Yet there were bounds beyond which one should not step, and one of those constraints was not to speak treason against the King. To gain a hearing of his resolutions, which were tantamount to treason, Henry alluded to the emotional issue of slavery. Not even the most dyed-in-the-wool Tory would want to be a slave. Henry's last argument, the appeal to God over King, could be compelling if he could prove that the issue admitted of no other solution.

The Narrative   Henry's *narratio* was a not-so-subtle negative portrayal of people for whom hope springs eternal. These people were the Tories and perhaps some neutrals, but definitely not Henry's partisans. He allowed that it was natural for such men "to indulge in illusions of hope" and to shut their eyes to a "painful truth." But a Tory or a neutral who did that ran the risk of listening to the song of the siren. This was an allusion to classical Greek mythology. Although many contemporary Americans would probably miss the allusion, members of Henry's audience, who had a strong classical education, would have understood the meaning immediately. The sirens were sea nymphs who sang sweet songs to lure sailors to destruction on the rock of Scylla. The enthymeme that Henry argued was that sailors should not be lured to destruction by the sirens: The sailors figuratively represented the Tories and the sirens were the King and Parliament.

But in case members of the audience did not assent to that classical allusion, Henry marshalled a series of rhetorical questions. If one considered oneself a wise man (and everyone fancies himself wise), Henry would have elicited the desired "No" from his audience when he asked: "Is this the part of wise men, engaged in a great and arduous struggle for liberty?" He also asked the rhetorical question (with biblical overtones) whether people had the ears to hear and the eyes to see their "temporal salvation?" The desired response would be "Yes."

Having motivated the audience to listen to the truth, Henry challenged them to abandon illusionary hope. In two short bursts, he exclaimed that he was willing "to know the whole truth" and "to provide for it!"

His transition to the arguments section was grounded in a traditional Virginian value. He knew "of no way of judging the future but by the past."

The Arguments   Thus far Henry had tried, and successfully so, to build his ethos with the audience. His narrative had further identified the classical and Biblical reasons for listening to him. But he still needed to prove his case.

This was his thesis: "I wish to know what there has been in the conduct of the British ministry for the last ten years which justifies those hopes with which gentlemen have been pleased to solace themselves and this house?"

He answered his thesis by using the method of residues.

The disjunct of the petition was dispatched with the aspersion toward King George III's "insidious smile." If one happened to be beguiled by that smile, Henry asked his audience not to be "betrayed with a kiss." Everyone would have understood that Biblical analogy because in it Henry likened King George to Judas Iscariot, who betrayed Jesus Christ to the Roman guards with a kiss.

The disjunct of the British fleets and armies was negated next. It was a fact that British warships and soldiers were sent to bully the colonies. Henry defined those facts as preparation for war. He used a string of rhetorical questions to argue thus: The army and navy are upon the colonies. No one can explain why British forces should be in the colonies, and Great Britain has no other enemies in the colonies. Therefore, Henry concluded, "They are meant for us! They can be meant for no other!"

The logical proof of Henry's confirmation was compelling. Even if one believed that petitions might yet save the day, which Henry believed was fanciful, he definitely proved by the method of residues that British armed forces were meant to subdue the rebellious colonists. In order to clinch the force of his logical reasoning, he once again referred to the emotional appeal of the freedom/slavery issue: "They are sent over to bind and rivet upon us those chains which the British ministry has been so long forging." Assuming that his audience would not like to be in chains, Henry asked, "And what have we to oppose them?" as a transition to his second argument.

Henry also used the method of residues for his second argument. For the disjunct of "Shall we try more argument?" he rightly claimed that nothing new had been thought of in the last ten years. The enthymeme at work here was that since argument had not worked in the past, there is no reason to believe it will work now or in the future.

For the disjunct of "Shall we resort to entreaty and humble supplication," Henry plaintively asked what else could be tried. The word choice of "humble supplication" was wise. With its connotation of a bowing and scraping servile posture, the term was probably repugnant to most of the proud Virginians in the audience.

He then summarized these disjuncts. He used anaphora in balanced phrasing: "We have petitioned . . . we have remonstrated . . . we have supplicated . . . we have prostrated ourselves before the throne." Juxtaposed to these colonial overtures, Henry used the style of antithesis to denigrate the British responses: "Our petitions have been slighted! Our remonstrances have produced additional violence and insult! Our supplications have been disregarded! We have been spurned, with contempt, from the foot of the throne!"

In summarizing his argument, Henry demonstrated the efficacy of the method of residues: "I repeat it, sir, we must fight! An appeal to arms and to the God of Hosts is all that is left us!"

The Refutation   Even if one were persuaded that the only avenue open to the Virginia convention was to fight the British, there would be at least one nagging doubt. Great Britain was one of the world's greatest military powers. Even if one believed Henry's argument that fighting was morally correct, perhaps one should not act on expedient grounds, i.e., one would likely lose! The refutation section is tailor-made for addressing such persuasive problems.

But before treating Henry's refutation, a caveat is in order. In the arguments section, Henry was at pains to support his claims with factual evidence. The audience accepted his interpretative history of negotiations with the British, and the deployment of British armed forces was public knowledge. This information served as logical appeals or evidence for his claims.

However, the critic looks in vain for evidence in Henry's refutation section. Here Henry relied on heavily freighted emotional appeals and God-is-on-our-side assertions to refute his opponent's reservations. If the British had won the Revolutionary War, an English rhetorical critic could have scorned Henry's lack of logical appeals for fighting the British.

The transition to the refutation section was "They tell us that we are weak, unable to cope with so formidable an adversary." Doubtless, sentiments of that nature had been uttered in the debate by the Tories and the neutrals.

Henry applied the method of residues in the refutation. He systematically negated reservations that might reside in the minds of his opponents. But he answered his opponent's question whether the colonies were strong enough to fight with a question. (Answering a question with a question is usually a giveaway that the person is trying to cover a weakness. The strategy is to divert attention from the original question to a new question more to the liking of the respondent.) In a series of four jabbing rhetorical questions, Henry asserted the colonies were not weak. But proof was lacking, although emotive language was not. Words and phrases, such as "totally disarmed," "British guard," "irresolution and inaction," and "lying supinely on our backs," effectively masked the issue of military ways and means for armed conflict with Great Britain. But not to worry, Henry rushed headlong into another disjunctive refutation.

God is on our side, claimed Henry. The "God of nature" had placed "means" —but Henry did not state what these means were—in the colony's power; the "holy cause of liberty" would make the colonies "invincible" against the British; and there was a "just God" who would "raise up friends to fight our battles for us." One wonders if Henry possessed preknowledge that the French would help the colonies to badger the British?

If one harbored any remaining doubts, Henry rolled over them in the last few sentences of his refutation. He recurred to the polarity of freedom versus slavery. Even if the Tories were "base enough" to desire to retreat, such a course was impossible. Henry applied the force of the method of residues as he exclaimed: "There is no retreat, but into submission and slavery! Our chains are forged! Their clanking may be heard on the plains of Boston! The war is inevitable—and let it come! I repeat! Let it come!"

The Conclusion   Henry's conclusion was succinct. It was a model conclusion because he achieved the high drama that one associates with a classical peroration.

He derided those who cried "Peace, peace" when there was no peace at all. He then lauded the patriotism of the Massachusetts colonists, shamed those Virginians who would not fight, and asked the convention to jump on the bandwagon of armed rebellion:

> The war is actually begun! The next gale that sweeps from the north will bring to our ears the clash of resounding arms! Our brethren are already in the field! Why stand we here idle? What is it that gentlemen wish? What would they have? Is life so dear, or peace so sweet, as to be purchased at the price of chains and slavery? Forbid it Almighty God!

This excerpt further illustrates Henry's tendency to polarize the issue between freedom and slavery, and it also resurrects the God-is-on-our-side appeal.

Every school girl and boy knows by heart Henry's final words: "I know not what course others may take, but as for me, give me liberty or give me death." The effect of the speech was "electrical." Judy Hample has listed all the effects that the speech had on persons who heard the speech as Henry delivered it. These eyewitness accounts of Henry's delivery would repay anyone who wished to read Hample's essay. Two of her researched quotations suffice here. A James Parker of Edinburgh, Scotland—although not a member of the convention, he was nevertheless there—wrote disparagingly of Henry: "You never heard anything more infamously insolent than P. Henry's speech: he called the K_____ a Tyrant, a fool, a puppet, and a tool of the ministry." On the other hand, John Roane, at ninety years of age, remembered that Henry's "voice, countenance, & gestures, gave an irresistible force to his words which no description could make intelligible to one who had never seen him, nor heard him speak."[6]

The Canon of *Elocutio*

Some comments have already been made in passing about Henry's *elocutio*. The focus here is on how Henry used an ornamented middle style.

Henry's style is commendable for its conversational diction. The speech is replete with personal pronouns. *I, my, we, our,* and *us* appear profusely throughout the address, and they enabled Henry to communicate directly and forcefully with his audience.

The speech also marched toward its goal with the active voice. Passive constructions are rare in the speech, and the various forms of the linking verb *is* are infrequent. Instead the verbs are forceful ones that energize the speech. Henry's use of short exclamations also prodded and pushed the audience toward his desired end. Henry even used the conjunction *and* to propel his speech. The word moved the audience from the narrative to the first, and then the second, part of the arguments; thus, Henry maintained the momentum of his speech.

The style was preeminently oral. True enough, the sentences in the introduction and the narration were longer than can be delivered in one breath. These would have required pacing by the speaker. Interestingly enough, eyewitnesses recalled that Henry began his speech in a calm manner.[7] However, in the arguments, refutation, and conclusion, most of the sentences are relatively short. The rhetorical questions are pithy, and the exclamations are concise. Thus, three of the five sections of the speech can be phrased easily in short, invigorated vocal pacing.

The speech was in the ornamented middle style. The vocabulary was neither grave nor simplistic. The Biblical and classical allusions gave the speech grace yet were readily understood by the audience. Using asyndeton, Henry left out the connectives to stress manly virtues: "the vigilant, the active, the brave." The rhetorical questions and the anaphora also set this speech apart from, but certainly not against or detached from, everyday parlance.

But perhaps Henry's greatest oratorical ability was to wed a strong style to a dynamic delivery, to which we now turn.

The Canon of *Actio*

Patrick Henry's "Liberty or Death" speech is a living example of how the classical canons of style and delivery are intertwined and interdependent. Neither is a veneer to the other.

As we have noted, Henry began his speech in a calm manner. His language corresponded to his delivery, or his delivery corresponded to his language: The point is that there was an appropriate fit. But as he warmed to his subject, auditors recalled that his rate increased and his voice became charged and louder. Thus, the synergism of delivery and style propelled the speech to greater emotional heights.

Eyewitnesses also recalled that Henry fit his gestures to his words. John Tyler wrote to his son, President John Tyler, that Henry was especially impressive in his peroration. When Henry spoke that he knew not what course others might take, Henry crossed his arms as if they were bound; when he shouted "Give me liberty . . . ," he broke his imaginary bonds; and when he cried out " . . . or give me death," he plunged a letter opener, which he had been holding in his hand, toward his heart with a dramatic gesture. Another auditor remembered that when Henry allowed that he did not know what course others might take, he looked toward where the Tories were sitting to confront them with their cowardice.[8]

The effect of Henry's delivery was profound. David McCants has demonstrated that the convention sat in silence for several minutes after Henry concluded, and Thomas Marshall, the father of Chief Justice John Marshall, told his son that Henry's speech was "one of the most bold, vehement, and animated pieces of eloquence that had ever been delivered."[9]

The Result

As famous as the speech has become, its success was not overwhelming, but Henry was triumphant. After he spoke, a vote was taken and his resolutions passed by a margin of sixty-five to sixty. How many minds he changed with his rhetoric is impossible to gauge, but it is safe to say that there were sixty Tories and their sympathizers who were not swayed by Henry's rhetoric. Although one could allege that his partisans, who included George Washington, Thomas Jefferson, and "Light Horse" Harry Lee, would have voted for Henry's resolutions anyway, one can observe that at least Henry did not lose them with his speech!

The closing words are left to Louis Mallory, who placed Henry's rhetoric in its persuasive perspective:

> [T]his reconstructed text is rhetorically superior to that of any other of Henry's reported speeches. It has a sustained literary quality that the others do not possess. There are a conciseness, a lack of repetition, a polish, a poetic quality, beside which much of the other texts seems almost commonplace. The speech rhythms of later texts reported in shorthand are for the most part much more those of ordinary conversation.[10]

Notes

1. See David A. McCants, "Patrick Henry," in *American Orators Before 1900: Critical Studies and Sources,* edited by Bernard K. Duffy and Halford R. Ryan (Westport, Conn.: Greenwood Press, 1987), pp. 219–227.
2. Judy Hample, "The Textual and Cultural Authenticity of Patrick Henry's 'Liberty or Death' Speech," *Quarterly Journal of Speech,* 63 (1977): 302.
3. David A. McCants, *Patrick Henry, The Orator,* (Westport, Conn.: Greenwood Press, 1990), pp. 123, 125–126.
4. McCants, *Patrick Henry, The Orator,* p. 57.
5. Hample, "Textual and Cultural Authenticity," p. 302.
6. Hample, "Textual and Cultural Authenticity" pp. 307–308.
7. Ibid, p. 306.
8. Ibid, pp. 306–307.
9. McCants, *Patrick Henry, The Orator,* p. 57.
10. Louis A. Mallory, "Patrick Henry," in *History and Criticism of American Public Address,* edited by William Norwood Brigance, 3 vols. (New York: Russell and Russell, 1960), II: 590.

Frederick Douglass's "What to the Slave Is the Fourth of July?"

Frederick Douglass (1818–1895). A former slave, reformer, and abolitionist, he was the foremost black speaker of the nineteenth century.

PREFACE

Frederick Douglass (1818–1895) was the preeminent black orator and black anti-slavery speaker of the nineteenth century. Not until the late nineteenth century did Booker T. Washington gain ascendancy as the foremost black spokesman.

Born into slavery in Maryland around 1818, Douglass escaped in 1838 and fled to Massachusetts. Racial prejudice in the Bay State forced him to work in a variety of menial jobs. But when he was asked to speak at an abolitionist meeting in 1841, he made such an impression on listeners that he was hired by the Massachusetts Anti-Slavery Society to deliver speeches on tour. The society sent strong speakers to address antislavery meetings throughout the North to reinforce the faithful and convert the uncommitted.

Douglass's mastery over the theory and practice of rhetoric was not a happenstance. As a youngster he taught himself how to read and write, although education was forbidden to slaves. As a teenager he was a hired slave in Baltimore. There he attended and often participated in debates sponsored by the East Baltimore Mental Improvement Society. This society was organized by free blacks in Baltimore. Douglass also devoured Caleb Bingham's *The Columbian Orator*, an anthology of oratorical masterpieces that taught politics and rhetoric. After his escape to Massachusetts, he continued to read widely, and to speak on issues that were important to blacks: abolition, racism, and social reform.[1]

Upon the publication of his *Narrative of the Life of Frederick Douglass* in 1845, he obtained a level of fame and financial success. Unfortunately, his acclaim also meant that his former owner could now find and reclaim him under the Fugitive Slave Act. Douglass fled to Great Britain, where he lectured on temperance and slavery. After friends bought his freedom, Douglass returned to Rochester, New York, in 1847. There, he founded a newspaper, the *North Star,* and continued to speak on abolition, as well as other reform topics, such as temperance and women's suffrage.

When Douglass spoke to an audience of abolitionists in Rochester's Corinthian Hall on July 5, 1852 [because the Fourth fell on a Sunday that year], he was an established speaker. He was well known on the abolition lecture trail, he had achieved international acclaim from his speaking in Great Britain, and faithful readers knew his views from his newspaper, which was now called *Frederick Douglass' Paper.* But this public speech would break new ground because he wanted to speak "boldly and clearly on behalf of abolition and equality."[2]

It is difficult to determine the effect of this speech. Those people who heard Douglass's address presumably were impressed with his oratory. Although the speech was quickly published as a pamphlet after its delivery, Ronald Reid has noted that the speech did not gain a national readership until the publication of Douglass's second autobiography, *My Bondage and My Freedom* in 1855. Douglass placed the speech in an appendix so that a national audience could read his masterful rhetoric.[3]

"WHAT TO THE SLAVE IS THE FOURTH OF JULY?": THE SPEECH

Delivered at Rochester, New York, July 5, 1852. Reprinted from Frederick Douglass, My Bondage and My Freedom *(New York: Miller, Orton and Mulligan, 1855), pp. 441–445.*

FELLOW-CITIZENS—Pardon me, and allow me to ask, why am I called upon to speak here to-day? What have I, or those I represent, to do with your national independence? Are the great principles of political freedom and of natural justice, embodied in that Declaration of Independence, extended to us? and am I, therefore, called upon to bring our humble offering to the national altar, and to confess the benefits, and express devout gratitude for the blessings, resulting from your independence to us?

Would to God, both for your sakes and ours, that an affirmative answer could be truthfully returned to these questions! Then would my task be light, and my burden easy and delightful. For who is there so cold that a nation's sympathy could not warm him? Who so obdurate and dead to the claims of gratitude, that would not thankfully acknowledge such priceless benefits? Who so stolid and selfish, that would not give his voice to swell the hallelujahs of a nation's jubilee, when the chains of servitude had been torn from his limbs?

I am not that man. In a case like that, the dumb might eloquently speak, and the "lame man leap as an hart."

But, such is not the state of the case. I say it with a sad sense of the disparity between us. I am not included within the pale of this glorious anniversary! Your high independence only reveals the immeasurable distance between us. The blessings in which you this day rejoice, are not enjoyed in common. The rich inheritance of justice, liberty, prosperity, and independence, bequeathed by your fathers, is shared by you, not by me. The sunlight that brought life and healing to you, has brought stripes and death to me. This Fourth of July is *yours*, not *mine. You* may rejoice, *I* must mourn. To drag a man in fetters into the grand illuminated temple of liberty, and call upon him to join you in joyous anthems, were inhuman mockery and sacrilegious irony. Do you mean, citizens, to mock me, by asking me to speak to-day? If so, there is a parallel to your conduct. And let me warn you that it is dangerous to copy the example of a nation whose crimes, towering up to heaven, were thrown down by the breath of the Almighty, burying that nation in irrecoverable ruin! I can today take up the plaintive lament of a peeled and woe-smitten people.

"By the rivers of Babylon, there we sat down. Yea! we wept when we remembered Zion. We hanged our harps upon the willows in the midst thereof. For there, they that carried us away captive, required of us a song; and they who wasted us required of us mirth, saying, Sing us one of the songs of Zion. How can we sing the Lord's song in a strange land? If I forget thee, O Jerusalem, let my right hand forget her cunning. If I do not remember thee, let my tongue cleave to the roof of my mouth."

Fellow-citizens, above your national, tumultuous joy, I hear the mournful wail of millions, whose chains, heavy and grievous yesterday, are today rendered more intolerable by the jubilant shouts that reach them. If I do forget, if I do not faithfully remember those bleeding children of sorrow this day, "may my right hand forget her cunning, and may my tongue cleave to the roof of my mouth!" To forget them, to pass lightly over their wrongs, and to chime in with the popular theme, would be treason most scandalous and shocking, and would make me a reproach before God and the world. My subject, then, fellow-citizens, is AMERICAN SLAVERY. I shall see this day and its popular characteristics from the slave's point of view. Standing there, identified with the American bondman, making his wrongs mine, I do not hesitate to declare, with all my soul, that the character and conduct of this nation never looked blacker to me than on this Fourth of July. Whether we turn to the declarations of the past, or to the professions of the present, the conduct of the nation seems equally hideous and revolting. America is false to the past, false to the present, and solemnly binds herself to be false to the future. Standing with God and the crushed and bleeding slave on this occasion, I will, in the name of humanity which is outraged, in the name of liberty which is fettered, in the name of the constitution and the bible, which are disregarded and trampled upon, dare to call in question and to denounce, with all the emphasis I can command, everything that serves to perpetuate slavery—the great sin and shame of America! "I will not equivocate; I will not excuse;" I will use the severest language I can command; and yet not one word shall escape me that any man, whose judgment is not blinded by prejudice, or who is not at heart a slaveholder, shall not confess to be right and just.

But I fancy I hear some one of my audience say, it is just in this circumstance that you and your brother abolitionists fail to make a favorable impression on the public mind. Would you argue more, and denounce less, would you persuade more and rebuke less, your cause would be much more likely to succeed. But, I submit, where all is plain there is nothing to be argued. What point in the antislavery creed would you have me argue? On what branch of the subject do the people of this country need light? Must I undertake to prove that the slave is a man? That point is conceded already. Nobody doubts it. The slaveholders themselves acknowledge it in the enactment of laws for their government. They acknowledge it when they punish disobedience on the part of the slave. There are seventy-two crimes in the state of Virginia, which, if committed by a black man, (no matter how ignorant he be,) subject him to the punishment of death; while only two of these same crimes will subject a white man to the like punishment. What is this but the acknowledgment that the slave is a moral, intellectual, and responsible being. The manhood of the slave is conceded. It is admitted in the fact that southern statute books are covered with enactments forbidding, under severe fines and penalties, the teaching of the slave to read or write. When you can point to any such laws, in reference to the beasts of the field, then I may consent to argue the manhood of the slave. When the dogs in your streets, when the fowls of the air, when the cattle on your hills, when the fish of the sea, and the reptiles that crawl, shall be unable to distinguish the slave from a brute, then will I argue with you that the slave is a man!

For the present, it is enough to affirm the equal manhood of the negro race. Is it not astonishing that, while we are plowing, planting, and reaping, using all kinds of mechanical tools, erecting houses, constructing bridges, building ships, working in metals of brass, iron, copper, silver, and gold; that, while we are reading, writing, and cyphering, acting as clerks, merchants, and secretaries, having among us lawyers, doctors, ministers, poets, authors, editors, orators, and teachers; that, while we are engaged in all manner of enterprises common to other men—digging gold in California, capturing the whale in the Pacific, feeding sheep and cattle on the hillside, living, moving, acting, thinking, planning, living in families as husbands, wives, and children, and, above all, confessing and worshiping the christian's God, and looking hopefully for life and immortality beyond the grave,—we are called upon to prove that we are men!

Would you have me argue that man is entitled to liberty? that he is the rightful owner of his own body? You have already declared it. Must I argue the wrongfulness of slavery? Is that a question for republicans? Is it to be settled by the rules of logic and argumentation, as a matter beset with great difficulty, involving a doubtful application of the principle of justice, hard to be understood? How should I look today in the presence of Americans, dividing and subdividing a discourse, to show that men have a natural right to feedom, speaking of it relatively and positively, negatively and affirmatively? To do so, would be to make myself ridiculous, and to offer an insult to your understanding. There is not a man beneath the canopy of heaven that does not know that slavery is wrong *for him*.

What! am I to argue that it is wrong to make men brutes, to rob them of their liberty, to work them without wages, to keep them ignorant of their relations to their fellowmen, to beat them with sticks, to flay their flesh with the lash, to load their limbs with irons, to hunt them with dogs, to sell them at auction, to sunder their families, to knock out their teeth, to burn their flesh, to starve them into obedience and submission to their masters? Must I argue that a system, thus marked with blood and stained with pollution, is wrong? No; I will not. I have better employment for my time and strength than such arguments would imply.

What, then, remains to be argued? Is it that slavery is not divine; that God did not establish it; that our doctors of divinity are mistaken? There is blasphemy in the thought. That which is inhuman cannot be divine. Who can reason on such a proposition! They that can, may; I cannot. The time for such argument is past.

At a time like this, scorching irony, not convincing argument, is needed. Oh! had I the ability, and could I reach the nation's ear, I would today pour out a fiery stream of biting ridicule, blasting reproach, withering sarcasm, and stern rebuke. For it is not light that is needed, but fire; it is not the gentle shower, but thunder. We need the storm, the whirlwind, and the earthquake. The feeling of the nation must be quickened; the conscience of the nation must be roused; the propriety of the nation must be startled; the hypocrisy of the nation must be exposed; and its crimes against God and man must be proclaimed and denounced.

What to the American slave is your Fourth of July? I answer, a day that reveals to him, more than all other days in the year, the gross injustice and cruelty to which he is the constant victim. To him, your celebration is a sham; your boasted liberty, an unholy license; your national greatness, swelling vanity; your sounds of rejoicing are empty and heartless; your denunciations of tyrants, brass-fronted impudence; your shouts of liberty and equality, hollow mockery; your prayers and hymns, your sermons and thanksgivings, with all your religious parade and solemnity, are to him mere bombast, fraud, deception, impiety, and hypocrisy—a thin veil to cover up crimes which would disgrace a nation of savages. There is not a nation on the earth guilty of practices more shocking and bloody, than are the people of these United States, at this very hour.

Go where you may, search where you will, roam through all the monarchies and despotisms of the old world, travel through South America, search out every abuse, and when you have found the last, lay your facts by the side of the everyday practices of this nation, and you will say with me, that, for revolting barbarity and shameless hypocrisy, America reigns without a rival.

ANALYSIS

As a genre of oratory, Frederick Douglass's speech seems to be epideictic because of its ceremonial nature. And, as Aristotle conceived an epideictic speech, the address was couched in the present. But surely the speech had deliberative elements in it as well. Rather than delivering the epideictic speech of praise generally associated with Fourth of July celebrations, Douglass used the occasion to blame the American political system for allowing slavery to exist. Implicit in the speech was Douglass's intent to reinforce partisans and possibly to win over some neutrals and perhaps even a few opponents. Douglass might have hoped that in the future the committed would work harder for abolitionism. Although he was surely under no illusion that the chains of bondage would be broken by this single speech, he may have hoped that a small number of neutrals and opponents might join the ranks.

One can reasonably assume that most of the persons in Douglass's Rochester audience were partisans, people already committed to the antislavery movement. Few opponents would have been likely to dignify the occasion with their presence. But one can assume that interested townspeople, probably somewhat neutral in their opinions, may have attended the speech, if for no other reason than to hear a famous black speaker, an uncommon happening in the mid-nineteenth century.

In light of the persuasive situation that Douglass confronted, he and his speech were more representative of the sophistic and philosophical strands of rhetoric. As we shall see, his speech was an exemplar of the technical strand of rhetoric that aimed for success. But, as we have already stated, Douglass doubtless recognized that he was for the most part preaching to the choir. Thus he employed the technical strand more for display, which is a function of the epideic-tic speech, than for moving his audience.

Douglass the speaker represented the sophistic strand. He stood on high moral ground. As a self-trained and self-taught black speaker, he stood on the public platform as the good person speaking well. This was an image to which his partisans reacted quite favorably.

Douglass's speech was in the philosophical strain. It communicated what the audience ought to believe and how the audience ought to act. Douglass argued that the audience ought to favor abolition because it would be good for black slaves and for white society. As he said in the conclusion of his speech, "There is not a nation on the earth guilty of practices more shocking and bloody, than are the people of these United States, at this very hour."

One may also infer that Douglass had in mind a larger readership for his speech. The fact that the speech was later issued in pamphlet form warrants the assumption. So, it is not unrealistic to suppose, as he composed his speech, that Douglass considered his rhetorical appeals in relationship to his immediate listen-ing audience and to his larger reading audience. But what to compose? what to say? what arguments to invent?

Douglass's *Inventio*

Douglass reacted to the rhetorical situation of the mid-nineteenth century as he found it. He based his arguments on the issues that pro- and antislavery forces had already developed. Inherent in nineteenth-century American culture were several basic tenets held by slave owners in the South and their sympathizers in the North.

The strongest argument for slavery was the constitutional argument. This was based on the stasis of fact. Slavery had existed in colonial times, and from 1789 forward it was the law of the land. The Constitution recognized the chattel nature of the slave. The slave was a piece of property, just like a cow, and the mas-ter owned the labor of the slave, just as he owned the cow's milk. The Constitu-tion counted a slave as only three-fifths of a person in determining the number of members a state would have in the House of Representatives. The Constitution guaranteed the right of masters to reclaim their fugitive slaves. That the U.S. Constitution recognized and supported slavery is an incontrovertible fact, which was finally overturned with the passage of the Thirteenth Amendment.

Negroes were assumed to be inferior to Caucasians. Committing the fallacy of *post hoc ergo propter hoc,* many nineteenth century whites assumed that blacks were innately stupid, else why could they not read or write, or rise above their lowly status? The reason, of course, was that the peculiar institution included a host of legal mechanisms that maintained the inferiority of slaves. For instance, in many Southern states it was illegal to teach slaves to read and to write. Before the Civil War the intellectual superiority of the white race over the black race was assumed, and many whites argued it was a demonstrable fact.

Southerners, as well as Northerners, took consolation from the fact that the Bible condoned slavery. Slavery was practiced in the Old Testament, and even God's chosen people had slaves. If slavery was so evil, Southerners slyly asked, why did God not proscribe it? (The enthymeme at work here was that since God did not proscribe it, slavery must be acceptable, and in the years just before the Civil War, Southern extremists even argued that slavery was a positive good.) As for the New Testament, slavery was a common practice in the Roman world. Jesus Christ never issued any prohibitions against Christian's holding slaves (in fact, most early Christians were slaves themselves), and St. Paul enjoined slaves to obey their masters.

The economic argument also reinforced slavery. Slaves were worth millions of dollars, and Americans whether from North or South, have always been loath to part with their material possessions.

Not surprisingly, Douglass wisely addressed all of these issues, except for the economic one, in his speech. He probably reasoned that people in his immediate Rochester audience, or in his Northern reading audience, did not have a direct economic interest in slavery; therefore, he did not need to treat that topic.

For the issues that he did address in his speech, Douglass evidently considered the three modes of proof. Although these will be treated in the next section from a traditional perspective, a word about Douglass-as-a-black-speaker is in order here.

Douglass had a unique ethos. He was living, breathing, speaking proof that a black man was both *homo* and *sapiens*. That Douglass, a black man and former slave, could speak before white people in public—and with considerable force and eloquence—was a profound statement in the mid-nineteenth century. That Douglass had a better command of the English language than most of his white contemporaries, was a striking proof of his good sense. That he valued the same political principles that whites held dear was a clear and positive indication of his good moral character.

That a black speaker could reason must have astounded some and annoyed others. That Douglass could logically organize a speech as white speakers did— that he could marshall reasoning and evidence for the various parts of his speech as whites did—was a living rebuke to those who believed in the black man's intellectual inferiority. In short, Douglass made an ethical, logical, and emotional impact on the audience before he ever opened his mouth. And he did not disappoint when he spoke.

Douglass's *Dispositio*

If beauty is in the eye of the beholder, surely an argument, or a refutation, is in the eye of the reader or the ear of the auditor. Frederick Douglass's use of the same sort of language that Patrick Henry had used in his Liberty or Death speech is a key to understanding his speech's success with his white audience.

Douglass employed the classical organizational pattern in his speech. The sections of the pattern will be explicated in their turn, but for now the focus is on how Douglass adapted the pattern to his audience. Douglass decided to delete a section, in this instance the arguments section, and to place all of his rhetorical eggs in the refutation basket. His doing so was a wise rhetorical adaptation. As the author of the *Rhetorica ad Herennium* maintained, the highest practice of the art is to know how and when to break the rules.

In terms of partisans, neutrals, and opponents, the refutation section functioned as an argument or as a refutation depending on the type of listener. For instance, the refutation of the proslavery position was an arguments section to Douglass's partisans, for they already believed in his position; the refutation persuasively reinforced the committed. Depending on the degree to which a neutral tilted toward or away from Douglass's thesis, the refutation could function as a refutation to one who had serious doubts about the abolitionist movement, or it could be an argument to one who tended to side with the antislavery position. For the opponents, the refutation section functioned in a straightforward fashion: Douglass used it to refute the reservations that opponents maintained against abolitionism.

The same kind of rhetorical reasoning is also applicable to the introduction, narrative, and conclusion. Depending on where one stood in relationship to Douglass's position, the introduction, narration, and conclusion could have the same effect. These sections should reinforce the partisans, move the neutrals, and entice some opponents to join the antislavery cause.

The Introduction   Douglass began his introduction with a series of rhetorical questions. The gist of these questions was whether the black man benefited from the lofty principles expressed in the Declaration of Independence. Douglass knew partisans would answer no to themselves. Thus, from the opening of his speech, Douglass established the irony that black people born in the United States (all that is legally required for citizenship) were not free citizens! Indeed, Douglass reminded his audience that "Your high independence only reveals the immeasurable distance between us."

The enthymeme at work in the exordium was artfully implied. Since black slaves do not enjoy the freedoms guaranteed by the Declaration and celebrated on the Fourth, the audience should redouble its efforts for abolitionism. As a matter of fact, all the sections of the speech had that basic enthymematic argument in them.

The Narrative   Douglass began his narration by quoting a biblical lamentation of the ancient Israelites enslaved in Babylon. It was a theme that seemed to correspond to the condition of black slaves in the United States. Douglass announced to his audience that he would speak for black slaves: "My subject then, fellow-citizens, is AMERICAN SLAVERY. I shall see this day and its popular characteristics from the slave's point of view." And, artfully punning, he claimed that "the character and conduct of this nation never looked blacker to me than on the Fourth of July."

Douglass ended his narrative by quoting William Lloyd Garrison, the famous abolitionist who was equally hated by Southern slave owners. In the first edition of his antislavery newspaper, *The Liberator*, Garrison proclaimed on January 1, 1831*: "I am in earnest—I will not equivocate—I will not excuse—I will not retreat a single inch—AND I WILL BE HEARD [in original]." Most persons in the audience would have immediately recognized the source when Douglass stated: "I will not equivocate; I will not excuse."

The tenor of his introduction and narrative make it clear that these sections were targeted primarily to partisans and perhaps to some sympathetic neutrals. Partisans would have appreciated Douglass's ironical allusions to the Fourth of July and the Declaration of Independence versus the conditions of black slaves, whereas opponents would have thought to themselves that the Fourth and the Declaration were never intended for black slaves and everybody understood that from the very founding of the country. Too, the allusion to Garrison would have irretrievably alienated Southern whites.

The Refutation   The refutative nature of his stance in this section is warranted by Douglass's transitional device. Taking his opponent's words from their mouths, Douglass stated:

> But I fancy I hear some one of my audience say, it is just in this circumstance that you and your brother abolitionists fail to make a favorable impression on the public mind. Would you argue more, and denounce less, would you persuade more and rebuke less, your cause would be much more likely to succeed.

Therefore, Douglass decided to argue, or actually to refute, the issues that the proslavery forces used to justify black slavery.

REFUTATION 1: THE SLAVE IS A MAN.   As we have seen, the proslavery forces conceived the slave more as a piece of property or a work animal than a human being. Douglass introduced his first refutation with an ironic rhetorical question: "Must I undertake to prove that the slave is a man?" Partisans would have indignantly answered "No," but opponents would have answered, "Yes."

Douglass supported his refutation by marshalling copious examples of the slave's manhood. Laws in the South recognized crimes for which slaves could be executed; slaves could not be taught to read or to write; slaves did all the work that white people did; and they even looked to "immortality beyond the grave." None of these things were true of animals.

Douglass used **argumentum ad absurdum** in this refutation. He proved the reasonableness of his position by exposing the ridiculous assertion that the

---

* Although the abolitionist movement was alive and well long before this date, January 1, 1831, is generally marked as the beginning of the end for American slavery.

slave was not a human being. He argued by negation. Through proof by examples, he clearly demonstrated that the slave was a human being and decisively defeated the initial proslavery premise.

REFUTATION 2: THE SLAVE IS ENTITLED TO LIBERTY.   As we have seen, the proslavery forces were on firm constitutional grounds that explicitly and legally sanctioned black slavery. This refutation was at once Douglass's weakest and strongest effort. On the one hand, he asked a series of six rhetorical questions that begged the question. (Always beware of a speaker who answers questions with more questions.) Of course, partisans already believed in the wrongfulness of slavery. But for the opponents, Douglass offered no constitutional argument on why slaves were entitled to liberty, and they surely would have noticed that glaring omission. To give Douglass credit, how could he argue that the Constitution granted the black slave freedom when it clearly did not! However, the strongest refutation in the entire speech was merely one sentence: "There is not a man beneath the canopy of heaven that does not know that slavery is wrong *for him.*"

REFUTATION 3: THE SLAVE-CODE ARGUMENT.   As we have seen, the South had a series of laws, generically known as the slave-codes, that allowed the owner to treat the slave as a piece of property. Ultimately, the slave-codes were allowable under the Constitution.

Douglass was unable to argue the legality of these laws with traditional logical appeals. So he wisely resorted to highly charged emotional appeals to move his audience. Obviously, his partisans would have been persuaded by his appeals, and they surely must have affected neutrals. Only the most heartless slaver would have been unmoved by Douglass's emotionally laden language. Graphic images of beating with sticks, flaying the flesh, selling at auction, knocking out teeth, and burning flesh would certainly have touched the emotions of all but the most hardened humans. These emotional examples of commonplace events on plantations were harsh reminders of what slavery was really like. As this refutation demonstrated, Douglass excelled in using emotive language.

REFUTATION 4: THE BIBLICAL ARGUMENT.   As we have seen, Southerners held that the Bible sanctioned slavery. Again, Douglass used emotional assertions rather than proof. Abolitionists believed that God was against slavery, so they would have acquiesced in Douglass's assertions.

The problem was that neither Douglass nor the other abolitionists could demonstrate with Scriptural texts that God was against slavery. If the ground of belief is based on what the Bible says rather than what one thinks the Bible ought to say, the Southerners had substantive proof on their side just as they did in their Constitutional argument.

From a logical perspective, then, Douglass would not have convinced slaveholders that God was against slavery. Again, Douglass could not make the Bible something it was not.

Let us now summarize Douglass's four refutations. He certainly won the first issue that the slave was a man, for the proslavery position was absurd. As for the constitutional issue, surely the fact that no white would want to be a slave was a compelling argument. However, the Almighty Dollar convinced many Americans to replace a moral argument with a financial one, so the philosophical or moralistic strand of rhetoric will not always persuade obdurate listeners. His third refutation was a highly emotional one and ought to have moved partisans, neutrals, and opponents as well. His fourth refutation on the biblical issue was weak, but it was not Douglass's fault that the Bible sanctioned slavery.

If one can play the role of a 1850s listener, some general observations can be offered on the supposed effect of this speech. One can probably assume that opponents, if they bothered to listen to his speech or to read his pamphlet or book, would not have been moved by Douglass's speech for the aforementioned reasons. One could make a reasonable case that Douglass should have had some marginal successes with neutrals whose minds were not so closed. Presumably, Douglass reinforced his partisans. Could one ask more of an antislavery rhetorician in the early 1850s?

The Conclusion   The conclusion of the speech was clearly targeted for partisans more than opponents, which was also the case for the introduction. "What to the American slave is your Fourth of July?" was the cue that Douglass would conclude his address. In answering for the silent slave, Douglass made the tenor of the conclusion sarcastic and ironical. The sarcasm was targeted against proslavery forces and their sympathizers. Partisans would not have taken personal offense at Douglass's attacks because they knew that they already believed as Douglass did and that the attacks were meant for the enemy. Irony was a useful tool against opponents, too, because it highlighted the paradox of a so-called free country that sanctioned slavery.

Douglass pulled out all the stops in his conclusion. If he could not attack his opponents physically, he would do it verbally. He lambasted the proslavery forces with a barrage of verbiage, such as "gross injustice," "unholy license," "brass-fronted impudence," "mere bombast," and "hypocrisy." Obviously, such diction, and this was only the tip of the iceberg, would have emotionally moved partisans to rededicate themselves to abolition.

Douglass's *Elocutio*

In terms of style, Douglass's Fourth of July oration was replete with technical stylistic devices. The focus here is not to list all of them, but to highlight some of his better passages as illustrations of his practices.

Douglass employed anaphora to heighten the urgency of the antislavery movement. In the second paragraph of his introduction, Douglass used a slight variation of "Who so" three times in order to underscore the irony that whites shared in the blessing of the Declaration of Independence but that blacks did not. Later in the speech he also used the anaphora of "In the name of" to demonstrate how humanity, liberty, and the Bible and the Constitution needed his voice to denounce the practice of human slavery.

Douglass used alliteration sparingly. In the third paragraph of his introduction, he stressed the "s" sound: "But, such is not the state of the case. I say it with a sad sense of the disparity between us." Perhaps it was merely chance, but the final words in his speech were an example of alliteration: "America reigns without rival."

Antithesis was one of Douglass's favorite devices in the speech. On the macrolevel, the whole speech was antithetical because he juxtaposed free whites and bonded blacks. Inherent in this antithesis were also elements of irony and sarcasm: irony because it was difficult to explain how liberty squared with slavery in a free country, and sarcasm because anger could be expressed only in words, not in actions, for which blacks could be flogged or hanged in the South. At the microlevel Douglass used, whenever he could, antithesis, with its overtones of irony and sarcasm, to reinforce an antithetical Fourth of July for whites versus blacks. The following quotations are examples of antithesis:

This Fourth of July is *yours*, not *mine*. *You* may rejoice, *I* must mourn.

At a time like this, scorching irony, not convincing argument, is needed. . . . For it is not light that is needed, but fire; it is not the gentle shower, but thunder.

[Y]our national greatness, swelling vanity; your sounds of rejoicing are empty and heartless; your denunciations of tyrants, brass-fronted impudence; your shouts of liberty and equality, hollow mockery; your prayers and hymns, your sermons and thanksgiving, with all your religious parade and solemnity, are to him mere bombast, fraud, deception, impiety, and hypocrisy.

Douglass also used apophasis extensively. The use of affirmation-by-denial suited his purposes well. For instance, Douglass introduced his first refutation with apophasis: "Must I undertake to prove that the slave is a man? That point is conceded already." If so, then why did Douglass devote considerable effort in refuting what he claimed was already obvious? For his partisans, who already believed his thesis, the apophasis reinforced their conviction that a slave was indeed a man. To the opponents, whom he wished to persuade in this refutation section of the speech, the apophasis stated the very point in which they believed and against which he offered his counterproofs. The second, third, and fourth refutations were introduced with apophasis and for the same rhetorical reasoning.

Douglass used irony and sarcasm especially well in the conclusion of his speech. These stylistic devices were a logical continuation of the tone of his address, and he made them coalesce in his conclusion:

Go where you may, search where you will, roam through all the monarchies and despotisms of the old world, travel through South America, search out every abuse, and when you have found the last, lay your facts by the side of the every-day practices of this nation, and you will say with me, that, for revolting barbarity and shameless hypocrisy, America reigns without a rival.

The quotation also illustrates the periodic sentence, for one has to wait until the very end of the sentence before one realizes the sentence's full impact.

Douglass's *Actio* and *Memoria*

When Douglass finished his speech before the Rochester audience at Corinthian Hall, an audience from between five and six hundred listeners, who had paid 12½ cents to hear the address, gave Douglass "a universal burst of applause."[4] Aside from the subject matter of his speech, the audience probably reacted favorably to the manner in which Douglass presented his speech.

By all accounts, Douglass had a superb voice. William G. Allen, a professor of rhetoric at Central College in McGrawsville, New York, heard Douglass deliver a speech in 1852. Prof. White criticized Douglass's *actio* as follows:

When he rises to speak, there is a slight hesitancy in his manner, which disappears as he warms up to his subject. . . . He has a voice of terrific power, of great compass, and under the most admirable control.[5]

Other critics described Douglass's voice as "highly melodious" and as a "rich baritone."[6]

Douglass's gestures evidently would have pleased Quintilian, for he decried speakers who sawed the air with their arms. Douglass was described as a "sparing user of gesture."[7]

Concerning his *memoria*, Douglass probably varied his procedures. For some speeches, he evidently "eschewed a manuscript or any written notes, preferring to rely on his memory or to trust the inspiration of the moment."[8] However, for the Rochester speech, Douglass wrote a fellow abolitionist that he had spent two to three weeks writing the speech.[9] The speech was carefully organized, it was eloquently styled, and it lacked the rambling, discursive nature of the impromptu address, all of which strongly suggest that Douglass carefully prepared the address. As for the actual delivery of the address, Douglass may have learned his speech, in the process of writing and revising it, so that he relied little, if at all, on notes or a manuscript.

Douglass was the classic good person speaking well. As we have seen, he mastered the strand of technical rhetoric by employing a classical organizational strategy and stylistic devices. Douglass-as-a-black speaker was a living, speaking example of the sophistic strand of rhetoric, which was all the more remarkable because his expertise in oratory was largely self-taught. And as a practitioner of the philosophical strand of rhetoric, he contributed his voice to the rising nineteenth-century chorus of speakers, both men and women, blacks as well as whites, who preached the morality of abolitionism.

Notes

1. See Waldo E. Martin, Jr., "Frederick Douglass," in *American Orators Before 1900: Critical Studies and Sources,* edited by Bernard K. Duffy and Halford R. Ryan (Westport, Conn.: Greenwood Press, 1987), p. 139, and *Three Centuries of American Rhetorical Discourse,* edited by Ronald F. Reid (Prospect Heights, Ill.: Waveland Press, 1988), pp. 369–371.

2. Martin, "Frederick Douglass," p. 141.

3. Reid, *Three Centuries of American Rhetorical Discourse,* p. 371.

4. *The Frederick Douglass Papers,* edited by John W. Blassingame (New Haven, Conn.: Yale University Press, 1982), II: 359.

5. *Frederick Douglass,* edited by Benjamin Quarles (Englewood Cliffs, N.J.: Prentice-Hall Inc., 1968), p. 101.

6. See Arna Bontemps, *Free At Last* (New York: Dodd, Mead, 1971), p. 19, and Benjamin Quarles, *Frederick Douglass* (Washington, D.C.: Associated Publishers, 1948), p. 60.

7. Quarles, *Frederick Douglass,* p. 61.

8. Ibid., p. 61.

9. *The Frederick Douglass Papers,* p. 359.

Henry Ward Beecher's "Woman's Suffrage Man's Right"

Henry Ward Beecher (1813–1887). A reformer, abolitionist, Unionist, and Darwinist, he was one of America's most influential preachers.

PREFACE

The Reverend Henry Ward Beecher was the foremost preacher in the United States from the late 1850s to his death in 1887. He also ranked as one of America's greatest speakers during that period. Beecher was something of a stump speaker who stumbled into the pulpit. That Beecher was at home on the public platform as well as in the pulpit did not bother Americans of the nineteenth century anymore than it has bothered modern audiences that Martin Luther King, Jr., Billy Graham, Jerry Falwell, and Jesse Jackson have successfully addressed sacred as well as secular audiences. These preachers/speakers followed in Beecher's footsteps by wedding politics and religion. When people went to hear Beecher speak or lecture, they heard a speaker as much as a preacher. Indeed, Beecher traded briefly on his dual roles as speaker and preacher in his speech's introduction when he alluded to "heathenism" and "perdition," which was a vocabulary closely associated with men of the cloth. However, Beecher-the-preacher was soon forgotten as Beecher-the-speaker launched into his secular address.

Beecher's speech, delivered at the Cooper Institute in New York City on February 2, 1860, must be read in the context of its time. We take it for granted today that women vote, and no one denies their right to do so. It was not always so, and Beecher had to address the American audience as he found it. Beecher's is a nineteenth-century speech because he faced a nineteenth-century culture. Many of his arguments strike us as obvious, some of them as quaint and Victorian, and one or two of them as downright silly. But such was his audience. To belittle Beecher or his listeners is to miss the rhetorical effect of his speech on woman's suffrage. His address is anthologized and criticized as an example of how a successful speaker adapts to the audience, of how to apply various rhetorical techniques, of how to marshal rhetorical proofs, and of how to bend the rules in adapting the classical organizational pattern to the audience. His was no mean persuasive accomplishment.*

 ## "WOMAN SUFFRAGE MAN'S RIGHT": THE SPEECH

Delivered at Cooper Institute, New York City, February 2, 1860.

Woman suffrage will bring civilization into our primary meetings, and decency into our secondary ones; for we have heathenism here as rife as that in any other quarter of the globe. You do not need to go out of New York to see whatever barbarity or truculent heathenism is to be seen anywhere else. We keep specimens of everything this side of perdition, and some, I think, of things the other side.

If it were understood that, in every ward and neighborhood, the adult population—the whole of them, men and women—were to control the primary meetings, there would be no more trouble in these meetings than there is in our households. The restraint, the refining influence of woman, would make that orderly which is now like the tussling of dogs. And that which is true of primary meetings is still more significantly true of legislatures and national assemblies. Woman's influence, if introduced into public affairs, would work in the same direction there that it has worked, and is working, in social life, in literature, and in religious assemblies.

But let us attend to some of the objections that are made to such an introduction of woman's influence into public affairs. It strikes many, before reflection, and none more than women themselves, that a participation in suffrage would subject them to rudeness, and to an exposure painful to delicacy. As if that very rudeness were not the result of woman's absence! As if it were not her very office to carry with her whatever is seemly and decorous!

In the first place, it should be understood that, if women were to vote, there would be an end of indecent voting places. The polls would no longer be in vile precincts and in pestholes. If father and mother, husband and wife, brother and sister, man and woman, in-

---

* For a more detailed description of Beecher's speaking career, see "Henry Ward Beecher," in *American Orators Before 1900*, edited by Bernard K. Duffy and Halford R. Ryan (Westport, Conn.: Greenwood Press, 1987), pp. 35–46.

spired by the sanctity of patriotism, were to go forth together to vote, do you suppose that our elections would be characterized by the vulgarity and violence which now defile them?

What is there in depositing a vote that would subject a woman to such peculiar exposure? A woman, dropping a letter into the post office, is made more public, and is fully as indelicate, as in depositing her vote. A vote is the simplest, the neatest, the most unobtrusive thing imaginable. This white slip of paper drops as quietly and gently as a snowflake on the top of the alps; but, like them, when collected, they descend like avalanches. Woe be to the evil which they strike! Let the man who is the most fastidious, who prides himself most on his refinement, find fault, if he can, with the vote of a woman—a thing that is so easy, so simple, but that would carry into human affairs a power almost like the right hand of the Almighty.

But why this publicity? Why not remain at home, and exert an influence upon public affairs through husband, father, brother?

Because, while woman is excluded with contempt from political duties, her advice and influence at home must always be at the minimum. If once she began to accept public patriotic duties, she then would exert a tenfold indirect influence at home. But now, men take it for granted that women know nothing of public affairs, and that all their suggestions must, of course, be the result of an ignorant simplicity. A woman is not made a safe adviser by being kept at home in ignorance of all public affairs; and, if she informs herself intelligently, then why should she not act just as much as man? It is amusing to hear men, when pressed upon this point, enlarging upon the silent influence of woman, upon the sweetening home affections, upon their bland and gentle restraints, or excitements, and declaring a woman's home to be the only appropriate sphere of political influence; but the moment she takes him at his word, and endeavors to incline husband or brother to any political conduct, they turn with lordly authority upon her, saying, "My dear, your proper duties are in the nursery and kitchen. What do you understand of public affairs?"

Indeed, there is a large infusion of vulgar arrogance even in good men. They believe that woman was created solely or chiefly for the cradle, the bread-trough, and the needle. These complacent gentlemen suppose that God made man for thought, action, heroism, and woman as nurse, cook, and plaything.

But, I ask, why does not this argument in respect to woman's influence hold just as good in everything else as in public affairs? Why do you now say, "A woman ought not to be a schoolteacher; if she wishes to teach the race, let her influence her father and brothers and husband, and act through them"? Why not say, "A woman ought not to be an artist, and daub her fingers with paints; let her influence her father and brothers and husband to paint"? or, "A woman ought not to waste her strength in writing; let her influence her father and brothers and husband to write"? Why do you not say; in short, "Woman is a mere silent, interior, reserved force, and man is the universal engine to be set in operation by her"?

There is, undoubtedly, such a thing as indirect influence, as general influence; but I have noticed that men who wish things to remain as they are, are in favor always of general influences, in distinction from directly applied forces. It is open, direct, applied force, that abates evil or promotes good.

Nobody makes out a bank account under the general influence of commerce. Nobody farms on this principle. The general influence of husbandry never drained a swamp. It is the theory of cultivation applied that brings harvests. The general progress of health never cleaned a street; it is sanitary ideas applied that do this work. General influences are nothing but the sum of particular influences. If these men who propose leaving evils to be corrected by general influences were to talk to the clouds, they would say, "Oh, never rain! Leave all things to the general influence of diffused moisture."

It is further objected: "If woman were to vote, then, of course, she would be eligible to public offices." Well, why not? In every respect in which woman is known to have gifts of administration, why ought she not to exercise them? When a farmer dies, if the wife has executive power, she carries on the farm; when a merchant dies, if the wife has tact, she carries on the business; if an editor dies, if the wife is enterprising and able, she carries on the newspaper; if a schoolmaster dies, and the wife is competent, she carries on the school or academy; and nobody supposes but that it is perfectly right. All through society, in a sort of unasserting way, woman goes out of what is considered her sphere, and nobody thinks but that it is perfectly right. But I hold that it should be recognized as her right to engage in everything for which she is fitted, public affairs not excepted. No woman could be elected to the office of a justice of the peace unless there was a general conviction that she had peculiar gifts for its duties. This matter is surrounded with such safeguards of popular prejudice that no woman will be called to any office unless it is very apparent that she has a fitness for it. Wherever there are gifts, there should be liberty of exercise. Faculty always demands function. Every human being has a natural right to do whatever he or she can do well.

But it is objected that, by mingling in public affairs, women would soon extinguish that delicacy that now gives them both grace and influence. Are we, then, to believe that womanly qualities are God's gift, or only the result of accident and education? If God made woman with a genius of refinement, tenderness, and moral purity, it is not probable that the exercise of large public duty will efface the marks of her original constitution, and that an active patriotism will tarnish her purity, and that zeal for public justice will demoralize her nature.

We are not to forget that woman's participation in suffrage will at once change the conditions upon which they are to enter. When men ask, "Would it be wise that woman should enter the hurly-burly of the caucus, and mingle with the fanaticism of party fury?" I reply, that her presence would end these evils. Should a man, having an exquisite lamp, burning perfumed oil, refuse to carry it into an unlighted room, lest the darkness should contaminate the flame, all would smile at his ignorance, as if light were not, in its nature, the death of darkness.

And when it is asked, "Would you go among brutal rowdies with your wife and daughter, and subject these to their insults?" I reply, if it were understood to be not an intrusion, nor a violation of con-stituted law, but a thing in accordance with both custom and law, I would take my wife and daughter, and walk, I care not into what pre-cinct or neighborhood; and there is not, in the United States, a place where they would not be safe. Or, if there were one drunken creature to mistreat them, there would be five and twenty stalwart men to crush the miscreant! For, when it is once the custom for women to mingle in public affairs with men, there will not be found a class of men in our land that will not respect her presence. Now and then I see a man that walks in the street smoking, with a woman on his arm—but only now and then. Once in a while I see a man that rides in an omnibus smoking, when there is a woman in it—but only once in a while. These are exceptions. Men instinctively reverence women. Nor is this the peculiarity of men of cultivation or wealth. Men who toll at the blacksmith's forge, and in the various other departments of manual labor,—men whose hands are so hard that they would almost strike fire from steel,—have under their brawny ribs a heart that loves and reveres the purity of woman. And in whatever sphere her duties might call her, if she were admitted to it by custom or law, men would meet her as now they meet her in the sanctuary and in these halls.

But it is said, "It would draw woman from her appropriate sphere. Home is the place of her life." And I would like to know if public affairs do not draw man from his appropriate sphere just as much? Can any man attend to his duties as a citizen and not give time to them? And yet, does he injuriously abandon his store or his bank? It would not take any more of woman's time than it does of man's. But what is time given for but to be used in duty? Nay, it would save time to men and women, if a higher spirit could be infused into public affairs. It is sordidness and low ambitions that exact so much time and strength of good men in the conduct of affairs. And if men were morally elevated, they would strike for rectitude without all those struggles and tergiversations which now impede their progress. Attention to public affairs, then, would not draw woman from her appropriate sphere one whit more than it draws man from his.

I do not ask that every woman should be a candidate for office, or an officer. There is no danger that she would suddenly become wild and rampant, simply because a high moral duty devolved upon her. Intelligence and real moral power sober the silly passions, restrain vagrancy, give stability and discretion. And woman would be a more discreet stayer at home if she were taught wisely how to act in public duty away from home.

Again, it is said that women lose the charm and delicacy of their sex by mingling in public affairs. No, no; you do not believe any such thing. You do not believe it, who say it; or you say it without thinking. A great many women, having received from God the gift of song, sing in public; and no man ever thought of raising this objection in regard to them. Who ever thought of raising it in regard to Jenny Lind? On the appearance here of Madame Sontag, a kind invitation was sent to the clergymen of New York and Brooklyn to attend a preliminary exhibition of her powers in the old Tripler Hall. You may be sure that we were all there; and she sang as she ought to have sung before the assembled clergy of these two cities. When she had finished, Dr. Cox rose, and, with his inimitable eloquence, expressed our united thanks and admiration to her for what she had done; and blessed God that she had the gift and power exhibited. But not a word did he say about exposure, about her being unsexed, or about her being out of her sphere. It was taken for granted that, since God had given her such song-power, it was her duty not to silence it, but to use it for the good of the greatest number. But what peculiar right is there in Art to enfranchise woman, and make that delicate and proper which custom forbids to religion or public affairs? Is it right to sing and wrong to speak in public? Is it delicate for Jenny Lind to confront five thousand faces standing alone upon a platform, and indelicate upon her husband's arm to go forth to the duty of suffrage?

As the different elements of society have developed in succession, they have been obliged to pass through the contention of the democratic and the aristocratic elements. Woman herself is vibrating between these antagonistic forces. For ages, woman has been advanced to honor, influence, office, and the highest public trusts, if she will accept them in aristocratic forms. Women, as members of the ruling classes, are emancipated from many clogs which yet hinder those lower down in the social scale. If it be as a representative of a noble family, or of a public order, woman is permitted to take her place in public affairs. She may be an abbess, a countess, a queen.

Today, the proudest throne on the globe is honored by a woman. No person is shocked that she is at the head of empire. Every reason urged against a larger liberty for woman is illustriously confuted by the dignity, purity, and womanly propriety with which Victoria stands before her empire, and before the world.

It is only woman *without a title* that must have no privileges. Woman, in her own simple self, with nothing but what God gave her, plain, democratic woman, is not deemed worthy of honor and publicity. With a crown on her brow, she may enter parliaments, and govern empires. With only her own simple personal virtues, she may not lift up her hand to cast a vote. If she represents a power, a state, an art, a class, if she only stand upon an aristocratic base, she is indulged. But woman, in her own nature, and representing her own self, is disowned and rebuffed. Now, as a Christian democrat, I assert for her every right and every privilege that aristocracy accords her. That which is good enough for a queen is not too good for my wife. That which is noble in a duchess is honorable in my daughter.

This, then, is the sum of what I wished to say to you tonight. I have said it more in the expectation that it will work in you as a leaven than that it will bear immediate fruits. But, as the farmer sows seed in October that he does not expect to reap till July, so we must sow, and wait patiently for the harvest. I do not know that I shall see the day when woman will occupy her true position in society. My children may, if I do not; and I think that there will be some approach to it, even in my time; for thoughts move faster than they used to.

It is Guyot who says that plants have three periods of growth. The slowest and longest is that of the root; the next fastest is that of the stem; and the last and quickest is that of the blossom and fruit. I have been wont to think that the world grew by the root till the advent of Christ; that from the advent of Christ to our day, it has been growing by the stem; and that in the period in which we stand it is growing by the blossom and the fruit. Changes that formerly required a hundred years for accomplishment, now require scarcely a score. Things rush to their accomplishment. And I make this plea in behalf of women, not without hope that I may see, in my day, an improvement in her condition.

Men will think about this reform, and talk about it. You will accomplish it by talking first, and thinking before you talk, and remembering that we are advocating this change, not because woman needs it, *but because we need it more.*

I stand, tonight, the advocate of *man's rights.* Because we need it, woman should be eligible to all public trusts, and should have the same liberty of suffrage that man now has.

ANALYSIS

Henry Ward Beecher delivered this speech in 1860, probably under the auspices of the Women's National Loyal League, whose president was Susan B. Anthony. Clifford Clark characterized this address as a "major speech on women's suffrage."[1] However, Clark did not reveal the rhetorical techniques that Beecher employed in the speech nor examine the speaker's argumentative strategies on the suffrage question.

The major organizational pattern of the speech was topical. But how Beecher treated the topics within his address was related to the nature of the audience. Realizing that many committed followers would attend the speech, Beecher created materials that would reinforce partisan beliefs. Cognizant that probably neutrals and opponents would also attend, Beecher knew he needed to deal with their reservations. The rhetorical strategy he employed was to argue by negation; the speech was in reality an extended classical *refutatio.* That is, he took the reservations and objections that might reasonably reside in his opponent's minds and openly refuted them. At the same time he augmented adherents' allegiance to the cause. Thus Beecher persuaded two birds with one stone: He accomplished part of his persuasive goal by eight refutations of arguments advanced by men and women who opposed woman suffrage, and he accomplished the other part by demonstrating to his partisans, who would gauge his good sense and moral character even more highly, that the arguments against woman suffrage were bogus.

The Arguments for Suffrage

Although it is beyond the purview of this rhetorical criticism of Beecher's speech to delve deeply into the history of woman's suffrage, a passing knowledge of the major rhetorical arguments that women and men used is necessary. Female speakers, and male ones like Beecher, tended to employ two major arguments in advocating woman's suffrage.

Justice   Women initially argued from justice. Karlyn Kohrs Campbell noted that the argument from justice "was drawn from natural rights philosophy and affirmed the personhood of women and their right to all the civil and political privileges of citizenship."[2] Speakers argued that as citizens of the United States, who paid taxes and could own property, women should be given the vote for simple justice. Of course, we take this argument for granted today, but most men and many women in the nineteenth century did not accept the justice argument.

A persuasive problem arose when women argued from justice. Using any reason they could fetch to deny women the vote, men and some women complained that the suffragists were selfish. They only wanted the vote for themselves (as if men did not!). Thus, women, in urging a self-centered measure for themselves, did not fit into the "woman's sphere," which will be defined momentarily.

Expediency   Having failed to persuade with justice, suffragists began to argue from expediency. They said, in effect, give women the vote, and they will use it, not so much for themselves, but to benefit the nation. They would vote for the pro-hibition of alcohol; for various progressive measures, such as child protection laws and prison reform; and against slavery in the South. As Campbell noted, women would "bring to bear on politics their purity, piety, and domestic concerns, and thus purify government and make it more responsive to the needs of the home."[3]

These two arguments revolved around certain assumptions that Americans made in the nineteenth century. People believed in the "woman's sphere." The woman's sphere was the kitchen and home, religion, and the children. According to this scheme, women did not need the vote because they controlled areas that did not require a ballot. When they claimed the justice of the vote, they were per-ceived as moving beyond the boundaries of their sphere. Man's sphere was busi-ness and politics. Men needed the vote in this sphere, but women did not.

The argument from expediency was an adaptation to the woman's sphere. Women argued that schools, religion, and saloons, which impinged on the woman's sphere, could be affected by the vote. This was more palatable to many Americans who were reformed minded because the woman's vote was perceived by many as the only way to redress many nineteenth-century American problems.

With this overview in mind, we will analyze Beecher's lecture with regard to how he argued for woman suffrage. The particular focus is on the rhetorical techniques he used to adapt his speech to the audience.

Beecher's Argument

"Woman suffrage," Beecher announced to his audience, "will bring civilization into our primary meetings and decency into our secondary ones." This was an argument from expediency. Decrying the "heathenism" that infested New York City, Beecher doubtless induced the audience to laughter when he allowed that New Yorkers kept "specimens of everything this side of perdition, and some, I think, of things the other side." Having put the audience in a good mood, Beecher stated his thesis: "Woman's influence, if introduced into public affairs, would work in the same direction there that it has worked, and is working, in social life, in literature, and in religious assemblies." His thesis statement was also an enthymeme. Partisans supplied the proof in their own minds as they drew on their experiences in life and literature: In fact, women had aided in those fields and could be expected to continue to do so outside the traditional woman's sphere. Since opponents would not assent to his thesis, Beecher then turned to disproving their positions.

Refutation: The Focus of Beecher's Speech

His transition to the first refutation was "But let us attend to some of the objec-tions that are made." If women voted, opponents argued, they would be subjected "to rudeness and to an exposure painful to delicacy." Beecher handily turned the tables by warranting that that very rudeness was "the result of woman's absence" from polling places, which were in "vile precincts and in pestholes." Thus woman suffrage would improve society. As for delicacy, Beecher countered that in mailing letters at a post office women were "made more public" and "fully as indelicate as in depositing her vote." Having dispatched those scurrilous objections, Beecher claimed that giving the vote to women would carry into national life "a power almost like the right hand of the Almighty."

Next Beecher refuted the argument that women should stay at home and have an influence there through their male relatives. Here, he frontally attacked the woman's sphere argument in which supporters of the status quo comforted themselves in denying women the ballot. He used humor to debunk that position. Allowing that males praised "the sweetening home affections" of women in the home, Beecher found it ironical that when women did attempt to influence men, the men "turn with lordly authority" and announce that the woman's role is in "the nursery and kitchen." Indeed, Beecher held that there was "a large infusion of vulgar arrogance even in good men" who held that God made woman "as nurse, cook, and plaything." He then used *reductio ad absurdum* to demolish the opposition. Using the examples of female school teachers, artists, and writers, who were generally accepted in Victorian America, Beecher asked why those who opposed woman suffrage did not also argue that women should eschew these jobs, stay at home, and work through their male relatives to effect change. Beecher thus efficiently explicated the absurdity of his opponent's position.

By this time, it should be apparent that Beecher highly prized the rhetorical question. Technically correct, Beecher always phrased them to elicit the desired responses. Partisans would of course answer as asked. For his opponents, Beecher used enthymemes as the basis for his rhetorical questions. For instance, since most Americans of the time acknowledged that women could and should teach school, it was absurd to apply a strict woman's sphere argument to suggest that women should only teach in the home. Hence, he made it difficult for objectors to answer in any other way than he had suggested.

Beecher's third refutation dealt with the objection that if women could vote, they could also run for public office. At base, this was an argument from justice, but it was used to demonstrate women's extreme selfishness in wanting to hold political office. Never one to mince words, Beecher followed his own logic and proclaimed, "Well why not?" He again argued by example. Using homey analogies of a farmer, merchant, editor, and schoolmaster, with which listeners could easily identify, Beecher observed that no one objected to wives taking the place of dead husbands to carry on their work. He then argued the idea of natural rights, or justice, for women's rights:

> I hold that it should be recognized her rights to engage in everything for which she is fitted, public affairs not excepted. . . . Wherever there are gifts, there should be liberty of exercise. Faculty always demands function. Every human being has a natural right to do whatever he or she can do well.

Although Beecher's logic was compellingly sound, not all listeners are convinced with systematic logic, as Aristotle knew was often the case.

"But it is objected that," Beecher stated as he began his fourth refutation, "by mingling in public affairs, women would soon extinguish that delicacy that now gives them both grace and influence." In reality, this was a recapitulation of his first point, which dealt with the woman's sphere argument, but Beecher now refuted it differently. He constructed a compelling enthymematic argument for a Victorian audience. Starting with the premise that "womanly qualities are God's gift," to which most Americans would give assent, Beecher then concluded that God's gifts could not be subverted. By elevating women above men on a moral level, but beneath men on a political plane, the opponents of women's rights inadvertently invited Beecher, who was a clever debater, to beat them at their own game. He easily turned the tables on his opponents: "it is not probable that the exercise of large public duty will efface the marks of her original constitution, and that an active patriotism will tarnish her purity, and that zeal for public justice will demoralize her nature."

By now it should also be evident that Beecher enjoyed turning the tables on his opponents. When the speaker turns the tables, he or she takes an opponent's position and shoves it back on the opponent. For instance, in the above quotation, Beecher showed how silly the antisuffragists were. On the one hand they argued that God made women pure, but that somehow if women voted they would be impure. Beecher handily showed that if God purified women, He would surely look over them in public life! To argue otherwise would be to assert that Man is more powerful than God, and few in the audience would assent to that belief.

The fifth refutation concerned what would happen when one's wife and daughter were subjected to "brutal rowdies" in public places. Beecher contended that he could take his wife and children anyplace in the United States. He then allowed that most men respect a woman's presence. Only "now and then" did Beecher see men smoking as they walked with women on the public streets, and "only once in a while" did men smoke when a woman was on an omnibus (the precursor of streetcars and the modern bus). Beecher concluded that civilized men would treat women in public affairs as they treat "her in the sanctuary and in these halls."

The sixth refutation dealt again with the woman's sphere argument. Opponents charged that if women became active in politics, they would abandon the home, their true calling. Again Beecher constructed a telling argument, based on example, that turned the tables on his opponents and reduced their argument to absurdity. He wisely did not reject the woman's sphere argument, for this would have angered both partisans and opponents. He merely held that there was room in that sphere for political action. In reality his argument was based on the man's sphere/woman's sphere enthymeme, and he argued by **analogy.** Observing that men attend to the duties of citizenship and yet still operate banks and stores, Beecher concluded "It would not take any more of woman's time than it does of man's." As a matter of fact, he opined, women would benefit men (expediency):

And if men were morally elevated, they would strike for rectitude without all those struggles and tergiversations which now impede their progress. Attention to public affairs, then, would not draw woman from her appropriate sphere one whit more than it draws man from his.

Beecher's seventh refutation was a recapitulation of the delicacy argument that he developed in his first point. But the supporting examples were different. Beecher observed that men did not object to women singing in public. He reminded the audience that the English operatic singer Jenny Lind, who toured the United States in the early 1850s, was widely praised and well received, and that Madame Sontag, another vocalist, sang before the assembled clergy of New York City and Brooklyn and no one commented about her "exposure, about her being unsexed, or about her being out of her sphere."

Beecher's eighth and last refutation of the arguments against woman suffrage was brilliantly conceived. When he delivered this speech, Queen Victoria reigned on the British throne. He used this fact to support his contention that women could serve a public function. But Beecher turned the idea of class distinction, which supported the British aristocracy, to his rhetorical advantage. He argued that males in the United States should trust their democratic women as much or more than British males trusted their aristocratic women. He thus played on inherent American democratic values as juxtaposed to European monarchical practices. Observing that societies "have been obliged to pass through the contention of the democratic and the aristocratic elements," he stated that women through the ages had been given power and public trust if they would "accept them in aristocratic form" as an "abbess, a countess, a queen." However, women "lower down in the social scale" were hindered by being female. On the one hand, Beecher used Queen Victoria as a model for the positive potentiality of female power:

> Today, the proudest throne on the globe is honored by a woman. No person is shocked that she is at the head of empire. Every reason urged against a larger liberty for woman is illustriously confuted by the dignity, purity, and womanly propriety with which Victoria stands before her empire, and before the world.

On the other hand, he appealed to democratic values by arguing that Americans should eschew aristocratic attitudes toward women:

> It is only woman *without a title* that must have no privileges. Woman, in her own simple self, with nothing more but what God gave her, plain, democratic woman, is not deemed worthy of honor and publicity. With a crown on her head, she may enter parliaments, and govern empires. With only her own simple personal virtues, she may not lift up her hand to cast a vote.

To complete the irony, Beecher invoked the subtle dislike of democratic Americans for British aristocracy: "That which is good enough for a queen is not too good for my wife. That which is noble in a duchess is honorable in my daughter." If one did not agree with Beecher's conclusion, then one was left in the unenviable and undemocratic position of holding that British aristocratic women should be better off politically than their democratic counterparts in the United States.

The Conclusion

Beecher used a smooth transition to close his address: "This, then, is the sum of what I wished to say to you tonight." In keeping with the nature of his speech, which was epideictic, Beecher targeted his conclusion more toward contemplation than action. In one of his homey metaphors, he urged reflection rather than immediate endeavor: "I have said it more in the expectation that it will work in you as a leaven than that it will bear immediate fruits. But, as the farmer sows seed in October that he does not expect to reap till July, so we must sow, and wait patiently for the harvest." He allowed that he did not expect to see female suffrage in his lifetime, but expected that his children might see it because "thoughts move faster than they used to."

He then finished his speech with a metaphor that expressed the Victorian value of progress. Given that biologists believed that plants grew in three stages, Beecher held that the root of society, which takes the longest to develop, grew until the advent of Christ; the stem, which grows faster, had been growing from Christ's time to the present; and "that in the period in which we stand it is growing by the blossom and the fruit." (It evidently never dawned on Beecher to complete the metaphor: that the blossom and fruit wither and die in a relatively short time; therefore, progress would have to start all over again.) In his final words to the audience, Beecher restated the expediency argument by asserting that women should have the vote because "we [men] need it. . . ."

Beecher supported his argument for woman suffrage by negation. His main logical proofs were refutations of opposing arguments. He persuaded compellingly well. However, he suffered one major logical flaw in his speech. He never did prove how or why woman suffrage was man's right. Perceptive opponents might have noticed that omission, but Beecher's adherents probably took his position for granted. Neither did he prove it was a man's right by disproving the opponent's arguments against the female vote. A classical arguments section might have been beneficial because it would have adduced some reasons why man's condition could be improved by women's vote (expediency). The title of the speech, "Woman Suffrage Man's Right," was certainly a catchy come-on, but the real persuasion was accomplished by applying a classical *refutatio* to demolish the sham arguments with which nineteenth-century males barred women from voting.

Notes

1. Clifford E. Clark, Jr., *Henry Ward Beecher: Spokesman for a Middle-Class America* (Urbana: University of Illinois Press, 1978), p. 198.
2. Karlyn Kohrs Campbell, *Man Cannot Speak for Her,* 2 vols. (New York: Praeger Publishers, 1989), I: 14.
3. Ibid.

Harry Emerson Fosdick's "My Account with the Unknown Soldier"

Harry Emerson Fosdick (1878–1969). A preacher at the Riverside Church, he spoke against fundamentalism in the 1920s and for pacifism in the 1930s.

PREFACE

The Reverend Harry Emerson Fosdick delivered this sermon at the Riverside Church on November 12, 1933. Fosdick was the nation's foremost preacher from the 1920s until his retirement in 1946, and it is safe to say that Fosdick made the Riverside Church the nation's premier pulpit in the years before World War II. Fosdick (like Father Charles Coughlin) was also a pioneer in using the radio to address a national audience. Fosdick began broadcasting in 1925, and he continued his National Vespers program until 1946.

The two major issues that Fosdick addressed were fundamentalism and pacificism. Fosdick delivered "Shall the Fundamentalists Win?" in 1922. That sermon made him a national spokesman for the modernist forces that succeeded in discrediting the fundamentalist movement until its resurgence in the late 1970s and early 1980s.

Fosdick's other calling was pacificism. A member of the generation that felt betrayed by World War I, which had not made the world safe for democracy as President Woodrow Wilson promised it would, Fosdick used his pulpit to preach Christian pacifism. He wanted believers to renounce war as a method of solving international disputes. Even in the face of fascism, the pacificists were a force to contend with during the 1930s, and they helped enforce the U.S. policy of isolationism until the Japanese bombed Pearl Harbor in 1941.

Fosdick's "My Account with the Unknown Soldier" was his most eloquent address on pacificism. His sermon is anthologized for the primary purpose of demonstrating how a speaker skilled in the art of rhetoric could adapt a troublesome topic to an audience of partisans, neutrals, and opponents. If there is a secondary purpose, it would surely be that Fosdick still makes a compelling case for pacificism. It is for you, the reader, who may take the military-industrial complex for granted, to determine the extent to which and in what contexts Fosdick's ideas are viable in a world that clearly contains evil.

"MY ACCOUNT WITH THE UNKNOWN SOLDIER": THE SPEECH
Delivered at Riverside Church, New York, November 12, 1933.

It was an interesting idea to deposit the body of an unrecognized soldier in the national memorial of the Great War, and yet, when one stops to think of it, how strange it is! Yesterday, in Rome, Paris, London, Washington, and how many capitals beside, the most stirring military pageantry, decked with flags and exultant with music, centered about the bodies of unknown soldiers. That is strange. So this is the outcome of Western civilization, which for nearly two thousand years has worshipped Christ, and in which democracy and science have had their widest opportunity, that the whole nation pauses, its acclamations rise, its colorful pageantry centers, its patriotic oratory flourishes, around the unrecognizable body of a soldier blown to bits on the battlefield. That is strange.

It was the war lords themselves who picked him out as the symbol of war. So be it! As a symbol of war we accept him from their hands.

You may not say that I, being a Christian minister, did not know him. I knew him well. From the north of Scotland, where they planted the sea with mines, to the trenches of France, I lived with him and his fellows—British, Australian, New Zealand, French, American. The places where he fought, from Ypres through the Somme battlefield to the southern trenches, I saw while he still was there. I lived with him in his dugouts in the trenches, and on destroyers searching for submarines off the shores of France. Short of actual battle, from training camp to hospital, from the fleet to No Man's Land, I, a Christian minister, saw the war. Morover, I, a Christian minister, participated in it. I too was persuaded that it was a war to end war. I too was a gullible fool and thought that modern war could somehow make the world safe for democracy. They sent men like me to explain to the army the high meaning of war and, by every argument we could command, to strengthen their morale. I wonder if I ever spoke to the Unknown Soldier.

One night, in a ruined barn behind the lines, I spoke at sunset to a company of hand-grenaders who were going out that night to raid the German trenches. They told me that on the average no more than half a company came back from such a raid, and I, a minister of Christ, tried to nerve them for their suicidal and murderous endeavor. I wonder if the Unknown Soldier was in that barn that night.

Once in a dugout which in other days had been a French wine cellar I bade Godspeed at two in the morning to a detail of men going out on patrol in No Man's Land. They were a fine company of American boys fresh from home. I recall that, huddled in the dark, underground chamber, they sang:

> Lead, kindly Light, amid th' encircling gloom,
>   Lead thou me on.
> The night is dark, and I am far from home,—
>   Lead thou me on.

Then, with my admonitions in their ears, they went down from the second- to the first-line trenches and so out to No Man's Land. I wonder if the Unknown Soldier was in that dugout.

You here this morning may listen to the rest of this sermon or not, as you please. It makes much less difference to me than usual what you do or think. I have an account to settle in this pulpit today between my soul and the Unknown Soldier.

He is not so utterly unknown as we sometimes think. Of one thing we can be certain: He was sound of mind and body. We made sure of that. All primitive gods who demanded bloody sacrifices on their altars insisted that the animals should be the best, without mar or hurt. Turn to the Old Testament and you find it written there: "Whether male or female, he shall offer it without blemish before Jehovah." The god of war still maintains the old demand. These men to be sacrificed upon his altars were sound and strong. Once there might have been guessing about that. Not now. Now we have medical science, which tests the prospective soldier's body. Now we have psychiatry, which tests his mind. We used them both to make sure that these sacrifices for the god of war were without blemish. Of all insane and suicidal procedures, can you imagine anything madder than this, that all the nations should pick out their best, use their scientific skill to make certain that they are the best, and then in one mighty holocaust offer ten million of them on the battlefields of one war?

I have an account to settle between my soul and the Unknown Soldier. I deceived him. I deceived myself first, unwittingly, and then I deceived him, assuring him that good consequence could come out of that. As a matter of hard-headed, biological fact, what good can come out of that? Mad civilization, you cannot sacrifice on bloody altars the best of your breed and expect anything to compensate for the loss.

Of another thing we may be fairly sure concerning the Unknown Soldier—that he was a conscript. He may have been a volunteer but on an actuarial average he probably was a conscript. The long arm of the nation reached into his home, touched him on the shoulder, saying, You must go to France and fight. If some one asks why in this "land of the free" conscription was used, the answer is, of course, that it was necessary if we were to win the war. Certainly it was. And that reveals something terrific about modern war. We cannot get soldiers —not enough of them, not the right kinds of them—without forcing them. When a nation goes to war now, the entire nation must go. That means that the youth of the nation must be compelled, coerced, conscripted to fight.

When you stand in Arlington before the tomb of the Unknown Soldier on some occasions, let us say, when the panoply of military glory decks it with music and color, are you thrilled? I am not—not any more. I see there the memorial of one of the saddest things in American history, from the continued repetition of which may God deliver us!—the conscripted boy.

He was a son, the hope of the family, and the nation coerced him. He was, perchance, a lover and the deepest emotion of his life was not desire for military glory or hatred of another country or any other idiotic thing like that, but love of a girl and hope of a home. He was, maybe, a husband and a father, and already, by that slow and beautiful graduation which all fathers know, he had felt the deep ambitions of his heart being transferred from himself to his children. And the nation coerced him. I am not blaming him; he was conscripted. I am not blaming the nation; it never could have won the war without conscription. I am simply saying that that is modern war, not by accident but by necessity, and with every repetition that will be more and more the attribute of war.

Last time they coerced our sons. Next time, of course, they will coerce our daughters, and in any future war they will conscript property. Old-fashioned Americans, born out of the long traditon of liberty, some of us have trouble with these new coercions used as shortcuts to get things done, but nothing else compares with this inevitable, universal, national conscription in time of war. Repeated once or twice more, it will end everything in this nation that remotely approaches liberty.

If I blame anybody about this matter, it is men like myself who ought to have known better. We went out to the army and explained to these valiant men what a resplendent future they were preparing for their children by their heroic sacrifice. O Unknown Soldier, however can I make that right with you? For sometimes I think I hear you asking me about it:

Where is this great, new era that the war was to create? Where is it? They blew out my eyes in the Argonne. It is because of that that now from Arlington I strain them vainly to see the great gains of the war? If I could see the prosperity, plenty, and peace of my children for which this mangled body was laid down!

My friends, sometimes I do not want to believe in immortality. Sometimes I hope that the Unknown Soldier will never know.

Many of you here knew these men better, you may think, than I knew them, and already you may be relieving my presentation of the case by another picture. Probably, you say, the Unknown Soldier enjoyed soldiering and had a thrilling time in France. The Great War, you say, was the most exciting episode of our time. Some of us found in it emotional release unknown before or since. We escaped from ourselves. We were carried out of ourselves. Multitudes were picked up from a dull routine, lifted out of the drudgery of common days with which they were infinitely bored, and plunged into an exciting adventure which they remember yet as the most thrilling episode of their careers.

Indeed, you say, how could martial music be so stirring and martial poetry so exultant if there were not at the heart of war a lyric glory? Even in the churches you sing,

> Onward, Christian soldiers,
> Marching as to war.

You, too, when you wish to express or arouse ardor and courage, use war's symbolism. The Unknown Soldier, sound in mind and body—yes! The Unknown Soldier a conscript—probably! But be fair and add that the Unknown Soldier had a thrilling time in France.

To be sure, he may have had. Listen to this from a wounded American after a battle. "We went over the parapet at five o'clock and I was not hit till nine. They were the greatest four hours of my life." Quite so! Only let me talk to you a moment about that. That was the first time he went over the parapet. Anything risky, dangerous, tried for the first time, well handled, and now escaped from, is thrilling to an excitable and courageous soul. What about the second time and the third time and the fourth? What about the dreadful times between, the long-drawn-out, monotonous, dreary, muddy barrenness of war, concerning which one who knew said, "Nine-tenths of war is waiting"? The trouble with much familiar talk about the lyric glory of war is that it comes from people who never saw any soldiers except the American troops, fresh, resilient, who had time to go over the parapet about once. You ought to have seen the hardening-up camps of the armies which had been at the business since 1914. Did you ever see them? Did you look, as I have looked, into the faces of young men who had been over the top, wounded, hospitalized, hardened up—over the top, wounded, hospitalized, hardened up—four times, five times, six times? Never talk to a man who has seen that about the lyric glory of war.

Where does all this talk about the glory of war come from, anyway?

> "Charge, Chester, charge! On, Stanley, on!"
> Were the last words of Marmion.

That is Sir Walter Scott. Did he ever see war? Never.

> And how can man die better
>   Than facing fearful odds,
> For the ashes of his fathers,
>   And the temples of his Gods?

That is Macaulay. Did he ever see war? He was never near one.

> Storm'd at with shot and shell,
> Boldly they rode and well,
> Into the jaws of Death,
> Into the mouth of Hell,
> Rode the six hundred.

That is Tennyson. Did he ever see war? I should say not.

There is where the glory of war comes from. We have heard very little about it from the real soldiers of this last war. We have had from them the appalling opposite. They say what George Washington said: It is "a plague to mankind." The glory of war comes from poets, preachers, orators, the writers of martial music, statesmen preparing flowery proclamations for the people, who dress up war for other men to fight. They do not go to the trenches. They do not go over the top again and again and again.

Do you think that the Unknown Soldier would really believe in the lyric glory of war? I dare you; go to Arlington and tell him that now.

Nevertheless, some may say that while war is a grim and murderous business with no glory in it in the end, and while the Unknown Soldier doubtless knew that well, we have the right in our imagination to make him the symbol of whatever was most idealistic and courageous in the men who went out to fight. Of course we have. Now, let us do that! On the body of a French sergeant killed in battle was found a letter to his parents in which he said, "You know how I made the sacrifice of my life before leaving." So we think of our Unknown Soldier as an idealist, rising up in answer to a human call and making the sacrifice of his life before leaving. His country seemed to him like Christ himself, saying, "If any man would come after me, let him deny himself, and take up his cross daily, and follow me." Far from appealing to his worst, the war brought out his best—his loyalty, his courage, his venturesomeness, his care for the downtrodden, his capacity for self-sacrifice. The noblest qualities of his young manhood were aroused. He went out to France a flaming patriot and in secret quoted Rupert Brooke to his own soul:

> If I should die, think only this of me:
>   That there's some corner of a foreign field
>   That is for ever England.

There you say, is the Unknown Soldier.

Yes, indeed, did you suppose I never had met him? I talked with him many a time. When the words that I would speak about war are a blistering fury on my lips and the encouragement I gave to war is a deep self-condemnation in my heart, it is of that I think. For I watched war lay its hands on these strongest, loveliest things in men and use the noblest attributes of the human spirit for what ungodly deeds! Is there anything more infernal than this, to take the best that is in man and use it to do what war does? This is the ultimate description of war—it is the prostitution of the noblest powers of the human soul to the most dastardly deeds, the most abysmal cruelties of which our human nature is capable. That is war.

Granted, then, that the Unknown Soldier should be to us a symbol of everything most idealistic in a valiant warrior, I beg of you, be realistic and follow through what was made the Unknown Soldier do with his idealism. Here is one eyewitness speaking:

> Last night, at an officers' mess there was great laughter at the story of one of our men who had spent his last cartridge in defending an attack. 'Hand me down your spade, Mike,' he said, and as six Germans came one by one round the end of a traverse, he split each man's skull open with a beadly blow.

The war made the Unknown Soldier do that with his idealism.

"I can remember," says one infantry officer, "a pair of hands (nationality unknown) which protruded from the soaked ashen soil like the roots of a tree turned upside down; one hand seemed to be pointing at the sky with an accusing gesture. . . . Floating on the surface of the flooded trench was the mask of a human face which had detached itself from the skull." War harnessed the idealism of the Unknown Soldier to that!

Do I not have an account to settle between my soul and him? They sent men like me into the camps to awaken his idealism, to touch those secret, holy springs within him so that with devotion, fidelity, loyalty, and self-sacrifice he might go out to war. O war, I hate you most of all for this, that you do lay your hands on the noblest elements in human character, with which we might make a heaven on earth, and you use them to make a hell on earth instead! You take even our science, the fruit of our dedicated intelligence, by means of which we might build here the City of God, and, using it, you fill the earth instead with new ways of slaughtering men. You take our loyalty, our unselfishness, with which we might make the earth beautiful, and, using these our finest qualities, you make death fall from the sky and burst up from the sea and hurtle from unseen ambuscades sixty miles away; you blast fathers in the trenches with gas while you are starving their children at home by blockades; and you so bedevil the world that fifteen years after the armistice we cannot be sure who won the war, so sunk in the same disaster are victors and vanquished alike. If war were fought simply with evil things, like hate, it would be bad enough but, when one sees the deeds of war done with the loveliest faculties of the human spirit, he looks into the very pit of hell.

Suppose one thing more—that the Unknown Soldier was a Christian. Maybe he was not, but suppose he was, a Christian like Sergeant York, who at the beginning intended to take Jesus so seriously as to refuse to fight but afterward, otherwise persuaded, made a real soldier. For these Christians do make soldiers. Religion is a force. When religious faith supports war, when, as in the Crusades, the priests of Christ cry, "Deus Vult"—God wills it—and, confirming ordinary motives, the dynamic of Christian devotion is added, then an incalculable resource of confidence and power is released. No wonder the war departments wanted the churches behind them!

Suppose, then, that the Unknown Soldier was a Christian. I wonder what he thinks about war now. Practically all modern books about war emphasize the newness of it—new weapons, new horrors, new extensiveness. At times, however, it seems to me that still the worst things about war are the ancient elements. In the Bible we read terrible passages where the Hebrews thought they had command from Jehovah to slaughter the Amalekites, "both man and woman, infant and suckling, ox and sheep, camel and ass." Dreadful! we say, an ancient and appalling idea! Ancient? Appalling? Upon the contrary, that is war, and always will be. A military order, issued in our generation by an American general in the Philippines and publicly acknowledged by his counsel afterwards in a military court, commanded his soldiers to burn and kill, to exterminate all capable of bearing arms, and to make the island of Samar a howling wilderness. Moreover, his counsel acknowledged that he had specifically named the age of ten with instuctions to kill everyone over that. Far from launching into a denunciation of that American general, I am much more tempted to state his case for him. Why not? Cannot boys and girls of eleven fire a gun? Why not kill everything over ten? That is war, past, present, and future. All that our modern fashions have done is to make the necessity of slaughtering children not the comparatively simple and harmless matter of shooting some of them in Samar, one by one, but the wholesale destruction of children, starving them by millions, impoverishing them, spoiling the chances of unborn generations of them, as in the Great War.

My friends, I am not trying to make you sentimental about this. I want you to be hard-headed. We can have this monstrous thing or we can have Christ, but we cannot have both. O my country, stay out of war! Cooperate with the nations in every movement that has any hope for peace; enter the World Court, support the League of Nations, contend undiscourageably for disarmament, but set your face steadfastly and forever against being drawn into another war. O church of Christ, stay out of war! Withdraw from every alliance that maintains or encourages it. It was not a pacifist, it was Field-Marshal Earl Haig who said, "It is the business of the churches to make my business impossible." And O my soul, stay out of war!

At any rate, I will myself do the best I can to settle my account with the Unknown Soldier. I renounce war. I renounce war because of what it does to our own men. I have watched them coming gassed from the front-line trenches. I have seen the long, long hospital trains filled with their mutilated bodies. I have heard the cries of the crazed and the prayers of those who wanted to die and could not, and I remember the maimed and ruined men for whom the war is not yet over. I renounce war because of what it compels us to do to our enemies, bombing their mothers in villages, starving their children by blockades, laughing over our coffee cups about every damnable thing we have been able to do to them. I renounce war for its consequences, for the lies it lives on and propagates, for the undying hatreds it arouses, for the dictatorships it puts in the place of democracy, for the starvation that stalks after it. I renounce war and never again, directly or indirectly, will I sanction or support another! O Unknown Soldier, in penitent reparation I make you that pledge.

ANALYSIS

A major and recurring problem in Christianity is how one reconciles hate and killing with the gospel of love in the New Testament and the sixth commandment in the Old Testament.

During World War I, the Reverend Harry Emerson Fosdick, in company with other patriotic pastors and priests, had cooperated with the government by blessing the war effort and by giving succor to the Allied troops. Some years later, however, on the Sunday following Armistice Day, Fosdick delivered this sermon, which urged Americans to stop praying to God about war and exhorted them to become Christian pacifists.

Spoken during the rise of pacifism in the United States, particularly on college campuses in the 1930s, "My Account with the Unknown Soldier" was a kind of expiation for Fosdick's involvement in World War I. Not everyone agreed with Fosdick. Colonel H. P. Hobbs had recently characterized peace parades on college campuses "un-American" and a retired army major had said the pacifists were "either too yellow to fight or wanted to grab-off something."[1]

The Riverside sermon contains robust rhetoric because Fosdick faced a congregation that did not totally share his convictions. Notwithstanding the persuasive stance he took on pacifism (which will be analyzed in due course), the address excelled in four of the five classical canons of rhetoric: *inventio,* the creativity and inventiveness of the addrress; *dispositio,* the speech's organizational arrangement; *elocutio,* its style and diction; and *actio,* its delivery. Fosdick did not follow the fifth canon, *memoria,* the commitment to memory of an address. He delivered the speech from a manuscript, but that evidently had no appreciable negative effect on the reception of his address by his audience.

Fosdick also used an organizational pattern that suggested his indebtedness to classical rhetoric, which he probably learned in speech classes at Colgate University.

The Introduction

To arrest the attention of his audience, Fosdick used irony in his introduction. Alluding to Armistice Day, he said it was "interesting" that Christians, committed to the worship of Christ, should partake in the military and patriotic pageantry that surrounded the Unknown Soldier, whom Fosdick characterized with alliteration as the "unrecognizable body of a soldier blown to bits on the battlefield." Claiming that the "war lords" chose the Unknown Soldier as the symbol of war, Fosdick, for argumentative purposes, accepted the symbol "from their hands."

The Narrative

Fosdick used the narration to frame his participation as a clergyman in World War I in an unfavorable perspective. Acknowledging that he had been sent by the government to address the troops "to strengthen their morale," he wondered if he had steeled the Unknown Soldier to go on a suicidal grenade mission, from which only half the company came back, or had admonished the Unknown Soldier to go on a patrol in No Man's Land. For the Riverside audience, Fosdick then made a remarkable statement. Using the rhetorical technique of apophasis, wherein the orator affirms a point by appearing to deny it, he challenged his congregation to listen to his sermon by appearing indifferent to whether it did: "You here this morning may listen to the rest of this sermon or not, as you please. It makes much less difference to me than usual what you do or think. I have an account to settle in this pulpit today between my soul and the Unknown Soldier." Thus challenged, even an opponent would be motivated to listen if for no other reason than to refute Fosdick's contentions.

The Arguments

Fosdick began the arguments with a bitter irony. Reminding his audience that ancient gods and even Jehovah demanded the best animals for bloody sacrifice, Fosdick assured his audience that the Unknown Soldier was doubtlessly "sound of mind and body," that "The god of war still maintains the old demand." Scorning the uses toward which modern medicine and psychiatry were applied, he questioned whether "nations should pick out their best, use their scientific skill to make certain that they are the best, and then in one mighty holocaust offer ten million of them on the battlefields of one war?" The irony would have bolstered listeners who already believed his thesis, and must have affected even his opponents. Continuing in the vein that this was a personal sermon, he summarized the first argument with an emphasis on the pronoun *I*, which was also combined with anaphora, to stress his thesis:

> I have an account to settle between my soul and the Unknown Soldier. I
> deceived him. I deceived myself first, unwittingly, and then I deceived
> him, assuring him that good consequences could come out of that. As a
> matter of hard-headed, biological fact, what good can come out of that?
> Mad civilization, you cannot sacrifice on bloody altars the best of your
> breed and expect anything to compensate for the loss.

Although these words passed as an apparent soliloquy, Fosdick cleverly invited the audience to acknowledge it had been duped, as he had been, by President Wilson's promise to make World War I the war to end all wars.

The second argument in the Riverside sermon was an attack on conscription. Decrying the tautology that the reason the United States had to have conscription was because it was necessary to win the war, Fosdick placed that patriotic pabulum in an undesirable perspective: "We cannot get soldiers—not enough of them, not the right kind of them—without forcing them. When a nation goes to war now, the entire nation must go. That means that the youth of the nation must be compelled, coerced, conscripted to fight." To invoke sympathy with these young men, he used emotionally laden language to suggest how men loved girls rather than war, loved as young husbands or fathers rather than as fighters. To heighten the argument, he predicted that in the next war women would be coerced as well as property, and eventually liberty would be lost. Giving an artistic unity to this argument, he again subtly invited his audience to join him in soliloquizing to the Unknown Soldier: "If I blame anybody about this matter, it is men like myself who ought to have known better. We went out to the army and explained to these valiant men what a resplendent future they were preparing for their children by their heroic sacrifice. O Unknown Soldier, however can I make that right with you?" Amidst the Depression, with fascism drawing nourishment from the aftermath of the Treaty of Versailles, Fosdick's audience was surrounded by proof that the war had been fruitless.

Fosdick employed only these two major arguments. For those who would already assent to his thesis, this was probably sufficient argumentation. But two arguments would probably not be enough for listeners who held opposed beliefs. Therefore, Fosdick turned immediately to the refutation section of his speech.

The Refutation

Fosdick used a *refutatio* to confute objections and reservations in the minds of his listeners. Notwithstanding his protestation in the introduction about not caring whether they listened, Fosdick's refutation suggests that he was trying to persuade them.

Fosdick framed the first objection artfully. "Probably," he allowed to his audience, "you say, the Unknown Soldier enjoyed soldiering and had a thrilling time in France. . . . Indeed, you say, how could martial music be so stirring and martial poetry so exultant if there were not at the heart of war a lyric glory?" His reply was a devastating rebuttal to his opponents but a reinforcing argument for his adherents:

> The trouble with much familiar talk about the lyric glory of war is that it comes from people who never saw any soldiers. . . . You ought to have seen the hardening-up camps of the armies which had been at the business since 1914. Did you ever see them? Did you look, as I have looked, into the faces of young men who had been over the top, wounded, hospitalized, hardened-up—over the top, wounded, hospitalized, hardened-up—four times, five times, six times? Never talk to a man who has seen that about the lyric glory of war.

Fosdick offered more analysis to sustain his rebuttal. After quoting famous poems that extolled warfare, he claimed that the poets Sir Walter Scott, Thomas Macaulay, and Alfred, Lord Tennyson, never saw war. Turning to those who did know war firsthand, he quoted George Washington, who said war is "a plague to mankind." Then, in one of the most damning passages in the sermon, he condemned easy patriotism:

> The glory of war comes from poets, preachers, orators, the writers of martial music, statesmen preparing flowery proclamations for the people, who dress up war for other men to fight. They do not go to the trenches. They do not go over the top again and again and again.

He dared his congregation to go down to Arlington to tell the Unknown Soldier about the lyric glory of war "*now.*"

His second refutation concerned the supposed idealism surrounding war. He began by enunciating the soldierly characteristics associated with idealism: loyalty, courage, venturesomeness, care for the downtrodden, and capacity for self-sacrifice. In juxtaposition, he quoted eyewitnesses about the real horrors of battle. He dramatically used the **vocative** case to addressed a personified War, whom he accused of using men to make, rather than "a heaven on earth," a "hell on earth instead." Having stirred the emotions of his hearers, he concluded with a logical appeal: "fifteen years after the Armistice we cannot be sure who won the war, so sunk in the same disaster are victors and vanquished alike."

His third refutation for the Riverside audience was to ask them to suppose that the Unknown Soldier was a Christian. He noted that religion was a force and, when supplemented by Christian devotion, it became a source "of confidence and power." "No wonder," he exclaimed, "the war departments wanted the churches behind them!" He then cited the case of an American general who ordered his troops to kill everyone over the age of ten on the island of Samar in the Philippines during the Spanish-American war. Rather than condemning the general, Fosdick averred that he was tempted to state the general's case for him. Using the rhetorical technique of turning-the-tables, wherein the orator takes an opponent's position and turns it to the opponent's disadvantage, Fosdick rhetorically asked why not kill everyone over ten: "Cannot boys and girls of eleven fire a gun?" Fosdick doubtless realized the cold logic of his question was repulsive, yet he pressed the point to its revolting conclusion: "That is war, past, present, and future."

Before turning to Fosdick's moving conclusion, a slight digression is in order. If verbiage is any indication of persuasive intent, the relative allotment between the confirmation and refutation divisions in the Riverside sermon is instructive. Fosdick developed two major arguments and three refutations. But in terms of words, about 15 percent of the sermon was arguments and about 50 percent of it was refutation. This allocation of persuasive resources suggests that Fosdick had analyzed his audience. He evidently reasoned that his opponents needed more persuasive attention than his partisans. This apportionment is additional evidence that he truly wanted to persuade neutrals and opponents in his congregation.

The Conclusion

In his powerful conclusion, Fosdick reiterated his thesis: "We can have this monstrous thing or we can have Christ, but we cannot have both." Again Fosdick used the vocative to portray the voice crying in the wilderness: "O my country, stay out of war! . . . O church of Christ, stay out of war! . . . And O my soul, stay out of war!" The stylistic device of epistrophe, the ending of clauses or sentences with the same or similar words, lent elegance to his pleas.

Hopeful yet cognizant that his words might not have persuaded everyone at Riverside, Fosdick personalized the sermon by settling his account with the Unknown Soldier. In a series of declaratory sentences that began with the anaphora of "I renounce war," he listed the practices he reviled, including "the dictatorships it [war] puts in the place of democracy." His final words were an intimate expiation: "I renounce war and never again, directly or indirectly, will I sanction or support another! O Unknown Soldier, in penitent reparation I make you that pledge." In squaring his account with the Unknown Soldier, Fosdick cleverly asked his audience to settle vicariously their accounts by validating his renunciation of war. Thus, his conclusion would have worked for Fosdick's partisans in the Riverside congregation, would have perhaps lured some neutrals into his fold, and may have caused his opponents to pause and think.

Fosdick's Enduring Influence

The lasting effect of Fosdick's "Unknown Soldier" speech has been aptly summarized by Robert Clark:

> With his instinct for the dramatic, Fosdick placed himself at the head of the pacifists and, unwittingly, in the vanguard of the isolationists. He had excited a dream of a world of peace which the people who heard him could never forget, but it was a dream which took little account of the realities of the international scene.[2]

Clark correctly summarized the effects of Fosdick's rhetoric but was overly harsh on the preacher with regard to the reality of 1933–1934, which was not that of 1939–1941. Robert Miller rendered a more sympathetic, yet balanced, judgment of Fosdick's pacifism by suggesting that it was difficult, but not impossible, to criticize Fosdick's theology.[3]

The complication one encounters in pronouncing a verdict on Fosdick's pacifist rhetoric is similar to the onerous task that confronts professing Christians. Christ's way is not altogether easy or rational. Although there are cogent arguments for the just war and national self-defense, Fosdick constructed a sound theological and persuasive position for Christian ministers on war: Mars and Christ are irreconcilable. (Under Fosdick's direction, and to his credit, the Riverside Church throughout World War II aided servicemen at home and abroad in an extensive and meaningful outreach program. Even in his eighties, Fosdick played what role he could in the anti-Vietnam War movement.[4])

On the other hand, as humans who miss the mark, Christians still continue to kill fellow believers and nonbelievers as well. To Fosdick's credit, he did not excuse the sin by invoking patriotism: The Father was greater to Fosdick than the fatherland. How inconvenient a pragmatic application of Fosdick's rhetoric might be, he at least bore witness to the standards that humans strive for but cannot obtain.

Notes

1. "Fight on Pacifism Asked," *New York Times*, May 8, 1934, p. 7.
2. Robert D. Clark, "Harry Emerson Fosdick" in *History and Criticism of American Public Address*, edited by Marie Kathryn Hochmuth (New York: Russell and Russell, 1955), p. 432.
3. Robert Moats Miller, *Harry Emerson Fosdick: Preacher, Pastor, Prophet* (New York: Oxford University Press, 1985), pp. 490–532.
4. "Clergymen Score U.S. Aid to Diem," *New York Times*, August 15, 1963, p. 3.

Richard M. Nixon's "My Side of the Story"

Richard M. Nixon (1913–). A former senator and president of the United States, he delivered in 1952 the "Checkers" speech, the most successful political apologia ever addressed.

PREFACE

The ancients defined a type of speech set that still occurs in contemporary communications. They realized that a certain kind of speech could motivate a speech in response, and that both of these speeches had certain characteristics. These attributes recurred enough times in enough speeches over enough historical periods so that the speeches could be termed a genre, or kind, of rhetoric. Their classical names were *kategoria*, a speech of accusation, and *apologia*, a speech of self-defense.[1]

The major figures in classical rhetoric discussed these speeches. Plato divided rhetoric into the two genres of accusation and apology; Isocrates included accusation and apology in his four-part division of speeches; Aristotle divided forensic oratory into accusation and apology; and Quintilian wrote about the speech set:

> I cannot understand why some hold that the elaboration of speech originated in the fact that those who were in peril owing to some accusation being made against them, set themselves to speak with a studied care for the purpose of their own defense. This however, though a more honorable origin, cannot possibly be the earlier, for accusation necessarily precedes defense. You might as well assert that the sword was invented for the purpose of self-defense and not for aggression.[2]

The theory of the speech set is straightforward. It holds that a speech of accusation generally motivates a speech of self-defense. A speaker perceives a problem that he or she would seek to resolve by attacking another person, and that person understands that, once under attack, he or she had better respond, or else the attack will stand unchallenged. The ensuing encounter comprises the speech set of accusatory and apologetic rhetoric.[3]

Further, accusatory and apologetic rhetoric center on matters of policy and character, and the speech set rests on one or more of the classical stases of fact, definition, and quality. For illustrative purposes, let us assume the following speech set.

Speaker X delivers an accusatory speech, claiming that Y had crib notes for a final examination. The possession of the crib notes is the policy, and speaker X must assure the audience of that fact. Accusatory speaker X may wish to define those crib notes as "cheating," and to assert that such cheating is an undesirable quality. At the conclusion of X's accusation, Y has two choices. If Y remains silent, the audience could reasonably assume that the accusations were true, and Y could be expelled from school. Or Y could deliver a speech in self-defense.

Having decided to deliver an apologia, speaker Y could first deny the factual policy. Apologist Y could argue that he or she did not possess crib notes at all and produce proof for that position. Assuming that defensive posture was the extent of the apologetic speech, the audience would decide on the stasis of fact whether Y enacted the policy.

However, suppose Y did in fact take crib notes into the examination. Speaker Y could agree that he or she did possess crib notes, thus admitting the stasis of fact, but contend that he or she never used them, thus clashing on the stasis of definition, for possession does not necessarily imply use. In this instance, the audience would decide whether apologist Y actually used the notes in the definitional dispute over the action.

However, if Y did possess the crib notes, and did refer to them during the examination, the quality of the action would be the last stasis on which to stake Y's hope. Apologist Y could argue that he or she did not refer to the crib notes as often as X alleged, or that the number of answers that were actually obtained by the crib notes was very small. In these cases, apologist Y would try to persuade the audience that the quality or degree of the transgression was so small that it should not be punished or should be punished by some penalty less drastic than expulsion.

So far, the sample speech set has clashed over policy. The accusatory speaker could also stress matters of character. Having established the fact, definition, and quality of an act, X could also indict Y's ethos. For instance, in the 1988 presidential primary contests, several Democratic contenders found themselves objects of political accusations. Accusers attacked individual candidate's actions by focusing on various deeds that were defined as plagiarizing and womanizing. These acts by public figures revealed flawed characters because they would stoop to such practices; hence, they were defined as unfit to lead the United States of America. As may be expected, these candidates offered a variety of apologias for their policies and characters, but these self-defenses did not wash with the American people.

However, one famous political apology washed exceedingly well. It was Senator Richard Nixon's "My Side of the Story" speech. In this speech, broadcast nationwide over radio and television on September 23, 1952, Nixon employed technical rhetoric in using a vast array of rhetorical devices to clear his policy and character with the American radio and television audiences in 1952. His methods will be explained in the rhetorical criticism that follows the text of Nixon's speech. These rhetorical techniques are amoral because they can be used for truthful or untruthful purposes.

Nixon was a trained and skilled speaker, a master who could manipulate the art to the very limits of its ethical employment. In fact many critics have held that Nixon exceeded legitimate ethical boundaries in his speech. After you have read the speech and its accompanying rhetorical criticism, you can decide for yourself whether he did.

Critics have disagreed sharply about the philosophical strand of rhetoric in Nixon's speech. Of course, some contended, Nixon delivered his apologia so that the audience ought to believe the sanitized version of his policy and character; it was just that his side of the story was *not* what the American people *ought* to believe. Not so, others rejoined, for what Nixon did was both legal and moral in the political milieu of 1952. Whether the accusatory or apologetic critics were correct will be yours to decide.

You are empaneled on this jury as a rhetorical critic. First read Senator Nixon's speech, just as the American people heard and read it in 1952. Then read the rhetorical criticism, which also recounts how the public and the newspapers reacted to his address. Then decide whether Plato would have said, "I told you so!"

"MY SIDE OF THE STORY": THE SPEECH

Broadcast on national radio and television, September 23, 1952, from Los Angeles, California.

My Fellow Americans: I come before you tonight as a candidate for the Vice Presidency and as a man whose honesty and integrity have been questioned.

The usual political thing to do when charges are made against you is to either ignore them or to deny them without giving details.

I believe we've had enough of that in the United States, particularly with the present Administration in Washington, D.C. To me the office of the Vice Presidency of the United States is a great office, and I feel that the people have got to have confidence in the integrity of the men who run for that office and who might obtain it.

I have a theory, too, that the best and only answer to a smear or to an honest misunderstanding of the facts is to tell the truth. And that's why I'm here tonight. I want to tell you my side of the case.

I am sure that you have read the charge and you've heard that I, Senator Nixon, took $18,000 from a group of my supporters.

Now, was that wrong? And let me say that it was wrong—I'm saying, incidentally, that it was wrong and not just illegal. Because it isn't a question of whether it was legal or illegal, that isn't enough. The question is, was it morally wrong?

I say that it was morally wrong if any of that $18,000 went to Senator Nixon for my personal use. I say that it was morally wrong if it was secretly given and secretly handled. And I say that it was morally wrong if any of the contributors got special favors for the contributions that they made.

And now to answer those questions let me say this:

Not one cent of the $18,000 or any other money of that type ever went to me for my personal use. Every penny of it was used to pay for political expenses that I did not think should be charged to the taxpayers of the United States.

It was not a secret fund. As a matter of fact, when I was on "Meet the Press," some of you may have seen it last Sunday—Peter Edson came up to me after the program and he said, "Dick, what about this fund we hear about?" And I said, "Well, there's no secret about it. Go out and see Dana Smith, who was the administrator of the fund." And I gave him his address, and I said that you will find that the purpose of the fund simply was to defray political expenses that I did not feel should be charged to the Government.

And third, let me point out, and I want to make this particularly clear, that no contributor to this fund, no contributor to any of my campaign, has ever received any consideration that he would not have received as an ordinary constituent.

I just don't believe in that and I can say that never, while I have been in the Senate of the United States, as far as the people that contributed to this fund are concerned, have I made a telephone call for them to an agency, or have I gone down to an agency in their behalf. And the record will show that, the records which are in the hands of the Administration.

But then some of you will say and rightly, "Well, what did you use the fund for, Senator? Why did you have to have it?"

Let me tell you in just a word how a Senate office operates. First of all, a Senator gets $15,000 a year in salary. He gets enough money to pay for one trip a year, a round trip that is, for himself and his family between his home and Washington, D.C.

And then he gets an allowance to handle the people that work in his office, to handle his mail. And the allowance for my State of California is enough to hire thirteen people.

And let me say, incidentally, that that allowance is not paid to the

Senator—it's paid directly to the individuals that the Senator puts on his payroll, that all of these people and all of these allowances are for strictly official business. Business, for example, when a constituent writes in and wants you to go down to the Veterans Administration and get some information about his GI policy. Items of that type for example.

But there are other expenses which are not covered by the Government. And I think I can best discuss those expenses by asking you some questions. Do you think that when I or any other Senator makes a political speech, has it printed, should charge the printing of that speech and the mailing of that speech to the taxpayers?

Do you think, for example, when I or any other Senator makes a trip to his home state to make a purely political speech that the cost of that trip should be charged to the taxpayers?

Do you think when a Senator makes political broadcasts or political television broadcasts, radio or television, that the expense of those broadcasts should be charged to the taxpayers?

Well, I know what your answer is. The same answer that audiences give me whenever I discuss this particular problem. The answer is, "no." The taxpayers shouldn't be required to finance items which are not official business but which are primarily political business.

But then the question arises, you say, "Well, how do you pay for these and how can you do it legally?"

And there are several ways that it can be done, incidentally, and that it is done legally in the United States Senate and in the Congress.

The first way is to be a rich man. I don't happen to be a rich man so I couldn't use that.

Another way that is used is to put your wife on the payroll. Let me say, incidentally, my opponent, my opposite number for the Vice Presidency on the Democratic ticket, does have his wife on the payroll. And has had her on his payroll for the ten years—the past ten years.

Now just let me say this. That's his business and I'm not critical of him for doing that. You will have to pass judgment on that particular point. But I have never done that for this reason. I have found that there are so many deserving stenographers and secretaries in Washington that needed the work that I just didn't feel it was right to put my wife on the payroll.

My wife's sitting over here. She's a wonderful stenographer. She used to teach stenography and she used to teach shorthand in high school. That was when I met her. And I can tell you folks that she's worked many hours at night and many hours on Saturdays and Sundays in my office and she's done a fine job. And I'm proud to say tonight that in the six years I've been in the House and the Senate of the United States, Pat Nixon has never been on the Government payroll.

There are other ways that these finances can be taken care of. Some who are lawyers, and I happen to be a lawyer, continue to practice law. But I haven't been able to do that. I'm so far away from California that I've been so busy with my Senatorial work that I have not engaged in any legal practice.

And also as far as law practice is concerned, it seemed to me that the relationship between an attorney and the client was so personal that you couldn't possibly represent a man as an attorney and then have an unbiased view when he presented his case to you in the event that he had one before the Government.

And so I felt that the best way to handle these necessary political expenses of getting my message to the American people and the speeches I made, the speeches that I had printed, for the most part, concerned this one message—of exposing this Administration, the communism in it, the corruption in it—the only way that I could do that was to accept the aid which people in my home state of California who contributed to my campaign and who continued to make these contributions after I was elected were glad to make.

And let me say I am proud of the fact that not one of them has ever asked me for a special favor. I'm proud of the fact that not one of them has ever asked me to vote on a bill other than as my own conscience would dictate. And I am proud of the fact that taxpayers by subterfuge or otherwise have never paid one dime for expenses which I thought were political and shouldn't be charged to the taxpayers.

Let me say, incidentally, that some of you may say, "Well, that's all right Senator; that's your explanation, but have you got any proof?"

And I'd like to tell you this evening that just about an hour ago we received an independent audit of this entire fund.

I suggested to Gov. Sherman Adams, who is the chief of staff of the Dwight Eisenhower campaign, that an independent audit and legal report be obtained. And I have that audit here in my hand.

It's an audit made by the Price, Waterhouse & Co. firm, and the legal opinion of Gibson, Dunn & Crutcher, lawyers in Los Angeles, the biggest law firm and incidentally one of the best ones in Los Angeles.

I'm proud to be able to report to you tonight that this audit and this legal opinion is being forwarded to General Eisenhower. And I'd like to read to you the opinion that was prepared by Gibson, Dunn & Crutcher and based on all the pertinent laws and statutes, together with the audit report prepared by the certified public accountants.

"It is our conclusion that Senator Nixon did not obtain any financial gain from the collection and disbursement of the fund by Dana Smith; that Senator Nixon did not violate any Federal or state law by reason of the operation of the fund, and that neither the portion of the fund paid by Dana Smith directly to third persons nor the portion paid to Senator Nixon to reimburse him for designated office expenses constituted income to the Senator which was either report-able or taxable as income under applicable tax laws. (signed) Gibson, Dunn & Crutcher by Alma H. Conway."

Now that, my friends, is not Nixon speaking, but that's an inde-pendent audit which was requested because I want the American people to know all the facts and I'm not afraid of having independent people go in and check the facts, and that is exactly what they did.

But then I realize that there are still some who may say, and rightly so, and let me say that I recognize that some will continue to smear regardless of what the truth may be, but that there has been under-standably some honest misunderstanding on this matter, and there's some that will say:

"Well, maybe you were able, Senator, to fake this thing. How can we believe what you say? After all, is there a possibility that maybe you got some sums in cash? Is there a possibility that you may have feathered your own nest?"

And so now what I am going to do—and incidentally this is unprecedented in the history of American politics—I am going at this time to give this television and radio audience a complete finan-cial history; everything I've earned; everything I've spent; everything I owe. And I want you to know the facts. I'll have to start early.

I was born in 1913. Our family was one of modest circumstances and most of my early life was spent in a store out in East Whittier. It was a grocery store—one of those family enterprises. The only reason we were able to make it go was because my mother and dad had five boys and we all worked in the store.

I worked my way through college and to a great extent through law school. And then, in 1940, probably the best thing that ever hap-pened to me happened, I married Pat—sitting over here. We had a rather difficult time after we were married, like so many of the young couples who may be listening to us. I practiced law; she continued to teach School. I went into the service.

Let me say that my service record was not a particularly unusual one. I went to the South Pacific. I guess I'm entitled to a couple of bat-tle stars. I got a couple of letters of commendation but I was just there when the bombs were falling and then I returned. I returned to the United States and in 1946 I ran for the Congress.

When we came out of the war, Pat and I—Pat during the war had worked as a stenographer and in a bank and as an economist for a

Government agency—and when we came out the total of our savings from both my law practice, her teaching and all the time that I was in the war—the total for that entire period was just a little less than $10,000. Every cent of that, incidentally, was in Government bonds.

Well, that's where we start when I go into politics. Now what have I earned since I went into politics? Well, here it is—I jotted it down, let me read the notes. First of all I've had my salary as a Congressman and as a Senator. Second, I have received a total in this past six years of $1,600 from estates which were in my law firm at the time that I severed my connection with it.

And, incidentally, as I said before, I have not engaged in any legal practice and have not accepted any fees from business that came into the firm after I went into politics. I have made an average of approximately $1,500 a year from nonpolitical speaking engagements and lectures. And then, fortunately, we've inherited a little money. Pat sold her interest in her father's estate for $3,000 and I inherited $1,500 from my grandfather.

We live rather modestly. For four years we lived in an apartment in Park Fairfax, in Alexandria, Va. The rent was $80 a month. And we saved for the time that we could buy a house.

Now, that was what we took in. What did we do with this money? What do we have today to show for it? This will surprise you, because it is so little, I suppose, as standards generally go, of people in public life. First of all, we've got a house in Washington which cost $41,000 and on which we owe $20,000.

We have a house in Whittier, Calif., which cost $13,000 and on which we owe $10,000. My folks are living there at the present time.

I have just $4,000 in life insurance, plus my G.I. policy which I've never been able to convert and which will run out in two years. I have no insurance whatever on Pat. I have no life insurance on our two youngsters, Patricia and Julia. I own a 1950 Oldsmobile car. We have our furniture. We have no stocks and bonds of any type. We have no interest of any kind, direct or indirect, in any business.

Now, that's what we have. What do we owe? Well, in addition to the mortgage, the $20,000 mortgage on the house in Washington, the $10,000 one on the hourse in Whittier, I owe $4,500 to the Riggs Bank in Washington, D.C. with interest 4½ per cent.

I owe $3,500 to my parents and the interest on that loan which I pay regularly, because it's the part of the savings they made through the years they were working so hard, I pay regularly 4 percent interest. And then I have a $500 loan which I have on my life insurance.

Well, that's about it. That's what we have and that's what we owe. It isn't very much but Pat and I have the satisfaction that every dime that we've got is honestly ours. I should say this—that Pat doesn't have a mink coat. But she does have a respectable Republican cloth coat. And I always tell her that she'd look good in anything.

One other thing I probably should tell you because if we don't they'll probably be saying this about me too, we did get something—a gift— after the election. A man down in Texas heard Pat on the radio mention the fact that our two youngsters would like to have a dog. And, believe it or not, the day before we left on this campaign trip we got a message from Union Station in Baltimore saying they had a package for us. We went down to get it. You know what it was.

It was a little cocker spaniel dog in a crate that he sent all the way from Texas. Black and white spotted. And our little girl—Tricia, the 6-year-old—named it Checkers. And you know, the kids love the dog and I just want to say this right now, that regardless of what they say about it, we're gonna keep it.

It isn't easy to come before a nationwide audience and air your life as I've done. But I want to say some things before I conclude that I think most of you will agree on. Mr. Mitchell, the chairman of the Democratic National Committee, made the statement that if a man couldn't afford to be in the United States Senate he shouldn't run for the Senate.

And I just want to make my position clear. I don't agree with Mr. Mitchell when he says that only a rich man should serve his Government in the United States Senate or in the Congress.

I don't believe that represents the thinking of the Democratic party, and I know that it doesn't represent the thinking of the Republican Party.

I believe that it's fine that a man like Governor Stevenson who inherited a fortune from his father can run for President. But I also feel that it's essential in this country of ours that a man of modest means can also run for President. Because, you know, remember Abraham Lincoln, you remember what he said: "God must have loved the common people—he made so many of them."

And now I'm going to suggest some courses of conduct.

First of all, you have read in the papers about other funds now. Mr. Stevenson, apparently, had a couple. One of them in which a group of business people paid and helped to supplement the salaries of state employees. Here is where the money went directly into their pockets.

And I think that what Mr. Stevenson should do should be to come before the American people as I have, give the names of the people that have contributed to that fund; give the names of the people who put this money into their pockets at the same time that they were receiving money from their state government, and see what favors, if any, they gave out for that.

I don't condemn Mr. Stevenson for what he did. But until the facts are in there is a doubt that will be raised.

And as far as Mr. Sparkman is concerned, I would suggest the same thing. He's had his wife on the payroll. I don't condemn him for that. But I think that he should come before the American people and indicate what outside sources of income he has had.

I would suggest that under the circumstances both Mr. Sparkman and Mr. Stevenson should come before the American people as I have and make a complete financial statement as to their financial history. And if they don't it will be an admission that they have something to hide. And I think that you will agree with me.

Because, folks, remember, a man that's to be President of the United States, a man that's to be Vice President of the United States must have the confidence of all the people. And that's why I'm doing what I'm doing, and that's why I suggest that Mr. Stevenson and Mr. Sparkman since they are under attack should do what I am doing.

Now, let me say this: I know that this is not the last of the smears. In spite of my explanation tonight other smears will be made; others have been made in the past. And the purpose of the smears, I know, is this—to silence me, to make me let up.

Well, they just don't know who they're dealing with. I'm going to tell you this: I remember in the dark days of the Hiss case some of the same columnists, some of the same radio commentators who are attacking me now and misrepresenting my position were violently opposing me at the time I was after Alger Hiss.

But I continued the fight because I knew I was right. And I can say to this great television and radio audience that I have no apologies to the American people for my part in putting Alger Hiss where he is today.

And as far as this is concerned, I intend to continue the fight.

Why do I feel so deeply? Why do I feel that in spite of the smears, the misunderstandings, the necessities for a man to come up here and bare his soul as I have? Why is it necessary for me to continue this fight?

And I want to tell you why. Because, you see, I love my country. And I think my country is in danger. And I think that the only man that can save America at this time is the man that's running for President on my ticket—Dwight Eisenhower.

You say, "Why do I think it's in danger?" and I say look at the record. Seven years of the Truman-Acheson Administration and what's happened? Six hundred million people lost to the Communists, and a war in Korea in which we have lost 117,000 American casualties.

And I say to all of you that a policy that results in a loss of 600,000,000 to the Communists and a war which costs us 117,000 American casualties isn't good enough for America.

And I say that those in the State Department that made the mistakes which caused that war and which resulted in those losses should be kicked out of the State Department just as fast as we can get 'em out of there.

And let me say that I know Mr. Stevenson won't do that. Because he defends the Truman policy and I know that Dwight Eisenhower will do that, and that he will give America the leadership that it needs.

Take the problem of corruption. You've read about the mess in Washington. Mr. Stevenson can't clean it up because he was picked by the man, Truman, under whose Administration the mess was made. You wouldn't trust a man who made the mess to clean it up—that's Truman. And by the same token you can't trust the man who was picked by the man that made the mess to clean it up—and that's Stevenson.

And so I say, Eisenhower, who owes nothing to Truman, nothing to the big city bosses, he is the man that can clean up the mess in Washington.

Take Communism. I say that as far as that subject is concerned, the danger is great to America. In the Hiss case they got the secrets which enabled them to break the American secret State Department code. They got secrets in the atomic bomb case which enabled 'em to get the secret of the atomic bomb, five years before they would have gotten it by their own devices.

And I say that any man who called the Alger Hiss case a "red herring" isn't fit to be President of the United States. I say that a man who like Mr. Stevenson has pooh-poohed and ridiculed the Communist threat in the United States—he said that they are phantoms among ourselves; he's accused us that have attempted to expose the Communists of looking for Communists in the Bureau of Fisheries and Wildlife—I say that a man who says that isn't qualified to be President of the United States.

And I say that the only man who can lead us in this fight to rid the Government of both those who are Communists and those who have corrupted this Government is Eisenhower, because Eisenhower, you can be sure, recognizes the problem and he knows how to deal with it.

Now let me say that, finally, this evening I want to read to you just briefly excerpts from a letter which I received, a letter which, after all this is over, no one can take away from me. It reads as follows:

"Dear Senator Nixon,

"Since I'm only 19 years of age I can't vote in the Presidential election but believe me if I could you and General Eisenhower would certainly get my vote. My husband is in the Fleet Marines in Korea. He's a corpsman on the front lines and we have a two-month-old son he's never seen. And I feel confident that with great Americans like you and General Eisenhower in the White House, lonely Americans like myself will be united with their loved ones now in Korea.

"I only pray to God that you won't be too late. Enclosed is a small check to help you in your campaign. Living on $85 a month it is all I can afford at present. But let me know what else I can do."

Folks, it's a check for $10, and it's one that I will never cash.

And just let me say this. We hear a lot about prosperity these days but I say, why can't we have prosperity built on peace rather than prosperity built on war? Why can't we have prosperity and an honest government in Washington, D.C., at the same time. Believe me, we can. And Eisenhower is the man that can lead this crusade to bring us that kind of prosperity.

And, now, finally, I know that you wonder whether or not I am going to stay on the Republican ticket or resign.

Let me say this: I don't believe that I ought to quit because I'm not a quitter. And, incidentally, Pat's not a quitter. After all, her name was Patricia Ryan and she was born on St. Patrick's Day, and you know the Irish never quit.

But the decision, my friends, is not mine. I would do nothing that would harm the possibilities of Dwight Eisenhower to become President of the United States. And for that reason I am submitting to the Republican National Committee tonight through this television broadcast the decision which it is theirs to make.

Let them decide whether my position on the ticket will help or hurt. And I am going to ask you to help them decide. Wire and write the Republican National Committee whether you think I should stay on or whether I should get off. And whatever their decision is, I will abide by it.

But just let me say this last word. Regardless of what happens I'm going to continue this fight. I'm going to campaign up and down America until we drive the crooks and the Communists and those that defend them out of Washington. And remember, folks, Eisenhower is a great man. Believe me. He's a great man. And a vote for Eisenhower is a vote for what's good for America.

ANALYSIS

This essay originally appeared in Ryan, H., *Oratorical Encounters*, Greenwood Press, Westport, CT, 1988.

Senator Richard Nixon's "My Side of the Story" speech, delivered on national radio and television on September 23, 1952, was to apologetic discourse as Franklin D. Roosevelt's First Inaugural Address was to inaugural oratory, as FDR's 1944 Teamsters' Union or "Fala" speech was to campaign speaking, and as Harry S Truman's 1948 acceptance address was to convention oratory. All of these speeches were delivered during difficult situations, all were highly publicized persuasions, and all were pivotal addresses in their respective orator's career. Yet, one characteristic seems to sully Nixon's speech from those addresses. The "Checkers" speech, which nomenclature was a pejorative attempt by the speech's critics to demean it and Nixon, has come to symbolize the nadir of political communication in the 1952 presidential campaign and to reaffirm Plato's charge that rhetoric can make truth appear untruth and untruth the truth. Indeed, Nixon later complained that his speech "was labeled as the 'Checkers speech,' as though the mention of my dog was the only thing that saved my career."[4]

Nixon's complaint has merit. The fund speech contained the artful application of a number of persuasive devices—the mentioning of Checkers was only a minor one of them—that have not been explicated heretofore. Moreover, when the speech is treated *in situ* as a response to a series of charges, Nixon's address can be evaluated in terms of the rhetorical techniques he used to meet the crisis.

"The Fund": Charges Against Nixon's Policy and Character

The speech set began innocently enough. The story has been told in a number of places how some disgruntled contributors complained about Nixon's fund, how these complaints reached columnist Peter Edson, and how Edson interviewed, at Nixon's invitation, Dana Smith, the fund's trustee. Smith was remarkably candid in his conversations with Edson, who passed his findings to Leo Katcher of the *New York Post*. However, in openly cooperating with Edson, Smith inadvertently supplied the core materials for the accusation that ensued. Edson was on a fishing expedition, and the theory of the speech set would suggest that when one is under attack, one should not divulge gratuitous information that could be used later against oneself. Indeed, Stewart Alsop noted that Nixon and his people should have sensed the potential danger in the fund story.[5]

Based on Edson's findings, Leo Katcher composed the first accusation against Nixon. The irony of the *New York Post*'s *kategoria* on Thursday, September 18, 1952, was that Katcher's story was based on Smith's information. First, the fund was a fact by Smith's admission. Katcher characterized the fund with the now-famous charge: "Secret Rich Men's Trust Fund Keeps Nixon In Style Far Beyond His Salary." To support the definition of an elevated life-style, Katcher used testimony from an anonymous donor: "A contributor to the fund, a state official in California, said the appeal to him was based on the fact that Nixon needed a larger home, as befitted a Senator, and that the Nixon's could not even afford a maid"; moreover, he quoted two damaging admissions from Smith: "Dick didn't have enough money to do the kind of job he wanted to do and that we wanted him to do" and "his expenses for such items as entertainment and living expenses would necessarily be greater than before."[6] Although this evidence did not prove Nixon lived beyond his means, one could easily infer, if one did not read the article too closely or critically, that Nixon probably did live in an elevated style. Although the fund was not public knowledge, neither was it exactly a secret—Nixon and Smith's candor about it was not an instance of "stonewalling," to use a term from the Watergate era. But the gray area in which the fund was solicited and dispersed was conducive to Katcher's defining it as "secret" even if the fund were not exactly what the headline trumpeted. In all, the accusation employed enough sensational language, offered enough apparent evidence, and invited enough inferences to raise a doubt about Nixon's policy and character.

However, not all newspapers perceived a *prima facie* case against the senator. Republican newspapers tended to downplay the story or to bury it and the *Los Angeles Times* did not print it until Saturday. United Press International relayed the *New York Post*'s story immediately, but Associated Press (AP) did not at first feature the story. The *New York Post*, piqued that Republican papers and the AP did not give its scoop its just due, credited the other news media for disseminating the fund story: "We think radio and newscasts helped a lot; many radio and television commentators seemed far less inhibited than the newspapers."[7] Ironically, the medium that was significantly involved in transmitting the accusation was also the means by which Nixon appealed to the mass audience in order to save his political career.

The second accusation, based on the *New York Post* story, was made by Democratic National Chairman Stephen A. Mitchell on Thursday, September 18. He charged that Nixon had accepted "donations from wealthy California businessmen to supplement his salary as a Senator," and Mitchell defined that policy as morally wrong: "By no standards of public morals or of private morals can such conduct be condoned or explained away." Although a partisan attack, Mitchell's accusation was more focused and less flamboyant than the *New York Post*'s banner headline, and hence more probative. What has not been emphasized about Mitchell's accusation, however, is the fact that Eisenhower was attacked for his handling of the Nixon affair. Here was an attempt to get at Eisenhower through Nixon. Mitchell juxtaposed the general's "making a great show of indignation over corruption in demagogic speeches" with the loaded question would Eisenhower "gag and swallow" the revelation about the fund or would "he state clearly and firmly that he would not run" with Nixon.[8] Mitchell cleverly hoisted the general on the horns of a dilemma: Silence would condemn Ike, but Ike's requesting Nixon's resignation would come back to roost on Eisenhower and his campaign because he was associated with Nixon, and guilt by association was a powerful tool of indictment in the McCarthy era.

On Friday, September 19, Mitchell added another accusation. Again, the strategy was to attack Nixon and through him, Eisenhower. Mitchell wisely narrowed the charge by defining the fund as "a subsidy from persons with an interest in Federal legislation." He called on the senator to resign and then outflanked the general: "It is time for General Eisenhower to cast away either his principles or his running mate." Ike cleverly steered clear of this whirlpool that threatened to suck him into its vortex. The general supported Nixon just enough by noncommittal statements of the wait-to-see variety in order to keep him afloat but not so much that he could not jettison his running mate if it came to that. The onus was on Nixon to clear himself with the general's encouragement but not with his help.

In an obvious attempt to try to preempt a defense from Nixon, Mitchell framed his final accusation specifically and damningly. Hopefully, Nixon would not oblige by: "1. Telling the public exactly what persons gave him these gifts, and how much he got from each person. 2. Telling the people what he spent his money on. . . . " Mitchell then adroitly allowed that that information would enable the public to decide if Nixon failed to file proper tax returns or broke a federal law. His parting shot was a clever instance of *petitio principii*, or begging the question: "if he makes the full facts available to the public, voters can at least judge how serious is the Senator's wrongdoing."[9]

Such a strategy had its rhetorical strengths and weaknesses. On the one hand, Mitchell probably reasoned that Nixon could not or would not reveal the facts, so Nixon's silence would condemn him and taint Eisenhower. On the other hand, if Nixon did give the facts, that disclosure would certify the charge of wrongdoing, would embarrass the contributors, and would probably raise new questions that could fuel fresh accusations. Either choice would be a risky rhetorical route to defend.

Yet, there was a flaw in Mitchell's strategy of accusation. By stressing the policy aspects of the fund, Mitchell inadvertently invited Nixon to defend the fund on Mitchell's criteria: who gave what and how much and how it was spent. If Nixon could do that, Mitchell probably calculated he would not or could not, then Nixon would apparently answer the accusation satisfactorily. By not stressing the ethical qualities of the fund with reference to Nixon's character, Mitchell accidentally diverted attention away from the critical issues: the propriety of the fund's very existence and its relationship to Nixon's habits as a public servant. Mitchell missed the opportunity to make a critical linkage. The fact of the fund superceded policy considerations and went to the crux of the issue—was it an honorable habit to have the fund in the first place? But the real issues were clouded in the *New York Post's* story and in Mitchell's two accusations, and therefore Nixon was not obliged to clarify them in his apologia.

The Mitchell-Nixon analog is an example of how the theory of the speech set can help identify the pertinent issues from the sham ones. Since Mitchell's *kategoria* focused on factual matters, Nixon wisely accepted the accusation because he may have perceived that it skirted the real issues. In short, the Democratic national chairman actually facilitated Nixon's apologetic strategy of defending the policy's ancillary points (who gave what, how much, etc.) rather than forcing the senator to address the difficult two central issues of the fund's propriety and his habit of maintaining it.

Moreover, an examination of the motive-response relationships in the speech set is instructive. To Mitchell's first charge, Nixon merely released a statement that the fund was not secret and had not been used to defray his Senate expenses, but he did not identify the supporters who gave the money. That answer motivated Mitchell to demand in a second charge on the nineteenth that Nixon name donors and donations. Accordingly, Nixon released the names and figures for the fund that had grown from $16,000 to $18,235 with seventy-six contributors. The *New York Herald Tribune* opined that its "names read almost like a blue book of metropolitan Los Angeles business, professional and social leaders—prominent manufacturers, lawyers, and oil men." As a historical footnote, Nixon also made public a complete and detailed accounting of the fund by category and expenditure.[10]

In a purely technical sense, Nixon answered most of the charge—who gave what—and albeit a little late, how the money was spent. Mitchell issued no more accusations. In fact, the *New York Herald Tribune,* which was the Eisenhower-Nixon ticket's most influential supporter on the East coast, admitted that "On the basis of the revealed facts, Senator Nixon's personal honesty should not be impeached. We share with General Eisenhower a conviction of the Senator's integrity," but the paper perceptively noted "Yet to receive it [the fund] at all, especially when the source of the support was not publicly affirmed, is to have put the Senator in an ambiguous position."[11]

The newspaper assumed a strange posture. In one breath, it affirmed Nixon's honesty and integrity, but in a second breath, it held that he was in an ambiguous position and therefore called for his resignation with Eisenhower to decide whether to accept it. This was a blow to Nixon. The cloudiness of the accusation-apology speech set can account for some of the paper's lingering doubts about the propriety of the fund because Mitchell's accusation inadvertently allowed Nixon to obfuscate the real issues. But part of the paper's concern was to assure that its candidate, Eisenhower, would not be brought down by Nixon, who was expendable.

Why, then, did Nixon deliver a televised speech to clear himself? Ironically, Richard Nixon, the accused, had helped create an era of suspicion and mudslinging against people's policies and characters that culminated in the 1952 campaign. This was evident in his campaign in 1946 for Jerry Voorhis' seat in the House of Representatives, in the 1950 campaign against Helen Gahagan Douglas for the U.S. Senate, and in the battle to put Alger Hiss behind bars. These ephemeral attacks, which Senator Joseph McCarthy perfected, were difficult to refute. When the accused cut off an attack, another charge, Medusa-like, spawned anew and drew nourishment from the old one. Nixon evidently understood the political climate he helped to produce, and his rhetorical choices were limited. He could not deny his policy, the fund existed. His only available strategy was to make the fund acceptable by redefining it in a favorable light. The newspapers, even the ones who had supported him and Eisenhower before the fund story broke, would not do his work for him and were in fact calling for his resignation. Eisenhower, who was teetering on the brink of disaster, would not lend Nixon a hand lest he be pulled down should Nixon fall, nor could he prematurely jettison

Nixon—what if he were innocent? These events seemed to warrant a response from Nixon. Many jittery Republicans hoped for and advised a resignation speech, but Dick decided to deliver instead a defense.

The senator's decision to deliver a nationally televised apology may have been motivated in part by his apologetic successes before smaller live audiences. His first oratorical response to Mitchell's charge was at Marysville, California, on September 19. Countering that the accusation was a Communist smear tactic, Nixon told the crowd he had actually saved taxpayer's money by not charging the government for excess amounts, that he did not take "fat legal fees on the side," and that he did not have his wife on the payroll, but that Senator John Sparkman, Governor Adlai Stevenson's vice-presidential running mate, did have his wife on the payroll. The crowd applauded.[12]

Nixon did a dress rehearsal of his fund apology speech at Portland, Oregon, on Saturday night, September 20. In that address, he recited again about Pat, about Sparkman, and about how he saved taxpayer's money. Of special interest is how he turned to his advantage the *New York Post's* and Mitchell's accusations. In a remarkable preview of his famous fund speech, Nixon framed their accusations: "he didn't return it on his income tax, he hid this thing, didn't let the people know about it, it was illegal, it was unmoral, it was unethical"; he also asked two rhetorical questions that later appeared in the fund speech: "Do you think that when a Senator makes a purely political speech in his own state that the taxpayers ought to pay the bill . . . ? Do you think, for example, that when I make political broadcasts taxpayers should pay the bill . . . ?"; and he phrased a question in his inimitable style: "And now, you say, well, now, look Senator, why all this hullaba-loo . . . ?" The Portland speech was well received.[13]

The point is that Ralph De Toledano and Lawrence Rosenfield realized that portions of Nixon's fund speech were tried out successfully on smaller live audiences,[14] but neither critic indicated the relationship these rhetorical appeals had to the fund speech's final success, which will be discussed fully in the next section.

Neither has any rhetorical critic detected the logical fallacy Nixon commit-ted in his two early apologies and again in his final defense. The fallacy was this. According to Nixon, he "was saving you money rather than charging the expenses of my office, which were in excess of the amounts which were allowed by the tax-payers, and allowed under the law." How could Nixon "save" taxpayer's money when he had already spent his legal allowance? In case the math is confusing, Glen Lipscomb, the executive secretary of Nixon's Washington headquarters, told a reporter that "It is a private fund to be used to cover expenses of running Nixon's office that are not covered by his government allowance."[15] In other words, Nixon used the fund to pay for additional expenses that exceeded his allotment and not, as he skillfully implied, to "save" the taxpayer's money he could not legally spend anyway. Since Mitchell attacked Nixon by arguing *petitio principii*, then so could Nixon defend with that device. Nixon assumed the propriety of the fund without justifying its necessity. He only replied in kind.

"My Side of the Story"

Fifty-five million Americans watched Richard Nixon's *tour de force* on their newly acquired television sets, while an untold number tuned to their radios. This speech was the first personalized political crisis to be mediated by television, and Fawn Brodie observed that it gave "Nixon a sense of the power of television, and of his special talent in using it." The immediate success of the speech was phenomenal. Movie mogul Darryl Zanuck telephoned Nixon that his effort was the "most tremendous performance I have ever seen." Americans sent about two million telegrams and wrote almost three million letters to voice their positive reception of Nixon's drama, and he claimed in *Six Crises* that more than enough small contributions came in to his office to cover the $75,000 cost of the broadcast. After some *real politik* maneuvering by General Eisenhower, as he stalled for time to test the political winds and to await the decision of the Republican National Committee, whose technical decision it was to make whether Nixon should resign, he finally asked Nixon to meet him in Wheeling, West Virginia, in order to mend their political fences. The intricate details of the entire historical episode have been explicated elsewhere, and they are not a concern here. Rather, the purpose is to explain how the speech, which was described by Gary Allen as "one of the most effective political speeches ever delivered,"[16] worked as well as it did. For what has never been explained fully or adequately by the speech's critics was why the speech was so successful.

To be sure, Henry McGuckin examined the address and found that Nixon successfully employed a number of appeals that were designed to tap the audience's adherence to the "American value system" that Edward Steele and Charles Redding found inherent in American culture in the 1950s. For instance, Nixon appealed to Puritan morality by offering the audience proof of his hard work as a congressman and senator, and tapped patriotism when he demonstrated his ability to catch the alleged Communist spy, Alger Hiss. As thorough and compelling as McGuckin's analysis was, it is only a partial explanation of the speech's efficacy. Lawrence Rosenfield investigated the fund speech and succeeded among its critics in providing the best explanation to date.[17]

Yet, Nixon's speech may be reexamined. In his apologia, Nixon used several rhetorical techniques that John Mason Brown called "high school oratory . . . devices"; however, neither Brown nor other critics have identified these devices.[18] Moreover, no one has described how Nixon fashioned his delivery in order to present himself and his message in a compelling manner. Previous critics' failures to treat the senator's speech techniques and delivery are telling. In conjunction with his language, Nixon's *actio* was a significant factor in the overall success of the speech. The symbolism of a man under attack, who defended himself in a personal and direct fashion before such an intimate medium as television, was an image to which Americans reacted. Nixon was an archetype for televised political apology. Having no previous roles by which to assess the genre, the American people reacted to the visceral cues of his language and to the visual cues of his sincerity. Since Nixon gave careful attention to his delivery, it would behoove his critics to do the same.

In *Six Crises,* Nixon realized that he must accomplish three goals. First, he had to explain and defend the fund. Second, he wanted to ward off future attacks so that these would "fall on deaf ears." Since he had chosen the route Mitchell probably thought he would not select, Nixon wanted to assure that his apologia would spike any new accusations. Third, he wanted to launch a political counterattack in order to give the audience reasons to vote for his ticket. In his later memoirs, he stated that he divided the speech into four parts: the facts about the fund, an attack against Stevenson, praise for Eisenhower, and a request for action. Rosenfield determined that the speech had three sections: a denial of unethical conduct in maintaining the fund, a revelation of his financial history, and a counterattack on Sparkman and Stevenson.[19] Although these versions differ slightly, they all distill to certain objectives that Nixon obtained by using several rhetorical techniques. He employed the classical organizational pattern to defend the fund and to counterattack the Democrats, and *tu quoque, argumentum ad personam, petitio principii,* affirmation by denial, turning the tables, and inoculation to attain his other objectives.

The Classical Elements of the Speech

The classical pattern was originally invented by Corax, a Greek from the fifth century B.C., as an effective organizational strategy for courtroom oratory.[20] Rosenfield noted that "the appropriate argumentative strategy was clearly forensic" for Nixon's speech, but he did not identify Nixon's using the classical pattern.[21] In the *exordium* or introduction, the orator introduces himself and the speech in such a manner as to make the audience receptive to both; a *narratio* presents favorably the events under consideration; the *confirmatio* gives the arguments that support the speaker's stand; the *refutatio* offers a refutation against the opposition; and the *epilogus,* or conclusion, appeals to the audience for support. The rhetorical device of *tu quoque,* translated as "you also," is a retort that charges one's opponents with doing or saying the same thing as oneself. Nixon used this diversionary tactic to deflect attention from himself to his opponents. *Argumentum ad personam* is directed toward the person or character assassination. *Petitio principii* is begging the question. Affirmation by denial, one of Nixon's knacks, is a technique whereby the orator covertly affirms a point by overtly denying such intention. Turning the tables is a device by which the speaker takes a point made by the opponent and turns it back to harm the opponent. The concept of rhetorical inoculation is borrowed from the medical metaphor. As a physician gives a patient an inoculation to ward off a disease, so may an orator administer the audience a dose of a carefully constructed message to fend off future harmful communications from the opposition.

The Introduction   Senator Nixon set the tone of his apologia in the *exordium.*[22] He subtly indicated that his speech would be an offensive defense.

Admitting that he addressed the audience because his honesty and integrity had been attacked, he noted the usual political ploy was to ignore or deny such charges "without giving details." Nixon countercharged that "we've had enough of that in the United States, particularly with the present Administration in Washington, D.C." This *tu quoque* reminded the audience that the Democrats were not pristine.

The Narrative Nixon went quickly to the *narratio* where he endeavored to portray Mitchell's charges against himself in a favorable light. Not content with a legal definition of the fund, he asked "was it morally wrong?" He then answered his question by stating Mitchell's criteria that would justify the fund. This was a brilliant rhetorical maneuver because Nixon wisely controlled the narrow context in which he would exculpate himself. In response to the *New York Post* story and Mitchell's accusations, Nixon asserted that the $18,000 had not gone for his personal use, was not secretly given or handled, and that no contributor got any special political favors. But he rightly realized that his protestations, given without evidentiary support, from a man whose very credibility was under attack, would not suffice; therefore, he moved to the *confirmatio*, which comprised almost half of his address. The importance of the *narratio* was to give an appearance of answering the charges in order to make the audience receptive to him and his message. The strategy of the *confirmatio* was to reiterate his defense by developing in more detail the arguments for his side of the story.

The Arguments Within the *confirmatio* section, Nixon marshalled his main arguments by using the method of residues. The method is actually a rhetorical application of the disjunctive syllogism: either A, B, or C; not A, not B, therefore C. By discrediting in turn each allegation against himself, he systematically narrowed the audience's perceptions to the desired residue: His fund was not legally nor morally wrong. In conjunction with the method, Nixon used the rhetorical question, phrased in the manner he had tried out at Portland, Oregon. Each disjunct addressed the queries that might weigh against him in the minds of his listeners. For instance, he began the *confirmatio* with the first interrogatory disjunct: "But then some of you will say and rightly, 'Well, what did you use the fund for, Senator? Why did you have to have it?'" He justified the fund with an enlarged series of rhetorical questions, which he used in a truncated fashion at Marysville and Portland: Should taxpayers pay for the cost of printing and mailing political speeches? the costs of political trips? the costs of political broadcasts? Of course, as Nixon knew, any taxpayer would answer "no." He let his audience infer why would a senator who did not use taxpayer's dollars for political expenses use a fund for personal benefit? Nixon raised a doubt.

The second disjunct continued in this vein to discredit the charges while concomitantly enhancing Nixon's financial habits as a public servant. Senator Nixon pointedly phrased the next disjunct: "But then the question arises, you say, 'Well, how do you pay for these and how can you do it legally?'" He answered this question with yet another disjunctive application. (1) One could be a rich man, but Nixon was not. (2) Or one could put one's wife on the payroll, but Nixon did not have Pat on the payroll; however, he reminded his national audience that Sparkman had his wife on the payroll for the past ten years. To cover this frontal attack on his opponent's practice and character that was inappropriate while ostensibly defending himself, Nixon used affirmation by denial: "Now let me say this. That's his business and I'm not critical of him for doing that. You will have to pass judgment on that particular point." He affirmed his criticism of Sparkman and invited the audience to pass judgment on him by denying such an intent. (3) Or one could continue to practice law, as he said at Marysville, but Nixon did not do that because he realized an inherent conflict of interest that other politicians chose to ignore. (4) Or one could have a fund. The clear impression one had about Nixon at the end of this disjunct was that since he had not used any of the questionable practices others in his position had used, then surely the senator was not the kind of person who would misuse the fund. Moreover, one could easily infer, and perhaps that was exactly what Nixon hoped his audience would do, that the fund was moral: It allowed Nixon to communicate his political messages about K_1C_2, the chemical formula that came to satirize the issues in the 1952 campaign: Korea, Communism and Corruption, to the electorate without directly or indirectly charging those costs to the taxpayers.

Mindful that the audience might still harbor doubts about the fund, Nixon moved to the third disjunct: "Let me say, incidentally, that some of you may say, 'Well, that's all right, Senator; that's your explanation, but have you got any proof?'" The evidence he offered his audience was an audit by Price, Waterhouse & Co., and a legal opinion by Gibson, Dunn & Crutcher. In a nutshell, the opinion stated that Nixon "did not violate any federal or state law" in the operation of the fund nor did funds paid directly to Nixon for reimbursement of expenses "constitute income . . . either reportable or taxable as income under applicable tax laws." These findings were never challenged, and they cleared the air about the legality of the fund. Not wanting to sacrifice what he had just accomplished, Nixon inoculated at the end of this disjunct to ward off future attacks: "and let me say that I recognize that some will continue to smear regardless of what the truth may be."

With the audit and legal opinion in his favor, Nixon might have ended the argument section. But in what could be termed an exercise in overkill, he proceeded to his last disjunct: "Well, maybe you were able, Senator, to fake this thing. How can we believe what you say? After all, is there a possibility that you may have feathered your own nest?" In this disjunct, Nixon disclosed himself: his war record, how Pat had worked for the government, how they had all their savings in U.S. government bonds, how much their houses cost and how much they owed on them, how much they inherited, how much they owed in personal debt, *ad nauseam.* But two appeals warrant detailed attention. First, Nixon allowed that Pat did not own a mink coat, but that she did have a "respectable Republican cloth coat." The allusion is perhaps lost today but it was meaningful in 1952: A wife of a high figure in the Truman administration was allegedly given a mink coat as a political gift. Nixon effectively turned that table on his opponents. Second, Nixon called on Checkers to perform his tricks. The senator remembered the great success President Franklin D. Roosevelt had in his Teamsters' Union Address, September 23, 1944—delivered exactly eight years before Nixon's speech—in deflecting charges that he had sent a destroyer back to pick up his dog Fala, whose "Scotch soul was furious" at such charges. In *Six Crises*, Nixon wrote: "I decided to mention my own dog Checkers. Using the same ploy as FDR would irritate my opponents and delight my friends, I thought." In his memoirs, Nixon recorded that he was aware of the technique of turning the tables with Checkers because it would "infuriate my critics if I could turn this particular table on them." Brown believed the Checkers ploy "was the climaxing emotional appeal made by Richard Nixon."[23] What is not generally understood about the Checkers appeal was its efficacy as a rhetorical application of *reductio ad absurdum*. Therein, an orator runs an argument to an absurd conclusion, thereby suggesting that the initial assumption was absurd. Nixon's closing statement of the disjunct clearly implied the absurdity of the charge against the fund by comparing it to the straw issue that Nixon should be compelled to return the dog: "regardless of what they say about it, we're gonna keep it."

Before treating the nature of Nixon's *refutatio*, it is important to note several things about his *confirmatio*. In order to be logically sound, the method of residues must assay all of the disjuncts that reasonably apply to the issue at hand. Nixon defended the fund on three disjuncts: not for personal use, not secretly given or handled, and no special favors given. Barnet Baskerville believed that "Nixon's setting up his three criteria by which to test the morality of his actions was a commendably forthright approach." Actually, the criteria were Mitchell's and the *New York Post's*. His use of the method of residues gave the desired appearance of answering the accusations, but he did not address the critical issues. Granted, he did prove the fund was not for his personal income, and by letting the newspapers print donor's names and contributions, he adequately answered the secrecy issue, although he might have treated the topic more forthrightly in his speech. However, the senator did not offer any evidence, except for two unsubstantiated assertions, that he had never given political favors to contributors. "This matter of influence, therefore, being central," according to Baskerville, "deserved more attention than it received." Neither did he address the propriety of the fund, except to argue he needed it to "save" money that he had already spent. Therefore, the residue that the fund was moral, even given that he proved it was legal, cannot stand. Rosenfield realized there were merits in Nixon's organizational structure, but rightly complained: "Given such overpowering lead-ins there is little room for an auditor's imagination to function. His mind remains riveted as the argument unfolds. Viewed as a performance-in-time, the inferences are predetermined by the transitions, and the discourse stubbornly resists efforts by an auditor to participate independently in the communicative act." William Miller clearly understood the efficacy of Nixon's strategy: "Another debating device that can be learned from Mr. Nixon is that it is better to deal with an irrelevancy on which one can make an effective performance than with a relevant point on which one may be less compelling." But as a rhetorical technique to persuade people who do not listen or read too closely, the method allowed Nixon to give the impression that the charges were fully answered. It may be that if Mitchell had stressed the propriety of the fund and not the "facts," Nixon would have been constrained to address that question in his apologia.[24]

The Refutation   Nevertheless, Senator Nixon certainly gave his audience the assured impression that he had answered all of the accusations against him when he moved to the *refutatio*. In it, he left his defensive position and developed a posture of overt attack against his opponents. Having cleared himself, he counterattacked with *tu quoque* to shift the audience's attention to Stevenson, Sparkman, and the Truman administration. The *refutatio* comprised about one-fifth of his speech and it reeked of the offal that characterized oratory in the 1952 campaign. All of these character assassinations on the Democratic triumvirate were applications of *argumentum ad personam*, pejoratively known as "If you have no case, then abuse your opponent."

Nixon began the *refutatio* in an aggressive manner. He turned the tables on the chairman of the Democratic National Committee who made the ill-advised comment that if one could not afford to be in the Senate, one ought not run for it. Nixon handily capitalized on that gaffe by suggesting that that idea probably did not reflect the thinking of the Democratic party and certainly not that of the Republican party. Nixon then turned on Stevenson with another affirmation by denial: "I believe that it's fine that a man like Governor Stevenson who inherited a fortune from his father can run for President," but Nixon thought it was essential that men of modest means could also run for the office. Nixon next launched a major *tu quoque* attack against Sparkman and Stevenson. The senator charged that the governor had a fund, but again used affirmation by denial to malign Stevenson: "I don't condemn Mr. Stevenson for what he did. But until the facts are in there is a doubt that will be raised." Also, Sparkman had his wife on the payroll, but "I don't condemn him for that." With their feet to the fire, Nixon fanned the flames by placing Sparkman and Stevenson on the horns of a dilemma. He commanded them to come before the American people and tell about their finances, as he had done, "And if they don't it will be an admission that they have something to hide." If they confessed, they would confirm their guilt; if they did not confess, their silence would convict them.[25] In either case, Nixon would win because his *tu quoque* would have been substantiated and it would divert attention to them. Here, again, Nixon effectively turned the dilemma in which Mitchell had tried to place him. Moreover, one should note that Nixon asked Stevenson to "Give the names of people that have contributed to that fund." As he had been embarrassed on the defensive, so would Nixon, now on the offensive, embarrass Stevenson.

Having attacked his opponents, Nixon tried to assure that those attacks would not be redirected at him. He immediately used inoculation effectively:

"Now, let me say this: I know that this is not the last of the smears. In spite of my explanation tonight other smears will be made; others have been made in the past. And the purpose of the smears, I know, is this—to silence me, to make me let up." The people who smeared him were, of course, the leftist media people. So, Nixon counterattacked them. He argued a subtle and convincing inference: The people who were attacking him now were the same people who attacked him in his handling of the Alger Hiss case; since they were wrong in the Hiss case, Nixon let his audience infer they were wrong now. This treatment also used the rhetorical technique of victimage and scapegoat. Nixon portrayed himself as a victim of media attacks. By blaming the fund crisis on the media as scapegoat, he focused the audience's attention not on the fund but on the media that victimized him.

Richard Nixon then weighed in against what was standing on the political landscape, the Truman administration. He accused it of having lost six hundred million people to the Communists and 117,000 casualties in the Korean War. Having smitten the K of the political formula, Nixon raked the muck on C:

> Take the problems of corruption. You've read about the mess in Washington. Mr. Stevenson can't clean it up because he was picked by the man, Truman, under whose Administration the mess was made. You wouldn't trust a man who made the mess to clean it up—that's Truman. And by the same token you can't trust the man who was picked by the man that made the mess to clean it up—and that's Stevenson.

As for the second C, Nixon inveighed against the Communists. In what has to be the funniest line in the speech, Nixon attacked Stevenson as unfit for the presidency because he called the Alger Hiss case a "red herring": "He's [Stevenson] accused us that have attempted to expose the Communists of looking for Communists in the Bureau of Fisheries and Wildlife—I say that a man who says that isn't qualified to be President of the United States." While it cannot be determined if Nixon, or the American people, understood the ironic humor in Stevenson's comment, it is plainly evident that one should look for red herrings in the Bureau of Fisheries and Wildlife.

The last ploy Nixon used in the *refutatio* section has been overlooked by critics, but it, too, served an emotional function and it may be more pathetic than the Checkers appeal. Nixon read a letter from a nineteen-year-old woman whose husband was with the Marines in Korea and had not seen his two-month-old-son. Living on $85 a month, she sent Nixon a check for $10, but Nixon assured his audience he would never cash it. This letter served several salutary functions. It tapped the anti-Korean sentiment against Truman's handling of the war, thus bolstering Nixon's political persona. It served as an analogy for the other contributors to the fund: The audience could easily infer that as this well-meaning young woman had contributed to Nixon's campaign with the best of intentions, so had earlier contributors to Nixon's fund. And it suggested that as this young American had faith in Nixon, so should the rest of the American people. But Baskerville observed that even the letter had a flaw because it was "represented as an expression of confidence written *after* the fund disclosure, but which Nixon had actually received and used much earlier in his campaign."[26]

The *refutatio* section was as remarkable as was the *confirmatio*. The aggressive posture of attack, the character assassination of Sparkman and Stevenson, the hatchet attack on the Truman administration, the blatant appeals on K_1C_2, and the victimage and scapegoating on the media, all combined to direct attention from Nixon to his opponents. Except for the attack on the Stevenson fund, Nixon had rehearsed these themes in rear platform appearances on his whistle-stop speaking tour in California and at Portland. In terms of **kairos** the disclosure that Governor Stevenson had a slush fund was propitious. The accusation appeared on Tuesday, September 23, and Nixon wisely worked this late-breaking story into his address. The remarkable paradox about Nixon's speech was that that kind of scrappy campaign oratory found its way into a televised apologia. Yet, that was why the classical pattern was so useful. Since Myles Martel found that attack and defense were common strategies in presidential campaigns, the amenability of the classical pattern to the rhetorical situation in 1952 is readily apparent. It allowed Nixon to present his defensive arguments in the *confirmatio* and then to attack his opponents in the *refutatio*. The pattern does not guarantee success, but in the hands of a skilled orator such as Senator Richard Nixon, it proved persuasive.[27]

The Conclusion   In the *epilogus*, Nixon phrased the last question on peoples' minds: "And, now, finally, I know that you wonder whether or not I am going to stay on the Republican ticket or resign." Asserting that he did not believe he should quit because he was not a quitter (this is an example of *petitio principii*), and neither was Pat a quitter (he misrepresented for the Irish vote that Pat Ryan was born on St. Patrick's Day when she was actually born the day before), he acknowledged the decision was not his to make but was the Republican National Committee's. In an appeal over Eisenhower's head, which Wills believed was Nixon's way of nettling the General for his ambivalent attitude toward the Senator during the crisis,[28] Nixon asked for specific action by the audience: "And I am going to ask you to help them decide. Wire and write the Republican National Committee whether you think I should stay on or whether I should get off. And whatever their decision is, I will abide by it." This direct appeal channelled listeners' belief in his apologia into direct salutary support for the speaker.

Nixon's Delivery   Richard Nixon's delivery for this speech was extraordinarily effective. Harry S Truman might have believed Nixon was "a shifty-eyed goddamn liar," but there was none of that on September 23, 1952. Nixon's eye-contact was outstanding. He credited his experiences as a debater for Whittier College in preparing him to address audiences without notes.[29] He relied sparingly on his speech draft while he was seated at a desk through the *confirmatio* section. The only exception was when he picked up his manuscript to detail his personal finances. But even then, his looking at his notes reinforced the image of accuracy and honesty in the figures, and when he had finished with that part of the speech, he laid down his notes. When he arose from the desk in order to step out in front of the camera during the *refutatio,* he used no notes at all. His direct eye-contact with the home viewers' eyes as they watched their TV sets enhanced Nixon's credibility. He lifted from his desk the legal opinion and audit, and he also showed the letter and check from the young woman. Like the evangelist who holds aloft the Bible or Senator Joseph McCarthy who waived empty laundry lists that supposedly contained names of Communists in the State Department, Nixon's proffering these documents reinforced the legitimacy of his claims.

Nixon's gestures appeared slightly wooden, but they successfully emphasized and reinforced his language. His usual hand gesture was a clenched fist that chopped the air to punctuate his points. When discussing the problem of corruption in government, he implored his audience with open palms not to trust Stevenson or Truman. During the *refutatio,* he assumed a combative posture toward the camera that suited the temper of his language. He matched the assertiveness of his word choice by thrusting forward his head and body and by gesturing vigorously. Little wonder that Bruce Mazlish thought "the Checkers speech was, in fact, a highly aggressive defense."[30] However, in the conclusion of his speech, Nixon wisely placed his hands behind his back, to assume a more meek and modest image, as he asked (rather than commanded) his audience to wire and write the Republican National Committee.

Although McGuckin found emotional stress in Nixon's voice and demeanor, Brown noted that his manner showed "no strain, his voice no tension."[31] In fact, Nixon's voice was superbly modulated. When he admitted that he was not a rich man, he allowed his voice to trail off in a semiembarrassed fashion so that the audience would identify with him. He increased his loudness and punctuated each word when he told his audience they had "never paid one dime for expenses" so they would not miss the point. And his voice oozed with righteous indignation when he asserted he would not return Checkers. Withall, he superbly executed the delivery of his speech.

Lastly, Nixon's diction reinforced the way in which he delivered his apologia. He communicated with homey words such as "folks" and "you know," verbal fillers such as "well" and "now," personal pronouns such as "I," "you," and "we," and vocal contractions such as "get 'em" and "gonna." These words suggested a guileless stylist, a speaker without pretensions to affectations—as juxtaposed to Stevenson who was caricatured for his erudite word choice in his speeches. In short, whereas Stevenson professed to "talk sense to the American people," Nixon did.

Nixon's Rhetorical Art

"For all their victories and acclaim," wrote William Miller, "the champions in the art of persuasion, from the days of the sophists to our own, have been under a bit of shadow. After the applause has died down and a more reflective mood has set in, one is never sure just where conviction ended and sheer artistry began."[32]

Nixon's "My Side of the Story" was like a pointillist painting. Impressionists were more concerned with technique and representation than with reality. Like his apologia, their pictures were optimally viewed from some distance where they presented their best appearance. In reception to his address, a gallery of newspapers took that point of view. The *New York Herald Tribune* editorialized that "Senator Nixon acquitted himself admirably" but was more interested in defending General Eisenhower's handling of the whole episode. The *Kansas City Star* thought the facts and truth "had been given—most frankly, most dramatically and with rare courage"; the *Detroit Free Press* saw on "TV a personality of deep sincerity"; and the *New Orleans Times-Picayune* noted that Nixon "may have taken his own ticket off the defensive."[33]

Some newspapers were apparently persuaded by the artistry of Nixon's rhetorical techniques. The *Chicago Tribune* commented upon his turning the tables: "Nixon has turned adversity to advantage for his party." The *New York Times, New York World-Telegram, San Francisco Examiner, Washington Evening Star, Chicago Daily News,* and *Pittsburgh Press* noted, in one way or another, how Governor Stevenson was now under obligation to respond about his fund as Nixon had, and how the Democrats were now on the defensive as a result of the senator's major *tu quoque* attacks. That the newspapers did not respond to his usage of the classical pattern may be expected. In truth, Nixon's artistry with it was an exemplar of the ability for which Lysias, an ancient Greek logographer or speech writer, was noted—"the art of concealing the art." However, with regard to inoculation, the *Los Angeles Herald Express* sensed its efficacy: "Who will sneer at this report to the country by one who loves his country. Watch, mark them."[34]

However, some editorials examined the canvass closely by looking at the points rather than the picture. Of course, the *New York Post* thought it was a "soap opera." But on the question of the propriety of the fund, some were not beguiled by Nixon's utilization of the method of residues. The *New York Times* regretted "the lack of recognition by Sen. Nixon that he had made any sort of mistake in accepting these funds in the first place"; the *Washington Post* posited the central issue "whether any such private fund can be squared with our American ideals of representative government"; the *Philadelphia Bulletin* perceived the issue percisely: "If there were a flaw in Sen. Nixon's presentation last night, it lay in his representation that the motive for the use of private funds in his behalf was consideration of the taxpayers," and noted that although he gave a certificate of legality from a law firm, "He could present no documents on ethics. . . . "; the *Baltimore Evening Sun* observed that "Nixon . . . did not deal in any way with the underlying problem of propriety"; the *Miami Daily News* asked Nixon to admit that he had made a mistake or "Lacking that, Nixon will continue to appear morally insensitive"; and the *Newark Star-Ledger* noted "He did not, however, explain the weakness of his judgment."[35]

Of *kategoria* and *apologia*, Quintilian wrote: "accusation necessarily precedes defence. You might as well assert that the sword was invented for the purpose of self-defence and not for aggression."[36] The sword that Leo Katcher wielded in his *New York Post* story and that Stephen Mitchell honed in his two accusations was used to attack directly Nixon and indirectly Eisenhower. These men and the media commentators, in addition to many Republicans, not to mention the Democrats on whom the sword was turned, probably miscalculated Richard Nixon's mastery over the chosen weapons. Of his ability to use with finesse persuasive rhetorical techniques and delivery skills, a line from his "My Side of the Story" speech says it succinctly: "Well, they just don't know who they're dealing with."

Notes

1. For a text that contains eighteen studies of such speech sets, see *Oratorical Encounters: Selected Studies and Sources of Twentieth-Century Political Accusations and Apologies*, edited by Halford R. Ryan (Westport, Conn.: Greenwood Press, 1988).

2. See George Kennedy, *The Art of Persuasion in Greece* (Princeton, N.J.: Princeton University Press, 1963), p. 86; Aristotle, *Rhetoric*, translated by W. Rhys Roberts (New York: The Modern Library, 1954), 1358b10, 1358b16, 1368b1; Isocrates, *Helen* (Cambridge: Loeb Classical Library, 1945), III, 15; *The Institutio Oratoria of Quintillan*, translated by H.E. Butler (Cambridge: Harvard University Press, 1963), I, Book III ii,2; Henry George Liddell and Robert Scott, compilers, *A Greek-English Lexicon* (Oxford: Clarendon Press, 1968), pp. 207–208, 926–927; Halford Ross Ryan, "*Kategoria* and *Apologia*: On Their Rhetorical Criticism as a Speech Set," *Quarterly Journal of Speech* 68 (1982): 254–261.

3. See Halford R. Ryan, "*Kategoria* and *Apologia*: On Their Rhetorical Criticism as a Speech Set," *Quarterly Journal of Speech* 68 (1982): 254–261; Halford R. Ryan, "Baldwin vs. Edward VIII: A Case Study in *Kategoria* and *Apologia*," *Southern Speech Communication Journal* 49 (1984): 125–134.

4. Richard M. Nixon, *Six Crises* (New York: Pyramid Books, 1968), p. 134.

5. See Nixon, *Six Crises*, pp. 77–79; Fawn Brodie, *Richard Nixon: The Shaping of His Character* (New York: W.W. Norton, 1981), pp. 273–275; and Stewart Alsop, *Nixon and Rockefeller* (Garden City: Doubleday, 1960), p. 60.

6. "Secret Rich Men's Trust Fund Keeps Nixon In Style Far Beyond His Salary," *New York Post*, September 18, 1952, pp. 3, 26.

7. Editorial, *New York Post*, September 22, 1952, p. 25.

8. "Mitchell's Statement," *New York Herald Tribune*, September 19, 1952, p. 11.

9. "Mitchell Urges Nixon to Name Fund Donators," *New York Herald Tribune*, September 20, 1952, p. 6.

10. "Nixon's Fund Itemized; 76 Gave $18,235," *New York Herald Tribune*, September 21, 1952, p. 1; "Nixon Confirms $16,000 Fund to Help with Senate Expenses," *New York Herald Tribune*, September 19, 1952, p. 1; and "How Fund Was Dispersed," *New York Herald Tribune*, September 24, 1952, p. 1.

11. Editorial, "The General's Decision," *New York Herald Tribune*, September 24, 1952, p. 8.

12. "Nixon Phones to Assistants of Eisenhower," *New York Herald Tribune*, September 20, 1952, p. 7.

13. "Nixon Talk on Political Fund," *New York Herald Tribune*, September 20, 1952, p. 4.

14. See Ralph De Toledano, *One Man Alone: Richard Nixon* (New York: Funk and Wagnalls, 1969), p. 145, and L. W. Rosenfield, "A Case Study in Speech Criticism: The Nixon-Truman Analog," *Speech Monographs* 25 (1968): 442.

15. "Nixon Phones to Assistants of Eisenhower," p. 7; "Mitchell's Statement," p. 11.

16. Brodie, *Richard Nixon*, p. 289; quoted in De Toledano, *One Man Alone*, p. 151; Nixon, *Six Crises*, p. 127; Gary Wills, *Nixon Agonistes: The Crisis of the Self-Made Man* (Boston: Houghton Mifflin Co., 1970), pp. 97–99, 107–112; and Gary Allen, *Richard Nixon: The Man Behind the Mask* (Boston: Western Islands, 1971), p. 160.

17. See Henry E. McGuckin, Jr., "A Values Analysis of Richard Nixon's 1952 Campaign-Fund Speech," *Southern Speech Communication Journal* 33 (1968): 259–269; Edward D. Steele and W. Charles Redding, "The American Value System: Premises for Persuasion," *Western Speech* 26 (1962): 83–91; and Rosenfield, "A Case Study," pp. 435–450.

18. John Mason Brown, *Through These Men* (New York: Harper and Brothers, 1956), p. 102.

19. Nixon, *Six Crises*, p. 108; Richard Nixon, *RN, The Memoirs of Richard Nixon* (New York: Grosset and Dunlap, 1978), p. 104; Rosenfield, "A Case Study," p. 436.

20. See Kathleen Freeman, *The Murder of Herodes* (New York: W. W. Norton, 1963), p. 32, and George Kennedy, *The Art of Persuasion in Greece* (Princeton: Princeton University Press, 1963), p. 61.

21. Rosenfield, "A Case Study," p. 438.

22. For the text of Senator Nixon's speech, see *American Rhetoric from Roosevelt to Reagan: A Collection of Speeches and Critical Essays*, edited by Halford Ross Ryan (Prospect Heights, Ill.: Waveland Press, 1983), pp. 114–123, or *Vital Speeches of the Day*, October 15, 1952, pp. 11–15.

23. Nixon, *Six Crises*, p. 109; Nixon, *Memoirs*, p. 99; Brown, *Through These Men*, p. 102.

24. Barnet Baskerville, "The Vice-Presidential Candidates," in Frederick W. Haberman, ed., "The Election of 1952: A Symposium," *Quarterly Journal of Speech* 38 (1952): 407–408; Rosenfield, "A Case Study," p. 445; William Lee Miller, "The Debating Career of Richard M. Nixon," *The Reporter*, April 19, 1956, p. 13.

25. This rhetorical technique haunted President Nixon in the battle over the release of the Watergate tapes.

26. Baskerville, "The Vice-Presidential Candidates," p. 408.

27. See "Subsidy for Illinois Aides Charged; Eases 'Sacrifice,' Stevenson Says," *New York Times*, September 23, 1952, p. 1; Myles Martel, *Political Campaign Debates: Images, Strategies, and Tactics* (New York: Longmans, 1983), p. 62.

28. Wills, *Nixon Agonistes*, p. 109.

29. Merle Miller, *Plain Speaking: An Oral Biography of Harry S Truman* (New York: Putnam's, 1973), p. 178; Nixon, *Memoirs*, p. 17.

30. Bruce Mazlish, *In Search of Nixon: A Psychohistorical Inquiry* (New York: Basic Books, 1972), p. 100.

31. See McGuckin, "A Value Analysis," p. 69, and Brown, *Through These Men*, p. 102.

32. Miller, "The Debating Career of Richard Nixon," p. 12.

33. Editorial, "The Air is Cleared," *New York Herald Tribune*, September 25, 1952, p. 22; "Papers Give Opinions on Nixon's Speech," *New York Herald Tribune*, September 25, 1952, p. 16.

34. Ibid.

35. Ibid.

36. *The Institutio Oratoria of Quintilian*, translated by H. E. Butler (Cambridge: Harvard University Press, 1963), I, Book III, ii, 2.

Jimmy Carter's "The Panama Canal Treaties"

Jimmy Carter (1924–). A former governor of Georgia and president of the United States, he sought by his speeches to restore a sense of morals and ethics to the White House.

PREFACE

The rhetorical presidency is a concept that has been practiced by all chief executives since Franklin D. Roosevelt. The construct of the rhetorical presidency holds that the president delivers a programmatic speech to persuade the American people, and, if Congress is intransigent, to ask them to urge the Congress to support the president.

The rise of the mass media fostered the rhetorical presidency. Historically the president delivered speeches to relatively small audiences. To be sure, one could read the cold print of a speech text in a newspaper, but then one missed the energy of the presidential interaction with the audience. However, with the advent of the radio and the motion picture newsreels of the 1930s and 1940s and the emergence of television from the 1950s onward, a president could deliver a persuasive speech to the entire nation. No longer were his words mediated by newspaper and newsreel editors, for the president went directly to the people. Thus, the president became the *vox populi*, the voice of the people, who spoke for all Americans.

President Jimmy Carter's "Panama Canal Treaties" speech was an instance of the rhetorical presidency. Carter took his case to the American people on national television. He spoke to secure the people's support for his treaties, for not everyone thought the United States should give away the Panama Canal, and to unite the people behind him so that the Congress, especially the Senate, would ratify the treaties. Although never known as a great communicator, Carter at least successfully practiced the rhetorical presidency with regard to his "Panama Canal Treaties" speech.

"THE PANAMA CANAL TREATIES": THE SPEECH

Address to the Nation. February 1, 1978.

Good evening.

Seventy-five years ago our nation signed a treaty which gave us rights to build a canal across Panama, to take the historic step of joining the Atlantic and Pacific Oceans. The results of the agreement have been of great benefit to ourselves and to other nations throughout the world who navigate the high seas.

The building of the canal was one of the greatest engineering feats of history. Although massive in concept and construction, it's relatively simple in design and has been reliable and efficient in operation. We Americans are justly and deeply proud of this great achievement.

The canal has also been a source of pride and benefit to the people of Panama—but a cause of some continuing discontent. Because we have controlled a 10-mile-wide strip of land across the heart of their country and because they considered the original terms of the agreement to be unfair, the people of Panama have been dissatisfied with the treaty. It was drafted here in our country and was not signed by any Panamanian. Our own secretary of state who did sign the original treaty said it was "vastly advantageous to the United States and . . . not so advantageous to Panama."

In 1964, after consulting with former Presidents Truman and Eisenhower, President Johnson committed our nation to work toward a new treaty with the Republic of Panama. And last summer, after 14 years of negotiation under two Democratic Presidents and two Republican Presidents, we reached and signed an agreement that is fair and beneficial to both countries. The United States Senate will soon be debating whether these treaties should be ratified.

Throughout the negotiations, we were determined that our national security interests would be protected; that the canal would always be open and neutral and available to ships of all nations; that in time of need or emergency our warships would have the right to go to the head of the line for priority passage through the canal; and that our military forces would have the permanent right to defend the canal if it should ever be in danger. The new treaties meet all of the requirements.

Let me outline the terms of the agreement. There are two treaties —one covering the rest of this century, and the other guaranteeing the safety, openness, and neutrality of the canal after the year 1999, when Panama will be in charge of its operation.

For the rest of this century, we will operate the canal through a nine-person board of directors. Five members will be from the United States and four will be from Panama. Within the area of the present Canal Zone, we have the right to select whatever lands and waters our military and civilian forces need to maintain, to operate, and to defend the canal.

About 75 percent of those who now maintain and operate the canal are Panamanians; over the next 22 years, as we manage the canal together, this percentage will increase. The Americans who work on the canal will continue to have their rights of employment, promotion, and retirement carefully protected.

We will share with Panama some of the fees paid by shippers who use the canal. As in the past, the canal should continue to be self-supporting.

This is not a partisan issue. The treaties are strongly backed by President Gerald Ford and by Former Secretaries of State Dean Rusk and Henry Kissinger. They are endorsed by our business and professional leaders, especially those who recognize the benefits of good will and trade with other nations in this hemisphere. And they were endorsed overwhelmingly by the Senate Foreign Relations Committee which, this week, moved closer to ratification by approving the treaties, although with some recommended changes which we do not feel are needed.

And the treaties are supported enthusiastically by every member of the Joint Chiefs of Staff—General George Brown, the Chairman, General Bernard Rogers, Chief of Staff of the Army, Admiral James Holloway, Chief of Naval Operations, General David Jones, Chief of Staff of the Air Force, and General Louis Wilson, Commandant of the Marine Corps—responsible men whose profession is the defense of this nation and the preservation of our security.

The treaties also have been overwhelmingly supported throughout Latin America, but predictably, they are opposed abroad by some who are unfriendly to the United States and who would like to see disorder in Panama and a disruption of our political, economic, and military ties with our friends in Central and South America and in the Caribbean.

I know that the treaties also have been opposed by many Americans. Much of that opposition is based on misunderstanding and misinformation. I've found that when the full terms of the agreement are known, most people are convinced that the national interests of our country will be served best by ratifying the treaties.

Tonight, I want you to hear the facts. I want to answer the most serious questions and tell you why I feel the Panama Canal treaties should be approved.

The most important reason—the only reason—to ratify the treaties is that they are in the highest national interest of the United States and will strengthen our position in the world. Our security interests will be stronger. Our trade opportunities will be improved. We will demonstrate that as a large and powerful country, we are able to deal fairly and honorably with a proud but smaller sovereign nation. We will honor our commitment to those engaged in world commerce that the Panama Canal will be open and available for use by their ships—at a reasonable and competitive cost—both now and in the future.

Let me answer specifically the most common questions about the treaties.

Will our Nation have the right to protect and defend the canal against any armed attack or threat to the security of the canal or of ships going through it?

The answer is yes, and is contained in both treaties and also in the statement of understanding between the leaders of our two nations.

The first treaty says, and I quote: "The United States of America and the Republic of Panama commit themselves to protect and defend the Panama Canal. Each Party shall act, in accordance with its constitutional processes, to meet the danger resulting from an armed attack or other actions which threaten the security of the Panama Canal or [of] ships transiting it."

The neutrality treaty says, and I quote again: "The United States of America and the Republic of Panama agree to maintain the regime of neutrality established in this Treaty, which shall be maintained in order that the Canal shall remain permanently neutral. . . . "

And to explain exactly what that means, the statement of understanding says, and I quote again: "Under (the Neutrality Treaty), Panama and the United States have the responsibility to assure that the Panama Canal will remain open and secure to ships of all nations. The correct interpretation of this principle is that each of the two countries shall, in accordance with their respective constitutional processes, defend the Canal against any threat to the regime of neutrality, and consequently [shall] have the right to act against the Canal or against the peaceful transit of vessels through the Canal."

It is obvious that we can take whatever military action is necessary to make sure that the canal always remains open and safe.

Of course, this does not give the United States any right to intervene in the internal affairs of Panama, nor would our military action ever be directed against the territorial integrity or the political independence of Panama.

Military experts agree that even with the Panamanian Armed Forces joined with us as brothers against a common enemy, it would take a large number of American troops to ward off a heavy attack. I, as President, would not hesitate to deploy whatever armed forces are necessary to defend the canal, and I have no doubt that even in a sustained combat, that we would be successful. But there is a much better way than sending our sons and grandsons to fight in the jungles of Panama.

We would serve our interests better by implementing the new treaties, an action that will help to avoid any attack on the Panama Canal.

What we want is the permanent right to use the canal—and we can defend this right through the treaties—through real cooperation with Panama. The citizens of Panama and their government have already shown their support of the new partnership, and a protocol to the neutrality treaty will be signed by many other nations, thereby showing their strong approval.

The new treaties will naturally change Panama from a passive and sometimes deeply resentful bystander into an active and interested partner, whose vital interests will be served by a well-operated canal. This agreement leads to cooperation and not confrontation between our country and Panama.

Another question is: Why should we give away the Panama Canal Zone? As many people say, "We bought it, we paid for it, it's ours."

I must repeat a very important point: We do not own the Panama Canal Zone. We have never had sovereignty over it. We have only had the right to use it.

The Canal Zone cannot be compared with United States territory. We bought Alaska from the Russians, and no one has ever doubted that we own it. We bought the Louisiana Purchases—Territories from France, and that's an integral part of the United States.

From the beginning, we have made an annual payment to Panama to use their land. You do not pay rent on your own land. The Panama Canal Zone has always been Panamanian territory. The U.S. Supreme Court and previous American presidents have repeatedly acknowledged the sovereignty of Panama over the Canal Zone.

We've never needed to own the Panama Canal Zone, any more than we need to own a 10-mile-wide strip of land all the way through Canada from Alaska when we build an international gas pipeline.

The new treaties give us what we do need—not ownership of the canal, but the right to use it and to protect it. As the chairman of the Joint Chiefs of Staff has said, "The strategic value of the canal lies in its use."

There's another question: Can our naval ships, our warships, in time of need or emergency, get through the canal immediately instead of waiting in line?

The treaties answer that clearly by guaranteeing that our ships will always have expeditious transit through the canal. To make sure that there could be no possible disagreement about what these words mean, the joint statement says that expeditious transit, and I quote, "is intended . . . to assure the transit of such vessels through the Canal as quickly as possible, without any impediment, with expedited treatment, and in case of need or emergency, to go to the head of the line of vessels in order to transit the Canal rapidly."

Will the treaties affect our standing in Latin America? Will they create a so-called power vacuum, which our enemies might move in to fill? They will do just the opposite. The treaties will increase our nation's influence in this hemisphere, will help to reduce any mistrust and disagreement, and they will remove a major source of anti-American feeling.

The new agreement has already provided vivid proof to the people of this hemisphere that a new era of friendship and cooperation is beginning and that what they regard as the last remnant of alleged American colonialism is being removed.

Last fall, I met individually with the leaders of 18 countries in this hemisphere. Between the United States and Latin America there is already a new sense of equality, a new sense of trust and mutual respect that exists because of the Panama Canal treaties. This opens up a fine opportunity for us in good will, trade, jobs, exports, and political cooperation.

If the treaties should be rejected, this would all be lost, and disappointment and despair among our good neighbors and traditional friends would be severe.

In the peaceful struggle against alien ideologies like communism, these treaties are a step in the right direction. Nothing could strengthen our competitors and adversaries in this hemisphere more than for us to reject this agreement.

What if a new sea-level canal should be needed in the future? This question has been studied over and over throughout this century, from before the time the canal was built up through the last few years. Every study has reached the same conclusion—that the best place to build a sea-level canal is in Panama.

The treaties say that if we want to build such a canal, we will build it in Panama, and if any canal is to be built in Panama, that we, the United States, will have the right to participate in the project.

This is a clear benefit to us, for it ensures that, say, 10 or 20 years from now, no unfriendly but wealthy power will be able to purchase the right to build a sea-level canal, to bypass the existing canal, perhaps leaving that other nation in control of the only usable waterway across the isthmus.

Are we paying Panama to take the canal? We are not. Under the new treaty, any payments to Panama will come from tolls paid by ships which use the canal.

What about the present and the future stability and the capability of the Panamanian Government? Do the people of Panama themselves support the agreement?

Well, as you know, Panama and her people have been our historical allies and friends. The present leader of Panama has been in office for more than 9 years, and he heads a stable government which has encouraged the development of free enterprise in Panama. Democratic elections will be held this August to choose the members of the Panamanian Assembly, who will in turn elect a President and a Vice President by majority vote. In the past, regimes have changed in Panama, but for 75 years, no Panamanian government has ever wanted to close the canal.

Panama wants the canal open and neutral—perhaps even more than we do. The canal's continued operation is very important to us, but it is much more than that to Panama. To Panama, it's crucial. Much of her economy flows directly or indirectly from the canal. Panama would be no more likely to neglect or to close the canal than we would be to close the interstate highway system here in the United States.

In an open and free referendum last October, which was monitored very carefully by the United Nations, the people of Panama gave the new treaties their support.

The major threat to the canal comes not from any government of Panama, but from misguided persons who may try to fan the flames of dissatisfaction with the terms of the old treaty.

There's a final question—about the deeper meaning of the treaties themselves, to us and to Panama.

Recently, I discussed the treaties with David McCullough, author of "The Path Between the Seas," the great history of the Panama Canal. He believes that the canal is something that we built and have looked after these many years; it is "ours" in that sense, which is very different from just ownership.

So, when we talk of the canal, whether we are old, young, for or against the treaties, we are talking about very deep and elemental feelings about our own strength.

Still, we Americans want a more humane and stable world. We believe in good will and fairness, as well as strength. This agreement with Panama is something we want because we know it is right. This is not merely the surest way to protect and save the canal, it's a strong, positive act of a people who are still confident, still creative, still great.

This new partnership can become a source of national pride and self-respect in much the same way that building the canal was 75 years ago. It's the spirit in which we act that is so very important.

Theodore Roosevelt, who was President when America built the canal, saw history itself as a force, and the history of our own time and the changes it has brought would not be lost on him. He knew that change was inevitable and necessary. Change is growth. The true conservative, he once remarked, keeps his face to the future.

But if Theodore Roosevelt were to endorse the treaties, as I'm quite sure he would, it would be mainly because he could see the decision as one by which we are demonstrating the kind of great power we wish to be.

"We cannot avoid meeting great issues," Roosevelt said. "All that we can determine for ourselves is whether we shall meet them well or ill."

The Panama Canal is a vast, heroic expression of that age-old desire to bridge the divide and to bring people closer together. This is what the treaties are all about.

We can sense what Roosevelt called "the lift toward nobler things which marks a great and generous people."

In this historic decision, he would join us in our pride for being a great and generous people, with the national strength and wisdom to do what is right for us and what is fair to others.

Thank you very much.

ANALYSIS

Whether President Jimmy Carter should have proposed the Panama Canal Treaties and whether the United States Senate should have ratified the treaties are not the issues here. Nor at issue is how this speech confirms or confutes the theoretical construct of the rhetorical presidency, which holds that the chief executive uses speeches to persuade the American people to pressure Congress to support the president. The crux of this rhetorical criticism concerns how President Carter used the classical organizational pattern in his speech to present his persuasive case to the American people.

The focus is on how Carter organized his speech because it has already been criticized from other perspectives. Dan Hahn suggested that a critic could explicate this speech in terms of a rhetorical atonement: As one can make an act of reconciliation with God, the Senate's passing the treaties could put the United States "right with the world."[1] Ronald A. Sudol has criticized Carter's speech within the greater context of the Panama Canal treaties debate.[2] Sudol's findings will be used to reinforce the critical stance of this essay, but it is worth mentioning that Sudol did not examine the speech in terms of the classical organizational pattern.

Dispositio: The Classical Pattern

The Introduction   The speech had an introduction insofar as Carter began talking, but it lacked a good beginning. The speech needed an exordium that would have accomplished Cicero's concepts of making the audience attentive and teachable. Even a minimal exordium would have helped. For argument's sake, one could allow that Carter probably thought he already had the nation's attention, because his nationally televised speech had been previously advertised. Clearly, though, Carter did not effectively play the role of the teacher in the introduction. His opening words were a self-inflicted wound. He praised the Canal as an engineering marvel, claimed that Americans were justly proud of its accomplishments, and acknowledged that the United States had a treaty with Panama that "gave us rights to build a canal across Panama." If anything, Carter played the wrong role of teacher: He reinforced the opinions of his opponents, who held that the U.S. already had a treaty and therefore should not easily give up such a valuable prize. It was not an auspicious beginning.

The Narrative   Carter did try to teach, but rather lamely so, in his narration. Playing the role of the politics professor, Carter gave a thumbnail sketch of the history of the Panama Canal. But the history lecture was too short and it lacked detail.

If there was any valid reason for the Senate's signing the new treaties, it surely was due to the way the United States got the rights to a canal in the first place. President Theodore Roosevelt boasted in speeches that "I took the Canal Zone . . . and let Congress debate."[3] To oversimplify a complex political situation, Roosevelt, with the aid of the U.S. Navy, in an instance of gunboat diplomacy, encouraged Panama to secede from Colombia and sign a treaty with the United States. In a convenient political *quid pro quo*, Panama became a republic and the United States got its rights to the canal on Panamanian soil. The Colombians were justifiably irked, but there was little they could do about the matter short of going to war with the United States. The episode, in which imperialistic Americans congratulated themselves for their prowess, sparked the invention of one of the longest palindromes in the English language: A MAN, A PLAN, A CANAL, PANAMA.

A case can be made that Carter did not adapt well to his audience in the narration. The only line in the narration about how the United States got the original treaty was a statement that it was advantageous to the United States but not so advantageous to Panama. It was not enough information on which to build Carter's case for righting past wrongs.

It was probably a mistake to assume that the American people were substantially informed about the genesis and intricacies of the original treaty. Perhaps if Carter had better informed the American people about the sordid details of the original treaty in his narration, he could have preempted distortions of his position. At least he could have made it difficult for others to mislead concerning the original treaty. Nevertheless, presidential candidate Ronald Reagan scored heavily in the 1980 election by claiming, "we bought it, we paid for it, and it is ours." Sudol noted that other political candidates ducked the issue by using humor. Perhaps following the advice of Gorgias, one candidate countered a serious question with a humorous response by claiming: "We ought to hang on to the canal. We stole it fair and square."[4]

The narrative was a place where Carter should have preempted that kind of argumentation. (He did get around to it later in the speech.) For, in fact, the United States never bought the canal, it did pay for building and operating it but never owned it. But Carter was not at pains in the narrative to dispel any misconceptions about the original treaty. That persuasive task could have been efficiently accomplished in a longer narration that specified in greater detail why the Panamanians justifiably, at least from their perspective, wanted the treaty changed.

Carter did employ one useful rhetorical technique in the narration. He used the **bandwagon effect.** The bandwagon effect takes place when the speaker mentions other important figures that are already on the speaker's side. The implication is that the members of the audience should follow in other's footsteps and get on the bandwagon, too.

Carter implicitly asked his American audience to join his presidential bandwagon. He reminded listeners that the treaty process actually began with President Lyndon Johnson, who consulted with former presidents Harry Truman and Dwight Eisenhower. Carter indulged in presidential name-dropping, and used the bipartisan appeal to show that the treaties were not politically motivated. After negotiations under two Republican and two Democratic presidents, Carter claimed he at last had a treaty that should be signed. Oddly enough, Carter did not here mention by name presidents Richard Nixon and Gerald Ford, who were the two Republican presidents, that favored the new treaties. Carter also glided over the fact that he was one of the two Democratic presidents to favor the treaties. The presidential bandwagon was something less than Carter implied it was, but it gave the impression of complete and bipartisan presidential support.

The Partition   Carter used a classical partition to enumerate the treaties's strengths. He claimed that the treaties satisfied four salient issues:

1. U.S. security interests would be protected.
2. The canal would always be open to all, and neutral.
3. U.S. warships could go to the head of the line.
4. U.S. forces could defend the canal.

Using a transitional device of the preview, "Let me outline the terms of the agreement," Carter seemed to communicate that he would address these arguments in a straightforward fashion, that he would explain how the treaties would meet his four national security concerns, for these were the major stumbling blocks to the two treaties. Thus, it appeared that the arguments would be devoted to proving these four contentions.

The Arguments   Alas, Carter did not prove his contentions at all. Rather, he devoted several paragraphs to extraneous issues, such as who would sit on the oversight board, who would operate the canal, and how American jobs would be protected. These were certainly valid concerns, but they did not prove that the new treaties met the national security concerns that Carter had enumerated in the partition.

He did tangentially argue, in a rather oblique fashion, that U.S. security interests would not be harmed. He claimed that President Gerald Ford, Secretaries of State Dean Rusk, and Henry Kissinger, members of the Senate Foreign Relations Committee, and five generals, which represented the armed forces, supported his treaties. By again employing the bandwagon effect, Carter invited listeners to assume that if these important people believed the treaties were safe, then so should the American people.

As yet, Carted had not proved his four points that he claimed were the reasons why the treaties should be ratified. He adduced a semblance of argumentation with the bandwagon technique, but that was the extent of his persuasion, which lacked substantive proof.

The Refutation   Carter then acknowledged that many Americans opposed his treaties because of "misunderstanding and misinformation," which he was not at pains, thus far in the speech, to dispel. Claiming that when the people understood the treaties, then they would agree with him, Carter phrased a transitional device to his refutation: "Tonight I want you to hear the facts. I want to answer the most serious questions and tell you why I feel the Panama Canal treaties should be approved."

The first reason, Carter stated, was that the treaties were "in the highest national interest of the United States." However, this was not really a refutation, but a confirmation. Search in vain in this paragraph, for you will not ascertain how these treaties will accomplish the national security goal, which was also never proved in the confirmation. Little wonder that Sudol found that the defects of Carter's speech included "haphazard arrangement of facts and arguments [and] curious omissions."[5]

However, Carter finally got around to issues that belonged in the refutation.

1. The most common concern was whether the United States had the right to protect and defend the canal and ships going through it. If Carter tried to use the advice of the *Rhetorica ad Herennium* in starting the refutation with a strong point, he started strongly. Carter asserted the answer was yes, and then quoted substantial portions of the treaty for his proof. Any reasonably intelligent person would assume the treaties might say that, but any reasonably intelligent person knows that treaties can easily be broken. Perhaps realizing that he had not really answered objections, Carter then allowed, in a Machiavellian manner, that of course the U.S. could and would defend the canal.

   In case that analysis was not convincing enough, Carter ended his first refutation by coyly stating that the treaties would lead "to cooperation and not confrontation" between Panama and the United States. Yet this fear appeal contradicted his national security argument, for it suggested at some later date that Panama could be confrontational (weren't the treaties supposed to mollify Panama?). Hence, the U.S. could very well have a military problem on its hands. Little wonder that Sudol found this argumentation aroused "suspicion and confusion."[6] If Carter started this first refutation with a bang, it ended with a whimper.

2. Another objection was a paraphrase of Ronald Reagan's emerging campaign rhetoric: We bought it, we paid for it, it's ours. Carter did a credible job of refuting this. He used the examples of buying Alaska from Russia and the Louisiana purchase from France, but stated that the United States never bought anything from Panama. Carter rightly claimed that you do not pay rent on your own land. The Panama Canal, as the Supreme Court and previous presidents all acknowledged, has always been under Panamanian sovereignty.

3. Responding to the question whether U.S. ships could go to the head of the line in a crisis Carter claimed they could. He again quoted the treaties to that effect. If one bought Carter's previous assertions, then one would accept this refutation on its face value.

4. Carter then answered those who believed that the treaties would create a power vacuum into which our enemies would move. Carter claimed that just the opposite would occur. If the United States signed the treaties, this would please the Panamanians, he said, which would "remove a major source of anti-American feeling." On the contrary, failure to ratify the treaties would play into the Communist's hands. Unfortunately for Carter, his argumentation came back to haunt him. Many Americans did not accept his vision of a great country capitulating to a small country. He compounded this perception by never proving in the confirmation that the treaties were in the national interest. Refutation number four seemed to imply just the opposite. How could Panama keep the canal neutral while at the same time allowing the United States to defend it, which would end the canal's neutrality? The question keeps lurking in the background: Why not just keep the status quo?

5. Whether the United States could benefit from and partake in a new canal, if one were to be built, seemed to be a straw issue. Carter assured his audience that the United States had rights to such a canal, but, even if he won this point, it had little to do with national security issues.

6. Some people were concerned that the United States would have to pay Panama to take the canal, which was like adding insult to injury. Carter correctly responded that Panama would only receive the tolls.

7. Carter finally got around to a pressing issue. What about the stability of the Panamanian government? Carter wisely skirted that issue, and argued his case from expediency. The Panamanians, never mind who ran the government, would want to keep the canal open because it contributed greatly to its country's coffers. He argued a compelling analogy when he claimed that Panama would no more want to close the canal than the United States would want to shut down its interstate highway system—either act would be an instance of the proverbial shot in the foot.

8. His last refutation concerned the deeper meaning of the treaties to the United States. But Carter made a curious reply. He claimed the canal was "ours" and that Americans have "very deep and elemental feelings about our own strength." In contravention to these elemental feelings, Carter claimed that Americans should demonstrate good will toward Panama, should be fair, should support the treaty because it is a "positive act of a people who are still confident, still creative, still great." Granted, the treaty might be creative. But if the American people were still confident and still great, then why should they sign away the canal? The American people had trouble in assenting to Carter's implication that it was the right thing to do.

Carter clearly did not follow the advice of the *Rhetorica ad Herennium*, which counseled ending a section of the speech with a strong argument; Sudol, for example, found that Carter left "the audience recalling the old values more strongly than the arguments."[7]

At this point, we can now compare Carter's arguments with his refutation. In terms of verbiage, Carter spent considerably more time trying to overcome the objections to his treaties. Yet, even if he "won" these objections, few of them were relevant to the national security concerns expressed in the arguments. Only refutation numbers one and three directly addressed national security. The other six refutations were tangential to the crux of the issue. The arguments lacked a clear demonstration of how the treaties fulfilled the national security interests of the United States. This was a persuasive task that was not fulfilled by the confirmation or supported by the refutation.

The Conclusion   It is probably a misnomer to call Carter's conclusion a peroration. One hesitates to define this section of the speech as eloquent. It is hard even to determine where the conclusion actually began; it did not employ effective rhetorical proof; and it had no memorable phrases.

To have to quibble over where the conclusion begins is in itself an indication that the speech was not structured clearly. The conclusion appears to begin with the paragraph that begins with "This new partnership. . . ." It could begin a paragraph later. The point is that the audience was not forewarned that the speech would end soon; hence, it ended without flair or artistry.

The conclusion also botched the use of rhetorical proof. Carter tried to argue an unconvincing enthymeme. In attempting once again to use the bandwagon effect, Carter alleged that President Theodore Roosevelt would favor the Panama Canal Treaties. Since Roosevelt would support them, the implication was that the American people should support them, too. It is always risky business to assert that famous dead persons would favor one's proposal. After all, Roosevelt's recommendation could not be verified, and in fact, it is possible that Roosevelt would not have supported the treaties. In the minds of many Americans lies an image of Teddy Roosevelt, the big-game-hunting, "bully" president, who advocated the big stick in foreign policy. Why would he, who secured the Panama Canal by force, assent to signing it away? It was not very convincing to allege that Roosevelt would have supported the treaties.

Carter's word choice also contributed to a diminution of powerful language. Consider the following quotation from the conclusion:

> But if Theodore Roosevelt were to endorse the treaties, as I'm sure he would, it would be mainly because he could see the decision as one by which we are demonstrating the kind of great power we wish to be.

Note the tenuousness of the language. "But if" tacitly admits the possibility that Roosevelt might not endorse the treaties. "[A]s I'm quite sure he would" is unconvincing, for obviously Carter would think so, even if no one else would. And then Carter asked the American audience to assent to another strange enthymeme. The normal definition of a great power is one that wields its weight in the world. Carter asked the American people to define a great power as one that made concessions to small powers.

The penultimate sentence was indicative of the persuasive problem that plagued the entire address. Carter implicitly asked the American people to join him "with a national strength and wisdom to do what is right for us and what is fair to others." Again Carter juxtaposed incongruent images. "[N]ational strength and wisdom" does not usually denote giving away valuable military assets. And, although Carter may have proved that the treaties were fair to the Panamanians, he failed to prove that the treaties were "right" for the United States. Indeed, many people thought they were wrong for the United States, an attack that Ronald Reagan leveled against Carter throughout the 1980 presidential campaign.[8]

Carter matched his delivery to the rhetorical situation. Heretofore, he had been infamous for using the presidential podium more for preaching than for speaking. But for this address, the *New York Times* observed, Carter's "tone was subdued, as though he was trying to convince his audience of the merits of the treaties more by gentle persuasion than exhortation."[9]

Carter's Persuasive Effect

It is very difficult to determine the effect of Carter's presidential persuasion on the people or on the senators. To be sure, he used his twenty-two-minute televised address to turn public opinion toward his position. Presumably the speech had some effect, but polls do not directly link this speech to changes in opinion. The United States Senate voted separately on the two treaties, and the vote was sixty-eight to thirty-two on March 16 and April 18, 1978.[10] This close partisan vote probably reflected the power of Carter's political IOU's rather than the impact of the speech.

But whether the speech persuaded, and to what degree, is not the focus here. Our purpose here was to determine how Carter used the classical organizational pattern. From this perspective, Carter's speech lacked artistic technique, irrespective of whether it persuaded.

The persuasive efficacy of the classical pattern rests on some workable combination of the arguments and refutation sections. With respect to different rhetorical situations, the refutation may be longer and more substantive than the arguments. In Carter's case, he was wise to adapt to the audience by treating extensively their objections to the treaties.

Carter's refutation was reasonably strong. He presented a "point-by-point rebuttal of the main objections raised by the critics of the treaties."[11] But however compelling the refutation was, it needed to function in tandem with the arguments, for a strong refutation cannot substitute for a weak arguments section.

Carter needed to use the confirmation section to demonstrate arguments that would impel Americans to support the treaties. As we have seen, the speech was deficient in presenting reasons, which supported his four national security issues, for signing the treaties. In short, Carter succeeded in telling people why they should have no fears in sustaining the treaties, but he failed to tell them why they should actively support the treaties.

Notes

1. Dan Hahn, "The Rhetoric of Jimmy Carter," *Presidential Studies Quarterly*, 14 (1984): 278, 287 n. 101.

2. Ronald A. Sudol, "The Rhetoric of Strategic Retreat: Carter and the Panama Canal Debate," *Quarterly Journal of Speech*, 65 (1979): 379–391.

3. Quoted in *The President in the 20th Century*, edited by Louis Filler (Englewood, N.J.: Jerome S. Ozer, Publisher, 1983), p. 39.

4. Sudol, "The Rhetoric of Strategic Retreat," p. 388.

5. Ibid, p. 381.

6. Ibid, p. 389.

7. Ibid, p. 385.

8. Jimmy Carter, *Keeping Faith: Memoirs of a President* (Toronto: Bantam Books, 1982), p. 161.

9. "Carter, In TV Talk, Asks Canal Backing," *New York Times*, February 2, 1978, p. 1.

10. Charles O. Jones, *The Trusteeship Presidency* (Baton Rouge: Louisiana State University Press, 1988), p. 159.

11. "Carter, In TV Talk, Asks Canal Backing," p. 1.

Barbara Bush's "Choices and Change"

Barbara Bush (1925–). Currently First Lady, Barbara Bush espouses traditional values for the betterment of the country.

PREFACE

The role of first lady is usually defined by a number of factors. As wife of the president of the United States, she must fulfill normative expectations. But at the same time, there is considerable latitude in which each first lady can develop a persona of her own. Some, such as Jacqueline Kennedy and Lady Bird Johnson, have preferred to play an active part in politics and to have a visible public life; some were closely identified with controversial issues that were not in vogue at the time, such as Eleanor Roosevelt, who championed civil rights; some have been trusted presidential advisers, such as Roselynn Carter; and some have assumed a more conventional wifely role, such as Bess Truman, Mamie Eisenhower, and Barbara Bush.

Barbara Bush brought to the White House a less glamorous but a more traditional kind of first lady. Satiated with the gospel of greed and selfishness of the 1980s, the American people welcomed her homey attributes of caring and concern for others. Proud of being foremost a wife and a mother, she was unembarrassed about her white hair and faux pearls. Indeed, if President Dwight D. Eisenhower seemed to be everybody's grandfather in the 1950s, then Barbara Bush has a similar role as the nation's grandmother in the 1990s, a persona that seems to suit her and the nation's expectations of her.

However, just as presidents never really speak for everybody—although they fancy themselves the *vox populi*—so Barbara Bush was not every woman's ideal. Some graduating seniors at Wellesley College believed that Bush's mother-and-wife role was too traditional, too self-effacing, too uncharacteristic of the politically correct feminism of the late twentieth century. They attemtped to block Wellesley's invitation to Mrs. Bush to speak at their commencement. In the address that follows, Bush proved her mettle. In this epideictic speech, delivered at Wellesley College in Massachusetts on June 1, 1990, she demonstrated that a traditional woman could use traditional rhetoric to defend her philosophy of life.

"CHOICES AND CHANGE": THE SPEECH

Delivered at Wellesley College, Wellesley, Massachusetts, June 1, 1990.

Thank you President Keohane, Mrs. Gorbachev, trustees, faculty, parents, Julie Porer, Christine Bicknell and the Class of 1990. I am thrilled to be with you today, and very excited, as I know you must all be, that Mrs. Gorbachev could join us.

More than ten years ago when I was invited here to talk about our experiences in the People's Republic of China, I was struck by both the natural beauty of your campus and the spirit of this place.

Wellesley, you see, is not just a place, but an idea, an experiment in excellence in which diversity is not just tolerated, but is embraced.

The essence of this spirit was captured in a moving speech about tolerance given last year by the student body president of one of your sister colleges. She related the story by Robert Fulghum about a young pastor who, finding himself in charge of some very energetic children, hit upon a game called "Giants, Wizards and Dwarfs." "You have to decide now," the pastor instructed the children, "Which you are . . . a giant, a wizard or a dwarf?" At that, a small girl tugging on his pants leg, asked, "But where do the mermaids stand?"

The pastor told her there are *no* mermaids. "Oh yes there are," she said. "I am a mermaid."

This little girl knew what she was and she was not about to give up on either her identity *or* the game. She intended to take her place wherever mermaids fit into the scheme of things. Where *do* the mermaids stand . . . all those who are different, those who do not fit the boxes and the pigeonholes? "Answer that question," wrote Fulghum, "And you can build a school, a nation, or a whole world on it."

As that very wise young woman said . . . "Diversity, like anything worth having requires *effort*." Effort to learn about and respect the difference, to be compassionate with one another, and to cherish our own identity, and to accept unconditonally the same in all others.

You should all be very proud that this is the Wellesley spirit. Now I know your first choice for today was Alice Walker, known for *The Color Purple*. Instead you got me—known for the color of my hair! Of

course, Alice Walker's book has a special resonance here. At Wellesley, each class is known by a special color, and for four years the class
of '90 has worn the color purple. Today you meet on Severance Green
to say goodbye to all that, to begin a new and very personal journey,
a search for your own true colors.

In the world that awaits you beyond the shore of Lake Waban, no
one can say what your true colors will be. But this I know: You have
a first class education from a first class school. And so you need not,
probably cannot, live a "paint-by-numbers" life. Decisions are not
irrevocable. Choices do come back. As you set off from Wellesley, I hope
that many of you will consider making three very special choices.

The first is to believe in something larger than yourself, to get
involved in some of the big ideas of your time. I chose literacy because
I honestly believe that if more people could read, write, and comprehend, we would be that much closer to solving so many of the problems plaguing our society.

Early on I made another choice which I hope you will make as
well. Whether you are talking about education, career, or service, you
are talking about life, and life must have joy. It's supposed to be fun!

One of the reasons I made the most important decision of my life,
to marry George Bush, is because he made me laugh. It's true, sometimes we've laughed through our tears, but that shared laughter has
been one of our strongest bonds. Find the joy in life, because as Ferris
Bueller said on his day off

"Life moves pretty fast. Ya don't stop and look around once in a while,
ya gonna miss it!"

The third choice that must not be missed is to cherish your
human connections: your relationships with friends and family. For several years, you've had impressed upon you the importance to your career
of dedication and hard work. This is true, but as important as your obli-
gations as a doctor, lawyer, or business leader will be, you are a human
being first and those human connections, with spouses, with children,
with friends, are the most important investments you will ever make.

At the end of your life, you will never regret not having passed
one more test, not winning one more verdict, or not closing one more
deal. You will regret the time not spent with a husband, a friend, a
child, or a parent.

We are in a transitional period right now, fascinating and exhila-
rating times, learning to adjust to the changes and the choices we,
men and women, are facing. I remember what a friend said, on hearing her husband lament to his buddies that he had to babysit. Quickly
setting him straight, my friend told her husband that when it's your
own kids, it's not called babysitting!

Maybe we should adjust faster, maybe slower. But whatever the era, whatever the times, one thing will never change: fathers and mothers, if you have children, they must come first. Your success as a family, our success as a society, depends *not* on what happens at the White House, but on what happens inside your house.

For over fifty years, it was said that the winner of Wellesley's annual hoop race would be the first to get married. Now they say the winner will be the first to become a C.E.O. Both of these stereotypes show too little tolerance for those who want to know where the mermaids stand. So I offer you today a new legend: The winner of the hoop race will be the first to realize her dream, not society's dream, her own personal dream. And who knows? Somewhere out in this audience may even be someone who will one day follow in my footsteps, and preside over the White House as the president's spouse. I wish him well!

The controversy ends here. But our conversation is only beginning. And a worthwhile conversation it is. So as you leave Wellesley today, take with you deep thanks for the courtesy and honor you have shared with Mrs. Gorbachev and me. Thank you. God bless you. And may your future be worthy of your dreams.

ANALYSIS

In 1916, D. W. Griffith produced a landmark film entitled *Intolerance*, in which Griffith wove four story lines about the effects of intolerance on individuals and their societies. A continent away from Hollywood and nearly a century later, the first lady of the United States, confronted intolerance with a speech in Massachusetts. Intolerance had reared its head in the rarefied atmosphere of Wellesley College. In one of the most select and privileged undergraduate institutions in the United States, some students had demonstrated that intolerance cuts across social, economic, and gender lines. The issue was who would give a commencement address at one of the most prestigious colleges for women in America. The conflict was whether Barbara Bush, First Lady of the United States, should address the graduating class of 1990. Alice Walker, author of the best-selling novel *The Color Purple*, had been many senior's first choice to address their graduating class. Instead, the first lady was asked to deliver the commencement address.

Some of the young women of Wellesley complained that Mrs. Bush was neither their first choice nor the role model they envisioned for their newer generation of professional women. A petition, signed by some one hundred and fifty seniors, allowed that they were "enraged" because Mrs. Bush did not represent the type of career woman that Wellesley sought to educate;[1] moreover, some students felt that Mrs. Bush did not possess "the self-affirming qualities of a Wellesley graduate."[2] In short, some of them did not want Mrs. Bush to speak.

The Rhetorical Situation

Barbara Bush's address is a fascinating study in rhetorical adaptation. It is a thoroughly modern speech that illustrates the classical nexus between speaker, speech, and audience.

The speech was, in Aristotelian terms, clearly epideictic. Focusing primarily on the present in a ceremonial setting, the formal purpose was to praise the accomplishments of the Wellesley graduates. But, according to Aristotle, epideictic speeches could also blame. At first glance, this was clearly not Mrs. Bush's purpose, nor would it have been appropriate for the commencement situation. However, as this rhetorical criticism will unfold, it will become clear that she expertly and astutely wove a thread of blame through the fabric of her speech. *Time* noticed her hidden motives: "her unofficial mission is to convince a new generation of women that there is honor and a deep, sustaining pleasure in motherhood, that life-style is no substitute for life."[3] That the first lady met audience expectations—praise of Wellesley graduates—and at the same time presented her own agenda was one of the major rhetorical accomplishments in this speech.

Mrs. Bush had several rhetorical choices. These responses converged around the controversy surrounding her invitation to speak. She could ignore the fact that she was second choice. A lesser speaker might have. Yet for the first lady of the United States, to accept tacitly a secondary position—a kind of snub that was public knowledge—without comment, might appear to demean the unofficial office of first lady of the land. Moreover, some observers thought that the Wellesley women wanted to embarrass Mrs. Bush. This was a slight that a person in her position could not blithely ignore.

At the other extreme, she could lash out at the pettiness of some of the seniors at Wellesley. There would have been some support for that approach because many people perceived the girls as spoiled and selfish. And the attack on President Bush's wife appeared to others to be politically motivated. Yet, such a reply-in-kind, a fight-fire-with-fire response, would have been unseemly. If she chose such a reaction, she would forfeit the high moral ground on which Americans expect their leaders to stand.

Somewhere between these two extremes was the Greek concept of the golden mean. Barbara Bush found the middle way. She satisfied the formal requirements of the generic situation, yet she politely made her point.

The Invention

The logographer for this speech was Ed NcNally. He drafted the speech in consultation with Mrs. Bush as the controversy unfolded. At this writing, little else is known about how the speech was conceived, except that the anecdote about babysitting was contributed by an aide.[4]

The Disposition

The speech followed no discernible classical organizational pattern. It had an introduction, a body, and a conclusion. If pushed, one could opine that it was organized topically, because the body of the speech had three main heads.

The introduction served effectively from a Ciceronian perspective. In *De Inventione*, Cicero observed that an exordium should make the audience well disposed, attentive, and teachable. Figuring that the first lady of the United States probably already had the audience's attention, although it could be easily lost after the first few minutes, the speech writer had Bush focus on making her audience well disposed and teachable. Bush accomplished these two important rhetorical tasks by devoting about half of the speech to the introduction.

Under normal circumstances, an introduction that comprised almost half the speech would be too long. But for a polarized audience at Wellesley, it was a wise choice. This is an instance wherein the rules were broken for a persuasive purpose. In a well-crafted attempt to make the audience favorably disposed to her and her message, Bush relied on the techniques of reference to place, of complimenting the audience, and of using humor. These devices were often interconnected, and they were enlarged with verbiage beyond their usual length to make the audience receptive.

Barbara Bush referred to the place several times in her exordium. She mentioned that she had spoken at Wellesley ten years ago and that she was still struck by the beauty of the campus and its spirit. Her second mention of Wellesley was her allusion to the custom that each senior class selects a color to wear.

Bush was also effusive with her compliments. She observed that Wellesley was an "experiment in excellence [alliteration] in which diversity is not just tolerated, but is embraced." Note how she effectively linked the word *tolerated* to embracing excellence in an enthymeme. In taking the compliment, the audience would have to acquiesce to the enthymeme that equated excellence with tolerance. If one denied the spirit of tolerance, which some of the girls had, one did not embrace excellence. Few would admit to doing that. Later in the introduction, Bush allowed there was a "Wellesley spirit," and she praised the young women for having a "first class education from a first class school" (anaphora). The ample compliments surely ameliorated her slight needling of some of the undergraduates' intolerance.

But Mrs. Bush's best forays were in plying the audience with humor. This was an example of Gorgias's admonition to respond to your opponent's seriousness with humor, and your opponent's humor with seriousness. She wisely chose to counter her host's serious protests with several light-hearted rejoinders. The *New York Times* noted that she "softened her lecture on family values with wit."[5]

The first use of humor was the extended story in the introduction. She used this story to communicate a subtle analogy. Quoting a commencement speech by a class president of a sister college, Mrs. Bush related Robert Fulghum's story of a little girl who did not want to play the role in the game that an authority figure assigned her. The little girl wanted to be a mermaid. At a metaphorical level, the little girl was Barbara Bush. The game she refused to play was the one played by the Wellesley protesters' rules. She was the mermaid who insisted on her own role as mother and wife rather than career woman.

The second instance of humor followed on the heels of the first. Bush also managed a clever play on words with the title of a book. Allowing that she knew the senior's first choice was Alice Walker, who wrote *The Color Purple*, Bush humorously granted that the seniors got instead "me—known for the color of my hair!"

Mrs. Bush's techniques served an integral and necessary function in her introduction. They allowed her to broach her thesis without turning people off prematurely. She sprinkled some key words, which comprised her unstated thesis, throughout the introduction. Words, such as "diversity," "tolerated," "tolerance," "difference," and "a 'paint-by-numbers' life," were scattered about just enough to make manifest her intent, but not enough to produce an exercise in rhetorical overkill. The whole introduction led inexorably to her gentle point: "Today you meet on Severance Green to say goodbye to all that, to begin a new and very personal journey, a search for your own true colors. In the world that awaits you beyond the shores of Lake Waban, no one can say what your true colors will be." In this metaphor, which was also an enthymeme, Mrs. Bush asked the class to give up its monolithic color purple, to consider her color of silver as well as all the other colors, which represent different life goals.

Bush then made a transitional statement that adjusted her speech to the audience and the audience to the speech. She announced that she would ask the audience to make "three very special choices." The body of her speech was organized topically around these three main heads.

Mrs. Bush's initial main head was "to believe in something larger than yourself." She quietly built her ethos with the audience by allowing that she chose literacy as her major involvement.

Eschewing the one-two-three approach, Bush varied slightly the transition to her second point: "Early on I made another choice which I hope you will make as well." She linked her husband's ability to make her laugh with a humorous line from the movie *Ferris Buehler's Day Off*.

Main heads one and two were relatively brief ones. They were also innocuous enough. Bush saved her major appeals for her third point, which was introduced with a clear transition: "The third choice that must not be missed is to cherish your human connections."

Reacting to the kind of feminism that favored professional achievement over traditional roles, Mrs. Bush finally and frontally assaulted her detractors. This was the crux of her commencement address. Acknowledging that the young women could be doctors, lawyers, and business leaders, Bush asserted that the "most important investments" they would ever make would be with spouses, children, and friends. "At the end of your life, you will never regret not having passed one more test, not winning one more verdict, or not closing one more deal. You will regret time not spent with a husband, a friend, a child or a parent." Having openly challenged some cherished beliefs in the audience, she wisely leavened her attack with another humorous story about a wife who had to set her spouse straight about how a husband did not baby-sit his own children! This showed the audience that Bush sympathized with modern women's difficulties in getting their spouses to share parenting chores.

Bush ended the argument of her third main head by observing that the success of the nation depended on what happened in the nation's houses, not in the White House.

One could quibble over where the conclusion of the speech began. Perhaps this is a weakness in the speech, for it lacks any verbal cues of a summary nature. I take the conclusion to begin with the last two paragraphs.

The primary function of the first paragraph in the conclusion was to challenge the audience. Bush used the entire speech to appeal to the seniors to be open to a variety of role models for modern women. She continued this appeal into the conclusion, again adapting to the audience by acknowledging a Wellesley ritual. For fifty years, she noted, it was said that the winner of the annual hoop race would be the first woman to be married. Now, as a reflection of changing mores, it was said that the winner would be the first C.E.O. [chief executive officer]. In conjunction with her thesis, Bush stated that both stereotypes showed "too little tolerance" for those who wanted to differ from the roles imposed by societal expectations.

Then, Bush pulled off the major rhetorical coup in her speech. To demonstrate that she was not intolerant, she coyly constructed a classical periodic sentence: "Someone out in this audience may even be someone who will one day follow in my footsteps, and preside over the White House as the president's spouse. I wish him well!"

Her final paragraph in the conclusion was her vindication: "The controversy ends here." It did. With magnanimity and empathy Barbara Bush had resolved it.

The Style

Neither grand nor simple, the speech was written in a middle style. If pressed, one would have to admit that the style tilted toward simple expression. The speech was embellished with a few classical stylistic devices as indicated above. But given the fact that Mrs. Bush did not have a prior ethos as an eloquent speaker, forays into a polished style, which are appropriate to the genre of commencement addresses, would have seemed inappropriate.

The speech succeeded moderately well in meeting Aristotle's criterion of clarity. Except for the slightly unclear conclusion, the speech's overall structure was manifest. The choice of words was clean. No verbal stragglers cluttered the way, and no linguistic road blocks impeded the way. Although not ornate, the speech was lucid. All of the sections of the speech and its language marched to the thesis of tolerance.

Metaphor played a key role in adapting the speech to the audience. The metaphor of the little girl who insisted on being a mermaid, the play on the color purple, and the Wellesley hoop race served Mrs. Bush well. At the literal level, the first two devices communicated humor and the last one identified with the immediate audience. But in the context of the controversy, one could not help understanding the devices at the level Mrs. Bush invited the audience to perceive them. For the devices connected the speech to her; hence, the veritable artistry of the speech's style.

The speech's conversational style was intimate. Mrs. Bush used personal pronouns, such as *we, you, us,* and *I,* profusely throughout the speech to identify with the audience at the individual level. These words contributed to the oral style of the speech by investing it with the ambience of a one-to-one conversation between the speaker and the audience. The transitional devices also helped cue the audience to the major sections in the speech, thus making it easily understood.

The Delivery

In at least one instance, Mrs. Bush used delivery for maximum effect.

In rendering her most memorable and humorous line, she exhibited an excellent sense of rhetorical timing. "Someone out in this audience," Mrs. Bush said, "may even be someone who will one day follow in my footsteps, and preside over the White House as the president's spouse." In order to let the thought germinate in the audience's mind, she paused slightly and then delivered the punch line: "I wish him well!" The audience evidently appreciated her humor, her unexpected verbal twist, and her excellent vocal pacing, because the line elicited great cheers from her commencement audience of over five thousand.[6]

The Persuasive Effect

What the long-run effect of Mrs. Bush's speech is or will be is hard to discern. It did not solve the pressing problem of intolerance, and it would be foolish to expect that it could. It did not persuade all of the seniors (remember that Aristotle claimed that not everybody could be persuaded anyway). It probably did win "over most of her audience."[7] The speech did, and perhaps this is its forte, demonstrate that Barbara Bush had the boldness to face her detractors. The first lady skillfully turned the tables and managed both to educate and to conciliate the protesters. They, not she, were intolerant; she, not they, had the last word.

Notes

1. "Family First, Mrs. Bush Tells Friend and Foe at Wellesley," *New York Times,* June 2, 1990, p. 1.

2. "The End of Another Cold War," *Time,* June 11, 1990, p. 21.
3. Ibid.
4. "A Job Wellesley Done," *Newsweek,* June 11, 1990, p. 26.
5. "Family First," p. 1.
6. "The End of Another Cold War," p. 21.
7. "Family First," p. 5.

A Glossary of Rhetorical Terms, Classical Writers, and Their Works

actio: one of the five classical canons of rhetoric, concerned with the delivering of a speech for persuasive effect

agones: the Greek term for the arguments of a speech

alliteration: a figure of sound, the repetition of the same sound in successive phrases or sentences

analogy: a form of reasoning in which if two things agree with one another in some respects, then they will probably agree in other respects

anaphora: a figure of sound; parallelism at the beginning of successive phrases, clauses, and sentences

Antiphon: a Greek speech writer, noted for the plain style

antithesis: a figure of thought; the opposition of contrasting ideas, A:B

apologia: a speech in defense of one's policy and/or character

apophasis: a figure of thought; affirming the point by appearing to deny it; affirmation by denial

apostrophe: a figure of thought; turning away from the audience to address an imaginary figure or audience for rhetorical effect

argumentum ad absurdum: see *reductio ad absurdum*

argumentum ad personam: a fallacious argument that unethically attacks the person rather than the person's ideas

Aristotle: Greek writer of the Rhetoric, 330 B.C., student of Plato

Asian-Attic controversy: joined by Cicero, who favored the Asian or ornamented style versus the Attic style, which was plain and unornamented

Asian style: an ornamented style of speech, which was favored by Cicero

asyndeton: a figure of thought; not using connective conjunctions in phrases and clauses

Attic style: a plain style of speech, which was favored by some Roman theorists who disliked Cicero's ornamented Asian style

audience adaption: the adapting of the speech—its emotional, logical, and ethical appeals, as well as its organization, style, and delivery—to the audience

audience analysis: the determination of the audience's values and beliefs by polls and questionnaires

bandwagon effect: mentioning other people who believe or act as the speaker desires in the hope that others will act likewise, that is, get on the bandwagon

Brutus: written by Cicero, 46 B.C.; defended the Asian style in the Asian-Attic controversy

Burkeian pattern: speech organizational pattern that consists of Anger, Victim/Scapegoat, and Salvation steps

canon: a body of principles, rules, standards, or norms

chiasmus: a figure of thought; the inversion of words or ideas, A:B::B:A

Cicero: Roman orator and writer, first century B.C.

classical canons of rhetoric: invention, disposition, style, delivery, and memory

classical pattern: the introduction, narration, arguments, refutation, and conclusion; invented by Corax

conclusio: the summary or conclusion of a speech

confirmatio: a section of a classical speech in which the speaker gives the arguments and proofs for the address

confutatio: a section of a classical speech in which the speaker refutes opposing arguments

coniecturalis: a classical stasis; whether an action was done

Corax: a Greek traditionally credited with the first book on rhetoric, which was entitled **Techne**; fifth century B.C.

De Inventione: written by Cicero, 90 B.C.; developed the stasis theory

De Optimo Genere Oratorum: written by Cicero, 46 B.C.; stressed style in the Asian-Attic controversy

De Oratore: written by Cicero, 55 B.C.; stressed sophistic strand of rhetoric

De Partitione Oratoria: written by Cicero, 46 B.C.; was the father's oratorical advice to his son

deduction: reasoning from a premise to a specific conclusion

definitiva: a classical stasis; how an action is defined

Demosthenes: Greek orator and logographer, noted for the "Philippics," a series of speeches against Philip of Macedonia

deliberative oratory: legislative speaking toward action aimed at expediency

digressio: a section of a classical speech in which the speaker digresses from the main flow of the address

disjunctive syllogism: see *method of residues*

dispositio: one of the five classical canons of rhetoric; concerned with arranging the speech for persuasive effect

divisio: the division of a speech

elocutio: one of the five classical canons of rhetoric; concerned with styling the speech for persuasive effect

emotional appeal: language that appeals to the audience's emotions; pathos

encomium: a speech of praise

enthymeme: a rhetorical argument based on generally held beliefs that are not stated in the argument

epideictic oratory: ceremonial speaking that praises or blames, that focuses on the present, and establishes virtue or vice

epilogus: the concluding section of a classical speech

epistrophe: a figure of sound; parallelism at the ending of successive phrases, clauses, and sentences

ethical appeal: a speaker's credibility; ethos

ethopoeia: making the character of the speaker apparent in the style of the speech

ethos: an Aristotelian term for the speaker's good sense, goodwill, and good moral character

exordium: the introductory section of a classical speech, its aim is to gain the audience's attention and make the audience receptive

eye contact: a variable of delivery; looking directly at all members of the audience

figure of sound: a stylistic device that uses the sound of language for persuasive effect

figure of thought: a stylistic device that uses the meaning of words and language for persuasive effect

forensic oratory: judicial speaking that establishes justice with regard to the past

generalis: a classical stasis that indicates degree or kind

genre: a kind of oratory—deliberative, judicial, epideictic

Gorgias: a Greek orator and sophist

Gorgias: a Platonic dialogue on rhetoric, 387 B.C.

grand style: a heavy, turgid style of speech, sometimes associated with the Asian style

Hippias of Elis: A Greek sophist who taught mnemonic devices

induction: rhetorical reasoning from examples to a general conclusion

Institutio Oratoria: written by Quintilian, 90 A.D.; most complete Roman treatment of rhetoric

inventio: one of the five classical canons; the invention of a speech

irony: a figure of thought; using words in an opposite sense to their usual meaning

Isocrates: Greek orator and sophist

kairos: the right or propitious time to speak

kategoria: a speech of accusation against a policy and/or character

logical appeal: an appeal based on reasoning, evidence, statistics, and facts; logos

logographer: an ancient Greek speech writer

logos: an Aristotelian term for the logical appeals that a speaker uses in a speech

Lysias: Greek logographer, noted for the "art of concealing the art"

memoria: the classical canon of memory; the art of recalling the speech when delivering it

metaphor: a figure of thought, such as "He is a lion in battle"

method of residues: the rhetorical application of a disjunctive syllogism: either A, B, or C; not A, not B, therefore C

middle style: a compromise style that was neither grand nor plain, but was nevertheless ornamented

Monroe motivated sequence: an organizational pattern that consists of five steps: attention, need, satisfaction, visualization, and action

narratio: the narrative section of a classical speech

Orator: written by Cicero, 46 B.C.; stressed style in the Asian-Attic controversy

ornamented style: a middle style that uses figures of thought and sound

parallelism: see *anaphora* and *epistrophe*

partitio: a section of a classical speech in which the speaker states the issues in the speech

pathos: an Aristotelian term for the emotional appeals that a speaker uses in a speech

peroration: the conclusion of a speech; reaches for a heightened effect

persuasion: the act or process of changing an audience's values, attitudes, or beliefs

Phaedrus: a Platonic dialogue on rhetoric, 370 B.C.

philosophical rhetoric: the classical strand of rhetoric that stressed what the audience ought to do, the moral obligation of ethical rhetoric

pitch: the musical tone at which the speaker produces the sound of the voice, modulated for rhetorical emphasis and variety

plain style: a kind of everyday, street-corner style of speech

Plato: Greek philosopher who wrote two dialogues on rhetoric, the *Gorgias* and the *Phaedrus*

primacy effect: the principle that first arguments make a strong impression on the audience

problem-solution pattern: an organizational pattern consisting of main heads that detail the problem area and how the audience can solve the problem

pronuntiatio: the delivery of the speech

Protagoras: an early Greek sophist who stressed debating both sides of an issue

qualitas: a classical stasis; pertaining to quality or degree of an action

Quintilian: Roman writer of *Institutio Oratoria*, 90 A.D.

rate: the speed at which a speaker talks, normally about 125 words-per-minute, paced or phrased for rhetorical effect

recency effect: the principle that recent proofs make a lasting impression on the audience

reductio ad absurdum: taking an initial premise and running it to its absurd conclusion to demonstrate the absurdity of the initial premise

refutatio: a section of a classical speech in which the speaker confutes the opposition

Rhetorica ad Herennium: written by an unknown author, 90 B.C.; outlined the five canons of rhetoric; earliest Roman work on rhetoric

Rhetoric: written by Aristotle, 330 B.C.; most important Greek treatment of rhetoric

rhetorical question: a figure of thought; a question carefully constructed to elicit the desired response from an audience

sarcasm: a sharp, bitter, or cutting remark

simile: a figure of thought, such as "His rapierlike refutations cut the opponents to shreds"

Socrates: Greek philosopher; major figure in the Platonic dialogues; see *Plato*

sophist: a Greek teacher of rhetoric

sophistic rhetoric: the classical strand of rhetoric that emphasized the speaker's education for public address

stasis: the ancient concept of where the argument stands; see *coniecturalis, definitiva, qualitas,* and *translativa*

syllogism: a rhetorical argument from a general premise to a specific conclusion

Techne: the first Greek book on rhetoric, written by Corax in the fifth century B.C.

technical rhetoric: the classical strand of rhetoric that emphasized a successful effect for a speech

Thrasymachus: Greek sophist who taught skills in delivery

Tisias: early Greek rhetorician and student of Corax

Topica: written by Cicero, 44 B.C.; discussed stasis theory

translativa: a classical stasis; an appeal to a different jurisdiction or judge

tu quoque: "you also"; charging another with doing or saying the same thing you have (or have been accused of)

vocative: a stylistic device in which the speaker addresses the audience, as in "O you of little faith"

volume: the loudness in the speaker's voice, changed for rhetorical emphasis and variety

Index